ALASTAIR
SPECIAL PLACES TO STAY

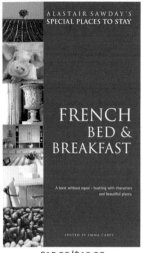

ALASTAIR SAWDAY'S
SPECIAL PLACES TO STAY

FRENCH
BED &
BREAKFAST

A book without equal – bursting with characters and beautiful places.

EDITED BY EMMA CAREY

£15.99/$19.95

ALASTAIR SAWDAY'S
SPECIAL PLACES TO STAY

FRENCH
HOTELS
CHÂTEAUX & OTHER PLACES

£14.99/$23.95

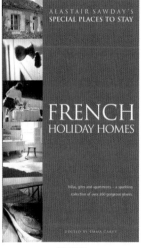

ALASTAIR SAWDAY'S
SPECIAL PLACES TO STAY

FRENCH
HOLIDAY HOMES

Villas, gîtes and apartments – a sparkling collection of over 260 gorgeous places.

EDITED BY EMMA CAREY

£12.99

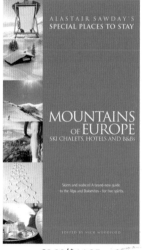

ALASTAIR SAWDAY'S
SPECIAL PLACES TO STAY

MOUNTAINS
OF EUROPE
SKI CHALETS, HOTELS AND B&Bs

Skiers and walkers! A brand-new guide to the Alps and Dolomites – for free spirits.

EDITED BY NICK WOODFORD

£9.99/$14.95

Credit card orders (free p&p) 01275 464891
www.specialplacestostay.com

In US: credit card orders (800) 243-0495, 9am–5pm EST,
24-hour fax (800) 820-2329 www.globepequot.com

Fourth edition
Copyright © 2006
Alastair Sawday Publishing Co. Ltd

Published in 2006
Alastair Sawday Publishing,
Yanley Lane, Long Ashton
Bristol BS41 9LR
Tel: +44 (0)1275 464891
Fax: +44 (0)1275 464887
Email: info@specialplacestostay.com
Web: www.specialplacestostay.com

The Globe Pequot Press
P. O. Box 480, Guilford,
Connecticut 06437, USA
Tel: +1 203 458 4500
Fax: +1 203 458 4601
Email: info@globepequot.com
Web: www.globepequot.com

Design:
Caroline King

Maps & Mapping:
Maidenhead Cartographic Services Ltd

Printing:
Butler & Tanner, Frome, UK

UK Distribution:
Penguin UK, 80 Strand, London

US Distribution:
The Globe Pequot Press, Guilford, CT 06437

ISBN 1-901970-61-2
       978-1-901970-61-6

Paper and Printing: We have sought the
lowest possible ecological 'footprint' from
the production of this book, using super-
efficient machinery, vegetable inks and high
environmental standards. Our printer is
ISO 14001-registered.

ALASTAIR SAWDAY'S
SPECIAL PLACES TO STAY

ITALY

Contents

Guide entries

Back

Alastair Sawday Publishing

We are the faceless toilers at the pit-face of publishing but, for us, the question of who we are and how we inter-react is important. For who we are shapes the books, the books shape your holidays, and thus are shaped the lives of people who own these 'special places'. So we are trying to be a little more than 'just a publishing company'.

New eco offices

By the end of 2005 we will have moved into our new eco offices. By introducing super-insulation, underfloor heating, a wood-pellet boiler, solar panels and a rainwater tank, we will have a working environment benign to ourselves and to the environment. Lighting will be low-energy, dark corners will be lit by sun-pipes and one building is of green oak. Carpet tiles are leased: some of recycled material, most of wool and some of natural fibres. We will sail through our environmental audit.

Environmental & ethical policies

We combine many other small gestures: company cars run on gas or recycled cooking oil; kitchen waste is composted and other waste recycled; cycling and car-sharing are encouraged; the company only buys organic or local food; we don't accept web links with companies we consider unethical; we use the ethical Triodos Bank for our deposit account.

We have used recycled paper for some books but have settled on selecting paper and printer for their low energy use. Our printer is British and ISO14001-certified and together we will reduce our environmental impact.

Thanks partially to our Green Team, we recently won a Business Commitment to the Environment Award – which has boosted our resolve to stick to our own green policies. Our flagship gesture, however, is carbon offsetting; we calculate our carbon emissions and plant trees to compensate as calculated by Future Forests. In 2006 we will support projects overseas that plant trees or reduce carbon use; our money will work better by going direct to projects.

Ethics

But why, you may ask, take these things so seriously? You are just a little publishing company, for heavens sake! Well, is there any good argument for not taking them seriously? The world, by the admission of the vast majority of scientists, is in trouble. If we do not change our ways urgently we will doom the planet and all its creatures – whether innocent or not – to a variety of possible catastrophes. To maintain the status quo is unacceptable. Business does much of the damage and should undo it, and provide new models.

Who are we?

Pressure on companies to produce Corporate Social Responsibility policies is mounting. We are trying to keep ahead of it all, yet still to be as informal and human as possible – the antithesis of 'corporate'. (We even have unofficial 'de-stress operatives' in the shape of several resident dogs.)

The books – and a dilemma

So, we have created fine books that do good work. They promote authenticity, individuality and high quality, local and organic food – a far cry from the now-dominant corporate culture. Rural economies, pubs, small farms, villages and hamlets all benefit. However, people use fossil fuel to get there. Should we aim to get our readers to offset their own carbon emissions, and the B&B and hotel owners too? That might have been a hopeless task a year or so ago, but less so now that the media has taken on board the enormity of the work ahead of us all.

We are slowly introducing green ideas into the books: the Fine Breakfast scheme that highlights British and Irish B&B owners who use local and organic food; celebrating those who make an extra effort; gently encouraging the use of public transport, cycling and walking. Next year we are publishing a book focusing on responsible travel and eco-projects around the globe.

Our Fragile Earth series

The 'hard' side of our environmental publishing is the Fragile Earth series: *The Little Earth Book*, *The Little Food Book* and *The Little Money Book*. They have been a great success. They consist of bite-sized essays, polemical and hard-hitting but well researched and methodical. They are a 'must have' for people from all walks of life – anyone who is confused and needs clarity about some of the key issues of our time.

Lastly – what is special?

The notion of 'special' is at the heart of what we do, and highly subjective. We discuss this in the Introduction. We take huge pleasure from finding people and places that do their own thing – brilliantly; places that are unusual and follow no trends; places of peace and beauty; people who are kind and interesting – and genuine.

We seem to have touched a raw nerve with thousands of readers; they obviously want to stay in special places rather than the dull corporate monstrosities that have disfigured so many of our cities and towns. Life is too short to be wasted in the wrong places. A night in a special place can be a transforming experience.

Alastair Sawday

Acknowledgements

Rarely can Italy have faced such a gentle and irresistible onslaught as that launched by Emma. She has immense charm and a wide appeal, and is as enthusiastic about her book as 'her' owners are about their work. She was brilliantly backed by Kate; it must have been hard to resist them both – hence the increase in numbers and the richer variety. No corner of Italy has escaped them, and they have developed an impressive feel for the peculiar fascination of the country.

They have, too, been largely autonomous. Emma, the editor, works in Leeds and only visits us occasionally. So she has worked alone for much of the time, with Kate manning the Italy desk here. They have worked with maximum imagination and integrity – backed to the hilt by Jo, who has tweaked and written her socks off. They should be as proud of this book as we are.

Alastair Sawday.

Series Editor Alastair Sawday

Editor Emma Carey

Assistant to Editor Kate Shepherd

Editorial Director Annie Shillito

Accounts Sheila Clifton,
Bridget Bishop, Christine Buxton,
Jenny Purdy, Sandra Hassell

Editorial Jackie King,
Jo Boissevain, Maria Serrano,
Rebecca Stevens, Danielle Williams

Production Julia Richardson,
Rachel Coe, Paul Groom,
Allys Williams, Philippa Rogers,
Kathy Purdy

Sales & Marketing & PR
Siobhán Flynn,
Andreea Petre-Goncalves,
Sarah Bolton

Web & IT Russell Wilkinson,
Chris Banks, Brian Kimberling

Writers Jo Boissevain, Viv Cripps,
Stephen Perry, Helen Pickles,
Aideen Reid, Allys Williams.

Inspections
Richard & Linda Armspach,
Emma Carey, Lois Ferguson,
Jill Greetham, Jo Lane, Sue Learner,
Aideen Reid, Philippa Rogers,
Kate Shepherd.

And many thanks to those people who did just a few inspections and helped with the writing.

Ideas seem to pour forth from Italy. They are 'can do' people: outline a problem and they will cast about for a solution, or just tell you that it can be done. Thus with the 'residenza', an Italian answer to the challenge of finding space for visitors in a city without many hotels. Reception may be a smart room in an apartment block, while the bedrooms are in the apartments available that night, scattered about the building according to the absences of their owners. It works brilliantly.

Now that *agriturismo* is thoroughly accepted in Italy, with thousands of farmhouses poised to welcome travellers, there has been an unleashing of Italian creativity into the B&B world. You can devour the finest food grown on the farm, drink the farmers' own wines, explore their gardens, admire their art work, learn to cook in their kitchens. They will arrange courses for you, take you to their favourite places, teach you Italian and bring you back to life after a dreary British winter.

Wherever you go with this book, to hotels, to spas, to mountains or to the plains, you will meet interesting people who are interested in you. They are humble, educated, grand, ex-professionals, simple, artistic,

musical – and somehow they seem to be among the most engaging of all the hosts in all our books.

This edition is bigger than ever, with new places in towns and cities and throughout the south especially. It is now so popular that it seduces people from all corners of Italy to want to join in with us. You have much to enjoy.

Alastair Sawday

Introduction

PLACES BULGING WITH HISTORY, FABULOUS FOOD, ART, SCENERY, ARCHITECTURE – EVERY REGION HAS IT ALL.

Italy's charms are well-charted and as seductive as ever. Places bulging with history, fabulous food, art, scenery, architecture – every region has it all.

If you can't make up your mind about what sort of place to stay in, this book is the answer. There's a sprinkling of just about everything here, from farmhouse B&Bs to Palladian villas to apartments in Venice. And as you scroll through these 340 pages, from Piedmont to Veneto to Puglia, the regional diversity of Italy unfurls, each region appearing more charming than the last. A guide-in-miniature to the country's landscape, history and culture, this book whets the appetite for the pleasures that are to come.

Most come for Tuscany. For the serene landscapes of Piero della Francesca, the Renaissance treasures of Florence, and the renowned food based on fine ingredients cooked with great delicacy and enjoyed always in company. Many, too, come for neighbouring Umbria, the little green heart of Italy, birthplace of St Francis of Assisi – all hill towns, truffles and churches.

Now the southern country cousins are catching up. The press is toasting Puglia and Sicily as the new 'in' places to go. In no European country is the north-south divide more marked than in Italy, but the areas below the 'poverty' line of Rome are rich in stunning beaches, untouched landscapes, Greco-Roman antiquities and delicacies garnered from the Calabrian coast. Hot dry Puglia is loved for its baroque palaces and churches, its conical (comical) stone houses, or *trulli* – meet some in this book – its soups, pastas and Arabic pastries. Sicily is known for its simplicity, exuberance and generosity. The first edition of this book did not penetrate the south; in this edition we have over 60 special places and flight paths are opening up, making Italy's 'heel' more accessible than ever.

Photo left Antica Locanda dei Mercanti, entry 23
Photo right Abbazia San Pietro in Valle, entry 213

Introduction

Hotels, inns, guesthouses are all well-represented here, as are *agriturismi* – your chance to stay on a farm. The *agriturismo* phenomenon, introduced to Tuscany in 1985, is creeping further south as farmers look for ways to supplement their income. Now there are 11,000 and the number is growing. For true *agriturismo* status, farms and estates must receive the bulk of their income through farming; the owners introduce their way of life to guests, while breakfast and dinner are a chance to taste their produce. Meals can be shared with the family round the kitchen table, or served in a restaurant that is open to the public as well as to guests.

The *residenza* idea is a more recent innovation – great for those seeking independence in cities and towns. In a central location you find a handful of B&B rooms or suites, someone on reception 8am-8pm, no room service but perhaps a shared sitting or breakfast room. You can come and go as you please, and there are sometimes self-catering apartments available, too. (See entry nos 128, 135, 137.)

More and more owners hear of us through the grapevine: perhaps their friends or members of their family are already in the book, or their guests – our readers – have passed on the word. The choice of special places to stay in this fourth edition is greater than ever.

What is a special place?

We look for owners, homes and hotels that we like – and are fiercely subjective in our choices. 'Special' for us is not about the number of comforts but relates to a multitude of elements that make a place 'work'. Certainly the way guests are treated comes as high on our list as the setting, the architecture, the atmosphere and the food.

How do we choose our Special Places?

We have selected the widest range of possibilities for you to choose from – castles, villas, city apartments, farmhouses, country

Photo Castello di Spaltenna, entry 186

inns, even a monastery or two. It might be breakfast under the frescoed ceiling of a Renaissance villa that is special, or a large and boisterous dinner in a farmhouse kitchen, or a life-enhancing view. We have selected not necessarily the most opulent places to stay, but the most interesting and satisfying. We include no star ratings in our guides; let our descriptions inform you.

What to expect

With Italy it's not always easy to distinguish myth from reality. For centuries poets and painters and almost everyone else who's ever been there has fallen in love with it. And because Italy has, to quote Lord Byron, "the fatal gift of beauty", it is easy to forget that in parts it can be ugly. Don't be put off when you discover that there are swathes of industrial plant (yes, even in Tuscany). These things can't be airbrushed out, but acknowledge that they exist and they won't spoil your fun.

Finding the right place for you

It's our job to help you find a place you like. We aim to give honest descriptions so you can glean from the write-ups what the owners or staff are like, and how formal or casual the place is. This edition also includes a large number of self-catering possibilities. Older properties may seem more

immediately appealing, but please don't overlook the more modern ones – they too have personality. It's always the owners and their staff who have the greatest influence on the atmosphere you experience.

Type of properties

Each entry is simply labelled (B&B, hotel, self-catering, *agriturismo*) to guide you, but the write-ups reveal several descriptive terms. This list serves as a rough guide to what you might expect to find.

Agriturismo Farm or estate with B&B rooms or apartments (see p.12)
Albergo Italian word for an inn, more personal than a hotel
Azienda Agrituristica Literally, 'agricultural business'

Introduction

Cà/Casa (Cà in Venetian dialect)
House
Cascina Farmhouse
Castello Castle
Corte Literally, a 'court'
Country House A new concept in
Italian hospitality, usually family-run
and akin to a villa
Dimora Dwelling
Fattoria Farm
Locanda Means 'inn', but sometimes
used to describe a restaurant only
Podere Farm or smallholding
Palazzo Literally a 'palace' but more
usually a mansion
Relais An imported French term
meaning 'inn'
Residenza An apartment or house
with rooms for guests (see p.12)
Tenuta Farm holding, or 'tenancy'
Villa Country residence

How to use this book

Map

Look at the map at the front of the
book to find your area, then the
detailed maps to find the places.
The numbers correspond to the page
numbers of the book. Our maps are
for guidance only; take a detailed
road map to find your way around.
Self-catering places are marked in
blue on the maps; others are marked
in red.

Rooms

We tell you about the range of
accommodation in singles, doubles,
twins, family rooms and suites as
well as apartments and whole
houses. A 'family' room is a loose
term because in Italy triples and
quadruples often sleep more than
the heading suggests; extra beds can
often be added for children, usually
with a charge. Check when booking.
Where an entry reads '4 + 2' this
means 4 B&B rooms plus 2 self-
catering apartments/villas/cottages.

Bathrooms

Assume that bathrooms are en suite
unless we say otherwise. Italian
bathrooms often have a shower only.

Symbols

There is an explanation of our
symbols on the inside of the back
cover. These are intended as a guide
rather than as an unequivocal
statement of fact; should an owner

Photo left Albergo Punta Regina, entry 290
Photo right Casa Palmira, entry 124

Introduction

not have the symbol that you're looking for, it's worth discussing your needs.

Practical matters
Prices
The prices we quote are the prices per night per room unless otherwise stated, breakfast included. For self-catering, we specify if the price is per week. For half-board, it may be per person (p.p.). Meal prices are always given per person; we try to give you an approximate price and specify if wine is included. Prices quoted are those given to us for 2006. We publish every two years so they cannot be current throughout the book's life. Treat them as a guideline rather than as infallible.

Photo Hotel Villa San Michele, entry 294

Phones and phone codes
From Italy to another country:
dial 00 followed by the country code and then the area code without the first 0. When dialling Alastair Sawday Publishing from Italy, the number 01275 464891 becomes 00 44 1275 464891.

From another country to Italy:
From the UK dial 00 then the full number given including the first 0.

From the USA dial 011 then the full number given including the first 0.

Within Italy: simply drop the country code (39) and dial the numbers given.

Italian mobile numbers start with 33.

Phone cards (*carte telefoniche*) can be bought from tobacconists, post offices and newspaper stands.

Meals
Eating in Italy is one of life's great pleasures. There is plenty of variety, and each region has its own specialities and its surprises. We used to have a symbol to show where food was organically grown, home-grown or locally grown. In Italy this is almost a given: so many owners use locally grown ingredients and more often than not have grown or produced some part of your meal.

Breakfast

What constitutes breakfast varies hugely from place to place. Many hotels don't offer it at all, especially in towns, where it is normal to walk to the nearest bar for your first espresso. (Prices double or triple as soon as you sit down, so if you want to save money, join the locals at the bar.) If you are confronted with a vacuum-packed breakfast it's because, in certain areas, B&Bs are only allowed to serve fresh ingredients if they meet certain strict regulations. On farms, however, you should find homemade jams and cakes as well as home-produced cheeses and fruit.

Dinner

Hotels and other places with restaurants usually offer the widest à la carte choice. Smaller places may offer a set dinner (at a set time) and you will need to book in advance. In family-run establishments you will sometimes find yourself eating in a separate dining room, served by a member of the family; in some cases, you will eat with the family. Small farms and inns often offer sumptuous dinners which are excellent value and delicious, so keep an open mind.

Vegetarians

There is so much fresh, seasonal food available that vegetarians should have no difficulty in Italy. Although main courses are often meaty, there are plenty of pasta dishes to suit vegetarians. Vegetables are the glory of southern Italian cooking, and are quite often eaten as a first or main course – or accompanied by rice, chickpeas, eggs, polenta.

Tipping

In bars you are given your change on a small saucer, and it is usual to leave a couple of small coins there. A cover charge on restaurant meals is standard. A small tip (*mancia*) in family-run establishments is also welcome, so leave one if you wish.

Photo Podere Le Mezzelune, entry 157

Introduction

Most families and even large companies take a holiday and head for the sea so some inland hotels consider August to be low season and prices go down accordingly.

1 January	New Year's Day *Capo d'Anno*
6 January	Epiphany *La Befana*
Easter	*Pasqua*
25 April	Liberation Day *Venticinque Aprile*
1 May	Labour Day *Primo Maggio*
15 August	Assumption of the Virgin *Ferragosto*
1 November	All Saints' Day *Tutti Santi*
8 December	Feast of the Immaculate *Festa dell'Immacolata* Conception
25 December	Christmas Day *Natale*
26 December	Boxing Day *Santo Stefano*

Note, each Italian town has its own patron saint who has his/her holiday, too.

Booking

Book well ahead if you plan to visit Italy during school holidays. Hotels will usually ask you for a credit card number for confirmation. Remember to let smaller places know if you are likely to be arriving late, and if you want dinner. There's a bilingual booking form at the back of the book. Hotels may send back a signed copy as confirmation but don't necessarily expect a speedy reply! Some of the major cities get very full around the time of trade fairs (eg. fashion fairs in Milan, the Biennale in Venice) – book well ahead.

Opening hours

Most shops are closed 1pm–4pm, and then stay open until 8pm. Restaurants are required to close for one day a week, often a Monday. Most museums, too, close one day a week. For many of the major art attractions – the Uffizi in Florence, the Last Supper in Milan, the Borghese in Rome – you need to book a ticket in advance, and a specific reservation time.

Seasons and Public Holidays

On the days before public holidays Italians like to stock up, so be prepared for long queues in the supermarket. *Ferragosto* marks the summer holiday for Italians and, for the week before and the week after, most places close down.

Photo above Villa i Bossi, entry 168
Photo right Pensione La Calcina, entry 51

Cancellation

Please give as much notice as possible. Cancellation charges will vary, so do check.

Registration

Visitors to Italy are obliged to carry some form of identification at all times. It is a good idea to take some form of ID other than your passport so that if you have handed your passport in at hotel reception on arrival, you can still prove who you are.

Payment

The most commonly accepted credit cards are Visa, Eurocard, MasterCard and Amex. Many places in this book don't take plastic because of high bank charges. Check the symbols at the bottom of each entry before you arrive, in case you are a long way from a cash dispenser!

Consider taking...

• Electrical adaptors: virtually all sockets now have two-pin plugs that run on 220/240 AC voltage
• A universal bath plug in case yours is missing
• Ear plugs could be useful for a light-sleeper driven mad by late-night Vespas
• A portable electric fan for your bedside in high summer could be a lifesaver

Italian Tourist Offices

www.italiantourism.com
UK: 1 Princes Street, London W1R 8AY. Tel: 0207 408 1254
USA: 630 Fifth Avenue, New York 10111. Tel: 212 245 5618

Subscriptions

Owners pay to appear in this guide. Their fee goes towards the cost of inspections (every entry has been inspected by a member of our team before being selected), of producing an all-colour book and of maintaining a sophisticated web site. We only include places and owners that we find positively special. It is not possible for anyone to buy their way into our guides.

Internet

www.specialplacestostay.com has online pages for all of the places featured here and from all our other books – around 5,000 Special Places in Britain, Ireland, France, Italy,

Photo left Il Giardino Segreto, entry 64
Photo right Villa Poggiano, entry 196

Spain, Portugal, India, Morocco, Turkey and Greece. There's a searchable database, a taster of the write-ups and colour photos.

Disclaimer

We make no claims to pure objectivity in choosing our Special Places to Stay. They are here because we like them. Our opinions and tastes are ours alone and this book is a statement of them; we hope that you will share them.

We have done our utmost to get our facts right but apologise unreservedly for any mistakes that may have crept in. Feedback from you is invaluable and we always act upon comments. With your help and our own inspections we can maintain our reputation for dependability.

You should know that we do not check such things as fire alarms, swimming pool security or any other regulation with which owners of properties receiving paying guests should comply. This is the responsibility of the owners.

And finally

We want to hear whether your stay was a triumph or not. If you are unhappy about something then try to speak to the owner or the manager while you are there. Many problems are best solved 'on the spot'. Please fill out the report form at the back of the book or email us at italy@sawdays.co.uk. We value your recommendations – for this, or any other book in the series. Do keep writing. If your recommendation results in the inclusion of a special place in any of our guides we'll send you a free copy.

Buon viaggio!
Emma Carey

General map

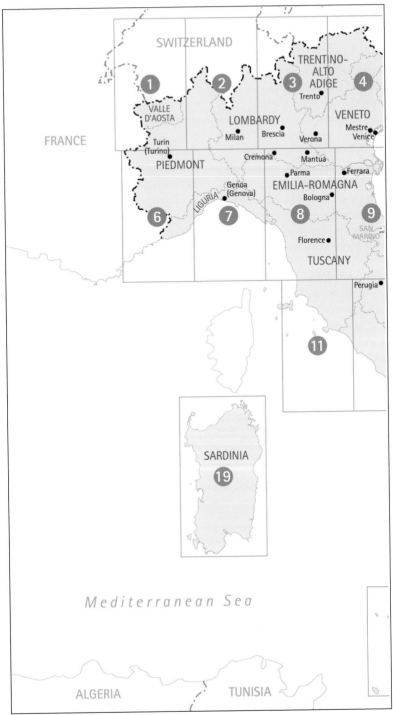

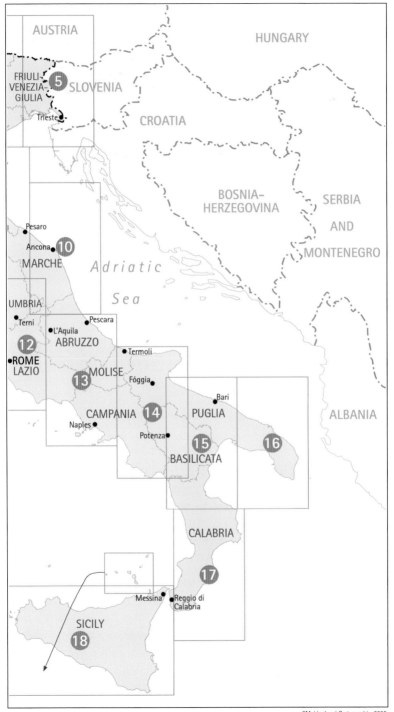

Map 1

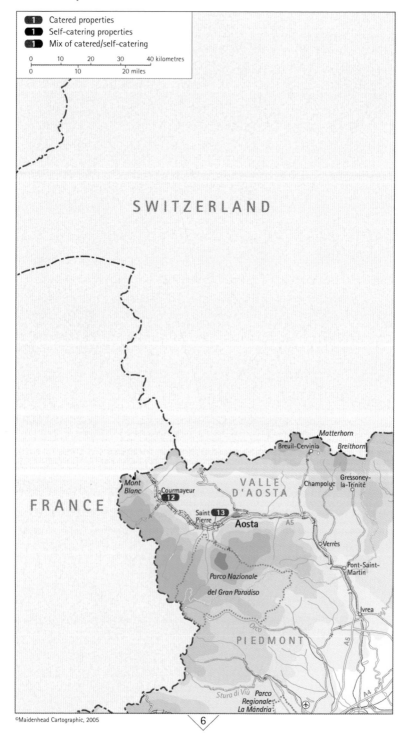

Catered properties
Self-catering properties
Mix of catered/self-catering

0   10   20   30   40 kilometres
0   10   20 miles

SWITZERLAND

Matterhorn
Breuil-Cervinia   Breithorn
Mont Blanc   VALLE   Champoluc   Gressoney-la-Trinité
Courmayeur   D'AOSTA
12
FRANCE   Saint Pierre   13
Aosta   A5
Verrès
Pont-Saint-Martin
Parco Nazionale
del Gran Paradiso
Ivrea
PIEDMONT
A5
A4
Stura di Viù   Parco
Regionale
La Mándria

Map 2

25

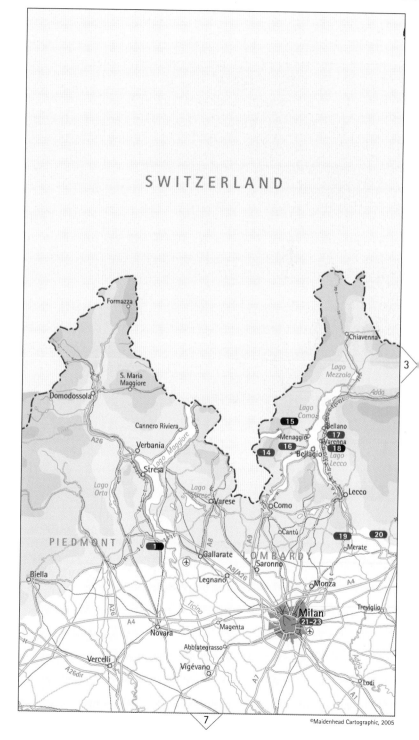

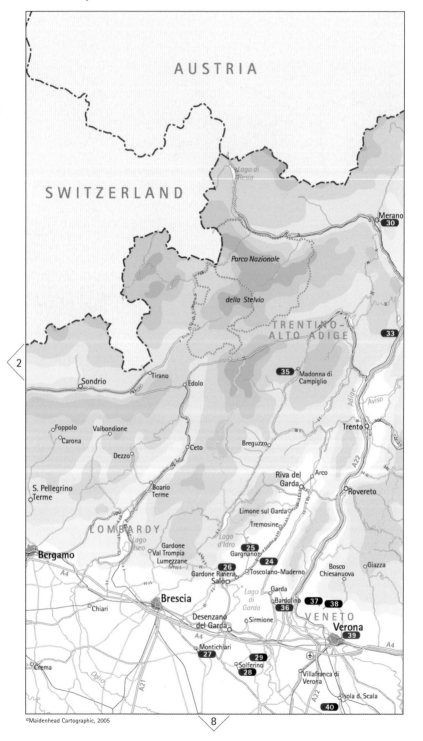

Map 4

27

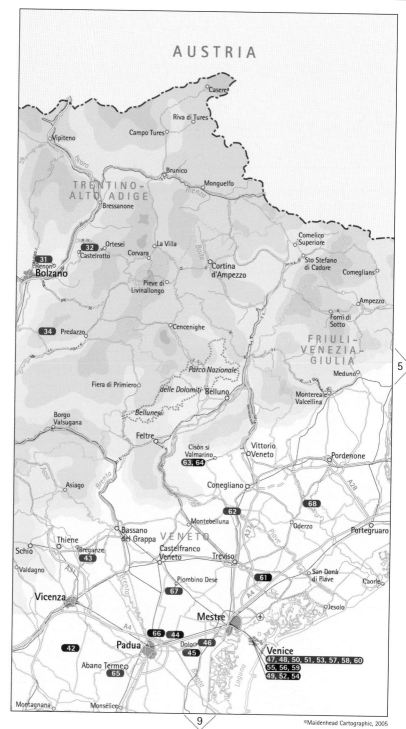

Map 5

Driving

Driving in Italy is challenging for the British driver; Italian drivers are skilled but scary and love nothing better than to sit on your tail. However, a car in remote areas is pretty much essential, and is great for exploring hill towns. Parking, mandatory theft insurance and tolls are expensive, but the more people you pack into a car or minibus, the cheaper it gets per person.

Here are a few pointers. Don't forget your driving licence; it is an offence to drive without it and, if you hire a car, you must show it. New legislation dictates that headlights have to be on at all times on motorway and main roads. And remember, you don't automatically have right of way on a roundabout in Italy: if the traffic coming from the right does not have a stop sign, you will have to stop on the roundabout, and give way.

The size and condition of each road varies from region to region.

Autostrada
Toll motorway, indicated with green road signs and numbers and preceded by 'A'. Generally indicated on maps by bold double black line.

Superstrada
Primary routes usually shown in bold red on maps and marked 'SS'.

Strada Statale
State roads, usually in finer red and also marked 'SS' or 'ss'.

Strada Provinciale
Secondary routes, marked in yellow and with numbers preceded by 'prov'. Marked 'SP'.

Strada Bianca
Unpaved roads, often with no number at all.

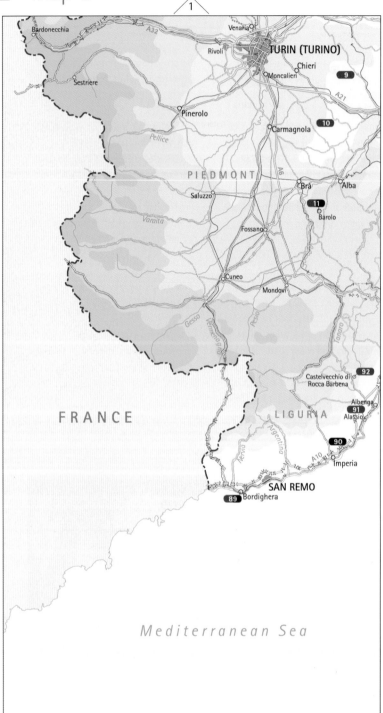

Map 7

31

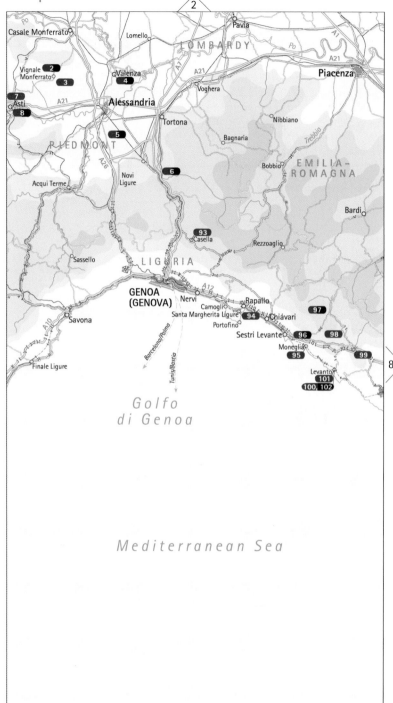

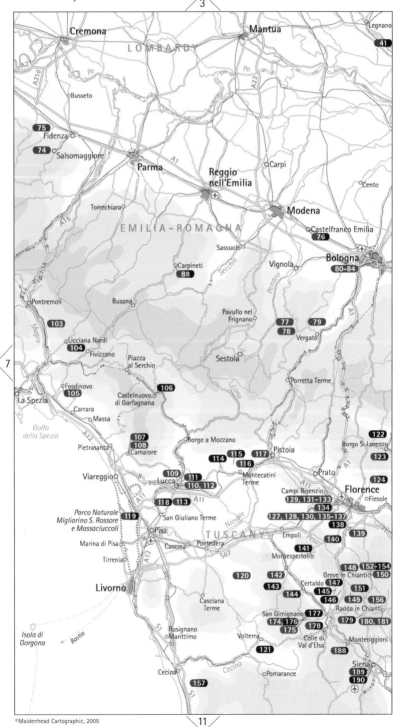

Map 9

33

Map 10

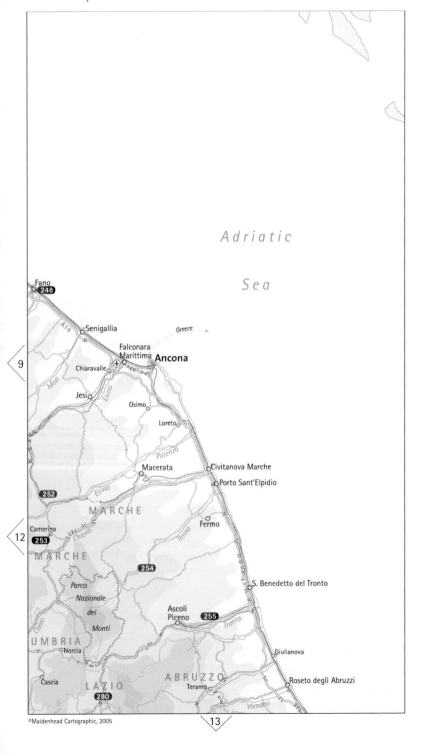

Adriatic

Sea

Fano
248

A14

Senigallia

Greece

Falconara
Marittima **Ancona**

9

Chiaravalle

Misa

Jesi

Esino

Osimo

Loreto

Potenzo

Macerata

Civitanova Marche

Porto Sant'Elpidio

252

Esino

M A R C H E

Camerino

12

253

Chienti

Fermo

Tenna

M A R C H E

254

Parco

Nazionale

S. Benedetto del Tronto

dei

Ascoli
Piceno

255

Monti

Tronto

Corno

U M B R I A

Norcia

Giulianova

Cascia

L A Z I O

A B R U Z Z O

Roseto degli Abruzzi

280

Teramo

Vomano

Public transport

Public transport is excellent in Italy, but do check times. It's frustrating to arrive somewhere at midday just as everything is shutting down for the all-important business of lunch. This is particularly true the further south you go.

Trains, give or take a strike or two (not uncommon), are an efficient and affordable way to get about. City-to-city travel is faster, easier and cheaper by train than car. Ferrovie dello Stato (FS) operates many different types of train: Inter Regionale (slow but cheap), Intercity (excellent) and the fast but relatively costly Eurostar (not to be confused with the London-Paris Eurostar). You pay per mile.

Seat reservations, compulsory on Eurostar, are strongly recommended on all routes at peak hours and in high season. Automatic ticket machines are plentiful in most major stations, but beware, you must validate ('convalida biglietto') your ticket by stamping it, either here or in the machines provided on platforms. If you don't, you'll get a fine.

Urban buses, metros, trains and trams are also reliable and cheap. Buy a day ticket in advance, at a ticket machine or at local news kiosks or *tabacchi*.

For up-to-date timetables, city and regional, go to **www.bus.it** - an all-Italian site – and **www.trenitalia.it** which has an English option.

Cycling

A few mainline and most regional trains in Italy now take bikes, and you need to purchase a ticket for the bike as well as the train. The bike ticket will be valid for 24 hours and can be used anywhere, so buy a few if you plan to cycle for several days. Usually there's a bike symbol on the bike carriage and, if you're lucky, a bike rack too. Hire a bike and pedal round the top of the old city walls of Lucca – or pit yourself against the thrilling terrain of the Amalfi coast. Temperatures are most perfect for cycling in Italy in April, May and October.

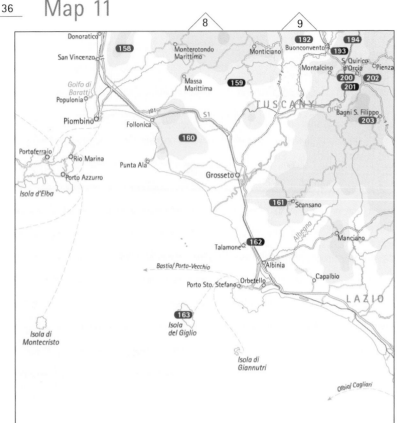

8   9

Donoratico

158

San Vincenzo

Monterotondo Marittimo

Monticiano

Buonconvento **192** **194** **193**

Montalcino

S. Quirico d'Orcia

Pienza

Golfo di Baratti

Populonia

Massa Marittima

159

TUSCANY

200 **202** **201**

Orcia

Bagni S. Filippo **203**

Piombino

Follonica

S1

160

Portoferraio

Rio Marina

Punta Ala

Grosseto

Porto Azzurro

Isola d'Elba

161 Scansano

Albegna

Manciano

Talamone **162**

Bastia/ Porto-Vecchio

Albinia

Porto Sto. Stefano

Orbetello

Capalbio

LAZIO

Isola di Montecristo

163

Isola del Giglio

Isola di Giannutri

Olbio/ Cagliari

Tyrrhenian Sea

Map 12

37

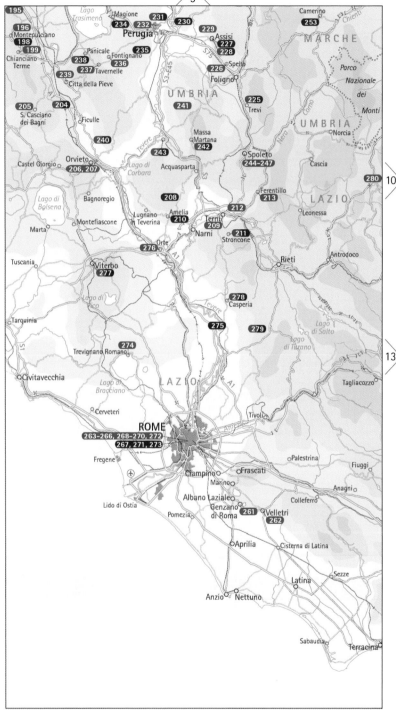

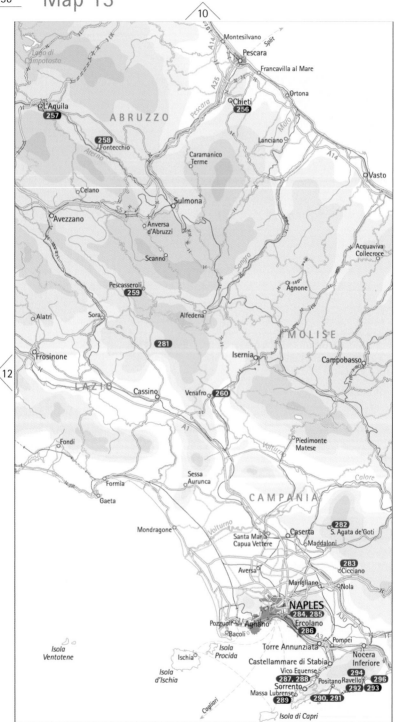

Map 14

39

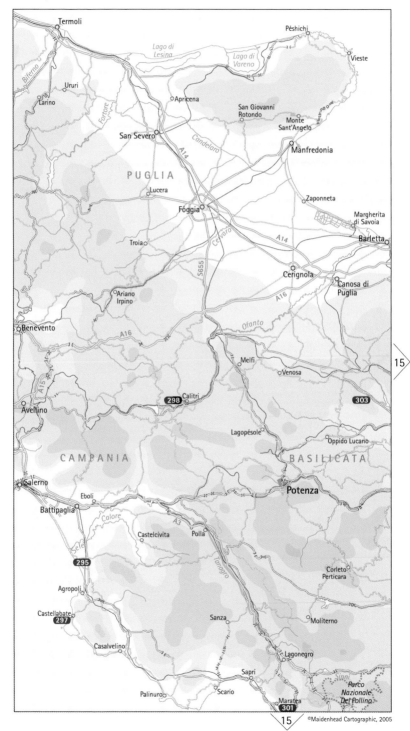

Map 16

41

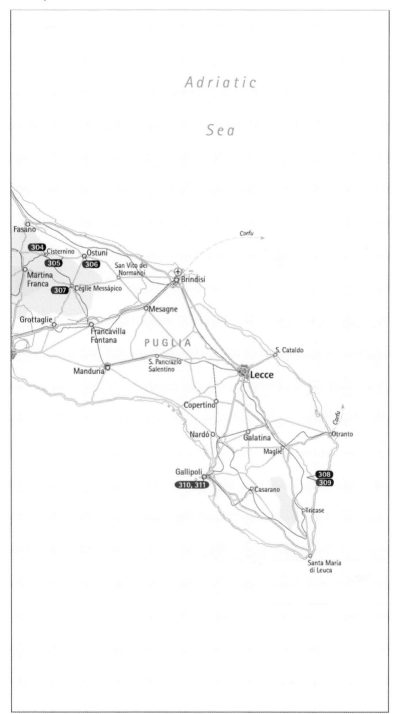

Map 17

Marina di
Fuscaldo

Páola

Rende

Cosenza

Lago
Cecita

Lese

Lago
Arvo

La   Sila

San Giovanni
in Flore

Strongolí

Marina di
Strongoli

Neto

Sta Severina

Crotone

Amantea

Savuto

Petilia
Policastro

Cutro

Isola di
Capo Rizzuto

Nocera
Terinese

Nicastro

Tiriolo

Catanzaro

Cape Rizzuto

Maida

Catanzaro
Lido

CALABRIA

Pizzo

Briático

Vibo Valentia

Soverato

Ancinale

Tropea

Morepotugua

Serra San Bruno

Alfaro

Monasterace Marina

Cinquefrondi

A3

Marro

Palmi

Roccella Iónica

Cosoleto

Gerace

Locri

Gambarie

la Verde

S Agata

18

Mélito di
Porto Salvo

Map 18

43

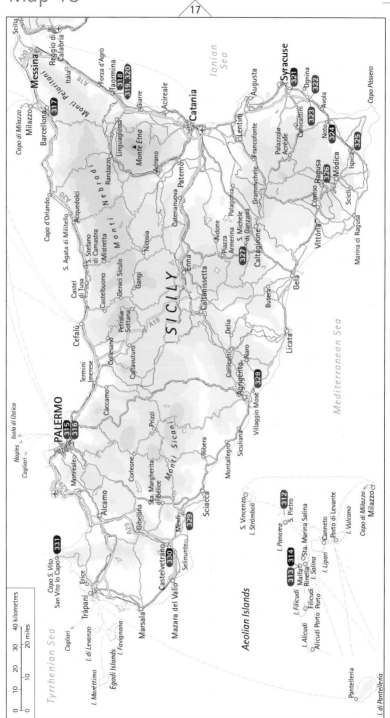

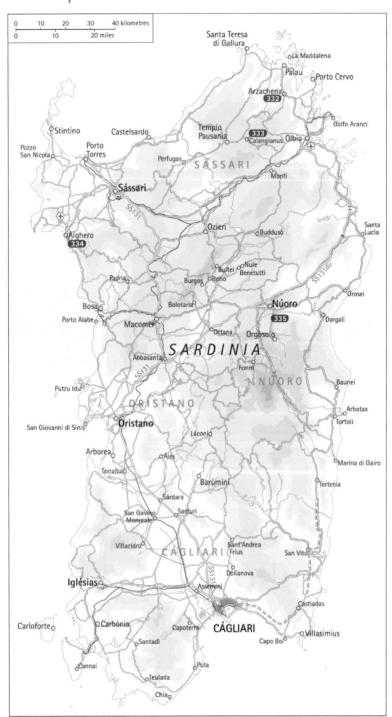

0   10   20   30   40 kilometres
0   10   20 miles

Santa Teresa
di Gallura

La Maddalena
Palau
Porto Cervo
Arzachena **332**

Stintino
Castelsardo
Tempio
Pausania
333
Calangianus Olbia
Golfo Aranci

Pozzo
San Nicola
Porto
Torres
Perfugas
S A S S A R I
Monti

Sássari
SS131

Ozieri
Buddusò
Santa
Lucia

Alghero
334

Padria
Bultei
Nule
Benetutti
Burgos Bono
SS131dir
Orosei

Bosa
Bolotaria
Núoro
Dorgali

Porto Alabe
Macomér
335

Ottana
Orgosolo

Abbasanta
S A R D I N I A
Fonni

Putzu Idu
N N U O R O
Baunei

O R I S T A N O
SS131

San Giovanni di Sinis
Oristano
Arbatax
Tortoli

Láconi

Arborea
Ales
Marina di Gairo

Terralba

Barúmini
Tertenia

Sárdara

San Gavino
Monreale
Samuri

Villacidro
Sant'Andrea
Frius
San Vito
C A G L I A R I

Dolianova
SS131

Iglésias
Assemini
Cástiadas

Carloforte
Carbónia
Capoterra
CAGLIARI
Villasimius
Capo Boi

Santadi

Cannai
Pula

Teulada

Chia

Photo Cascina Motto, entry 1

piedmont
valle d'aosta

Cascina Motto
via Marzabotto 7, 28010 Divignano

Flowers everywhere, spilling from the balcony, filling the patio, clasping the walls of the cottage... wisteria, vines, azaleas, roses. It's an immaculate garden, with lawns, spreading trees, boules court and a discreet summer pool. Roberta's lovely, too, so warm and friendly you are made at once to feel part of the family. They came here years ago – she and David, their daughters, Roberta's parents Sergio and Lilla, four dogs. They clearly love the house, which they've restored and filled with paintings and beautiful things. In a quiet street, in a quiet village, this is a happy and restful place to stay. The twin room has windows facing two ways – over the garden and towards Monte Rosa – plus whitewashed walls, blue cotton rugs, hand-painted beds, books, a comfy sofa, a big bathroom. The cottage, its bedroom in the hayloft, is bright, airy, charming, with country furniture, a well-equipped kitchenette, a balcony. It turns its back on the main house and is completely independent of it. A wonderful area, and the lakes of Orta and Maggiore are a 20-minute drive. *Minimum stay two nights.*

rooms	1 + 1: 1 twin. 1 cottage for 2-4.
price	€70. Cottage €80-€140.
meals	Restaurants 1km.
closed	December-February.
directions	From Milano A4 (Laghi); after Gallarate A26 for Alessandria exit Castelletto Ticino. Signs for Novara SS32, 3rd exit for Divignano (via Boschi di Sopra). At Divignano, 2nd left via Marzabotto.

	Roberta Plevani
tel	+39 0321 995350
fax	+39 0321 995350
email	cascinamotto@interfree.it
web	www.cascinamotto.com

B&B & Self-catering

Map 2 Entry 1

Il Mongetto Dré Castè

via Piave 2, 15049 Vignale Monferrato

The epitome of a grand Italian country house, Il Mongetto shows you two sides
of Italian life. Hidden behind a high wall, through a massive wooden gate…
a handsome 18th-century townhouse. Your jam at breakfast, however, is from
the farm a couple of miles away. Carlo, a moustachioed eccentric with a dry
sense of humour, is a fantastic host and produces wine, vegetables and fruit on his
organically farmed estate. Rooms are huge, old and regal, all frescoed ceilings and
heavy antiques. The two top-floor apartments are just as original, and private, too.
In winter, wood is left dry and chopped for you to burn in the open fireplaces.
In summer, you have breakfast outside on a terrace, as early or as late as you wish,
surrounded by rolling hills. Staff will come to cook you dinner on Friday and
Saturday nights and Sunday lunchtime, using produce from the farm; the food is
delicious. One warning: as the rice fields of Vercelli are not too far away, you will
need to take mosquito cream if the little beasts find you irresistible. *Minimum stay
two nights.*

rooms	3 + 2: 1 double; 2 doubles sharing bath. 2 apartments for 2.
price	€65–€75.
meals	Breakfast €6. Sunday lunch €26. Dinner Friday & Saturday, €26.
closed	Christmas, January, 15-31 August.
directions	In Vignale, through Piazza Mezzarda for Camagna. Entrance 200m on right through large archway with (usually closed) wooden doors.

	Signor Carlo Santopietro
tel	+39 0142 933442
fax	+39 0142 920921
email	info@mongetto.it
web	www.mongetto.it

B&B & Self-catering

Map 7 Entry 2

Cascina Alberta
loc. Ca' Prano 14, 15049 Vignale Monferrato

People rave about this attractive hilltop farmhouse in this famous wine-producing area. Marked by two stately cypress trees, the house is two kilometres from the town centre and has 360° views of the surrounding vineyards and hills – sensational. The business is run on agriturismo lines by smiling, capable Raffaella. Tiled guest bedrooms are extremely pretty: an old marble-topped table here, a country wardrobe there, beds painted duck-egg blue, walls in soft pastel and many pieces beautifully painted by Raffaella. Both the bedrooms and the frescoed dining room lie across the farmyard from the main house; here you dine at your own table on delicious Piedmontese dishes at very reasonable prices, and wines come from the estate – some of them have been aged in wooden barrels and are hard to find outside the area. Raffaella pours huge amounts of energy and love into her farmhouse-cosy *cascina*; she speaks excellent English and is happy to help guests get the most out of this enchanting area. Just an hour's drive from the coast.

rooms	5 doubles.
price	€60.
meals	Dinner €16.
closed	January & August.
directions	From Vignale, follow signs to Camagna. After 2km left at roadside chapel. Cascina Alberta is 400m on right.

	Signora Raffaella de Cristofaro
tel	+39 0142 933313
fax	+39 0142 933313
email	cascinalberta@netcomp.it

Agriturismo

Map 7 Entry 3

Cascina Nuova
strada per Pavia 2, 15048 Valenza

Beyond lightly wooded hills and fertile fields, a mile from thriving Valenza, you arrive to four jaunty silage towers painted in pretty colours, a bed of tall sunflowers and gaggles of chickens. The hard-working owners farm 300 acres of cereals and sunflowers, and have almost achieved their goal of becoming fully organic. There are two B&B rooms in the farmhouse and a further two in the stable block, specially designed for wheelchair use. The apartments are divided between the stables – opening to a lovely long terrace protected by green awnings – and five new designer-chic flats encased in old farm buildings. All are uniformly excellent. If you are self-catering, lively Valenza is nearby and there are organic eggs, vegetables, jams and home-baked breads to buy here. The region is not big on tourism but worth exploring, and you're only an hour from the splendours of Milan, Genoa and Turin. Hikers, bikers and birdwatchers will find plenty to do; families will love the pool, play area and babysitting (must book). *New pool for 2006.*

rooms	5 + 10: 4 doubles, 1 triple. 10 apartments for 2-4.
price	€60–€75. Extra bed €15. Apartments €300–€500 per week.
meals	Breakfast €8 for self-caterers.
closed	Rarely.
directions	From Milano & Casale for Pavia on SS494. Farm on right 1km out of town, after bridge over river.

	Signora Armanda Felli
tel	+39 0131 954763
fax	+39 0131 928553
email	cascinanuova@tin.it
web	www.cascinanuova.com

B&B & Self-catering

Map 7 Entry 4

Agriturismo Tenuta la Camilla

strada Mandrino 29, 15065 Frugarolo

Bowling along flat agricultural land, with crops as high as an elephant's eye… then the high faded ochre walls and the great open gate of the *tenuta* arise to welcome you. Once a refuge for soldiers fleeing the battle of Marengo, the family *masseria* with a hacienda-like feel now offers escape of a different sort. Pia, as warm and hospitable as her parents, oversees the apartments. Heavy front doors lead to light, airy rooms kept cool by ancient walls. Eclectic family furniture, cheerful contemporary cottons, tiled and speckled stone floors, firm beds and immaculate, old fashioned bathrooms, welcome and satisfy. Jugs of flowers and comfortable old sofas and extra beds (some in the sitting rooms) feel homely and uncontrived. As you might expect from the marriage of a young cookery journalist and venerable farm buildings, well-kitted kitchens range from enormous to bijou. En route to the shady garden, a pedigree herd welcomes you with soft sighs and organic charms. Swap deep peace, country smells and the odd mosquito for jaunts to Milan or the coast. Wonderful. *No washing machines.*

rooms	4 apartments: for 4, 5, 6, 8.
price	€300–€650 per week.
meals	Restaurants nearby.
closed	Rarely.
directions	A7, A21, A26 – exit Alessandria or Novi Ligure; follow signs for Bosco Marengo & Frugarolo; to Mandrino; just past Mandrino, signed.

	Pia Scavia
tel	+39 0131 296691
fax	+39 0131 2296032
email	info@agricamilla.com
web	www.agricamilla.com

Agriturismo & Self-catering

Map 7 Entry 5

La Traversina

Cascina La Traversina 109, 15060 Stazzano

Come for the roses – over 180 varieties – and the irises, and the hostas! They are Rosanna's passion. With drowsy shutters, buzzing bees and walls festooned in roses, the house and outbuildings appear to be in a permanent state of siesta. As do the seven cats, basking on warm windowsills and shady terraces. There's a touch of *The Secret Garden* about the half-hidden doors, enticing steps and riotous plants... the air is fragrant with lavender, oregano and roses, many from France. The house and farm, on a wooded hillside, have been in Rosanna's family for nearly 300 years; she gave up a career as an architect to create this paradise 40 minutes from Genoa. Large bedrooms have handsome furniture, books, pictures and a homely charm; bathrooms come with baskets of goodies. Everyone eats together at a long table in the conservatory or outside, where lights glow in the trees at night. Rosanna and Domenico are the friendliest, most delightful hosts and the home-grown food is a revelation: agriturismo at its best. Ask about courses on roses in February and May. *Children over 12 welcome.*

rooms	2 + 4: 1 double, 1 family. 4 apartments: 3 for 2, 1 for 4.
price	€84–€98. Half-board €60–€68 p.p. Apartments €105–€120.
meals	Dinner €20. Restaurant 6km.
closed	Rarely.
directions	A7 Milan-Genova exit Vignole Borbera for Stazzano; 4km; signs for La Traversina.

Rosanna & Domenico Varese

tel	+39 0143 613 77
fax	+39 0143 613 77
email	latraversina@latraversina.com
web	www.latraversina.com

Agriturismo & Self-catering

Map 7 Entry 6

La Violina
fraz. Mombarone 115, Monferrato, 14100 Asti

A frantic twist of the steering wheel, up a narrow winding road, past a few houses and you're there. This rather grand old farmhouse owns all that it surveys: vineyards, olive groves, orchards and, down in the valley, century-old woodland. What to discover first? The exquisite family chapel, the lawns, beds and urns sweeping up to the tennis court and pool? Or the rambling delights of the house: the sitting room with its acres of comfy sofas, thick Persian rugs, billiard table and magazines; the gilded, garlanded music room; the playroom, exercise room and sauna? The food is delicious, a resident chef cooking what is seasonal and best, fresh from the market or organically grown on the estate. The cellars groan with home-produced olive oil and Barbera d'Asti wine, made from the grapes that swell on the sunny hillside. Energetic, artistic, friendly Davide and Carla dine with you. They love antiques, books and art, and the traditional bedrooms, with charming wallpapers and comfortable rugs, reflect their eclectic tastes. Shower rooms are well-equipped. A charming, peaceful haven.

rooms	6: 4 doubles; 1 double, 1 single sharing shower room.
price	€130. Half-board €100 p.p.
meals	Dinner with wine €35-€40.
closed	Never.
directions	Exit Asti/Ovest; follow SS458 Asti-Chivasso; 7km; at roundabout, signed Valmonasca; house signed suddenly on right; climb narrow hill; on right.

	Davide & Carla Palazzetti
tel	+39 0141 294173
email	info@laviolina.it
web	www.laviolina.it

B&B

Map 7 Entry 7

Villa Sampaguita

Bricco Cravera, Valleandona 117, 14100 Asti

Laze in the garden and listen to the crickets. Potter in the woods or orchards and search for fossils. Then, when you're thoroughly rested, sally forth to explore the region's vineyards (Barolo, Barbaresco, Barbera and Moscato are the best known) and wonderful, baroque Turin, a 30-minute drive. The Villa is a modernised 18th-century *cascina* in an 11-hectare farm in the Val de Botto e Valleandona national park. Standing on a ridge just outside medieval Asti, it has fine views of the Monferrato hills – and, on a clear day, the Alps. Tim and Rina have converted their barn into a pleasant guest wing, furnished with fine farmhouse pieces. The bedrooms have French windows and a private balcony; the apartments, on the ground floor, open to verandas. There's also a large guest salon with a wood-burning stove and big windows overlooking the terrace. The area is full of fabulous Piedmontese restaurants but, if you don't feel like eating out, Rina loves cooking and uses home-grown organic produce in her Italian and Asian dishes. She's kind and charming, and Tim is a well-travelled and friendly host.

rooms	4 + 2: 4 doubles. 2 apartments: 1 for 2, 1 for 4.
price	€90-€110. Apartments €120-€160; €700-€1,025 per week.
meals	Dinner with wine €25.
closed	B&B closed 15 December-15 March.
directions	A21 Torino-Piacenza, Asti Ovest exit; 2km in opp. direction to Asti; just after Palucco, right at sign 'Valcoresa'; under autostrada to top of hill; signed right.

Tim Brewer

tel	+39 0141 295802
fax	+39 0141 295970
email	timbrewer@tele2.it.
web	www.villasampaguita.com

Agriturismo & Self-catering

Map 7 Entry 8

Cascina Piola
via Fontana 2, fraz. Serra, 14014 Capriglio

Raffaella and Piero are former teachers who left Turin many years ago to bring up their children in the country. Their village home is a late 19th-century farmhouse hidden away in a walled garden next to the church. The two guest bedrooms are warm, cheerful and homely, and have a country farmhouse feel; you have your own entrance so feel very private. Meals are served in a small guests' dining room at one table, and the food is good and generous – as are your hosts. Raffaella describes her style as regional home cooking and emphasises vegetarian dishes; ingredients, and wine, are entirely organic. With the produce from their smallholding they also make and sell large quantities of chutneys, preserves and jam. Surrounded by flat farmland you are off the beaten tourist track but you'll find plenty to do: walking, biking, horse riding… there are also some lovely old churches and castles to visit. It would be a shame to make this house a mere pit-stop – delightful hosts and good cooking ensure guests return again and again.

rooms	2 doubles, each with separate bath & shower.
price	€62. Half-board €52 p.p.
meals	Lunch or dinner, 5 courses, €27.
closed	15 June–5 July; 24 December–10 January.
directions	A21 exit Villanova d'Asti towards Buttigliera d'Asti to Colle Don Bosco Santuario, then towards Montafia for 1km. House in Serra di Capriglio, by white church.

	Signora Raffaella Firpo
tel	+39 0141 997447
fax	+39 0141 997447
email	cascinapiola@inwind.it

Agriturismo

Map 6 Entry 9

Cascina Papa Mora
via Ferrere 16, 14010 Cellarengo

Come for authentic agriturismo in northern Italy. Adriana runs grandmother's old house with her sister, speaks fluent English and makes you really welcome. The farm produces wine, vegetables and fruit; the pantry overflows with bottles of oil, wine, chutneys and jams. (This is one of Italy's top wine regions for Barbera, Dolcetto, aristocratic Bracchetto, cheap and cheerful Spumante.) We can't say that the farmhouse has been lovingly restored – more razed to the ground and rebuilt, then bedecked with simple stencils of flowers. Bedrooms have no-nonsense 1930s furniture and light floral spreads; those in the roof area, hot in summer, are the nicest. Shower rooms are spotless. Outside, a garden with roses, lavender and herbs slopes to the new pool and the stables. The sisters also run a restaurant here and are passionate about their organic credentials. Dinner is a feast of gnocchi and tagliatelle, pepperoni cream puffs, anchovies in almond sauce; all delicious, and fun. Breakfast on the veranda where the blossom is pretty, the hills surround you, the bread comes fresh from the wood oven.

rooms	6: 3 doubles/twins, 1 triple, 2 quadruples.
price	€60–€70. Triples €70–€85. Quadruples €80–€95. Singles €35–€40. Half-board €50–€60 p.p.
meals	Lunch or dinner €20–€25.
closed	2 January–February.
directions	A21 exit Villanova d'Asti & for Cellarengo. On outskirts of village left into via Ferrere, past small chapel to farm.

Adriana & Maria Teresa Bucco

tel	+39 0141 935126
fax	+39 0141 935444
email	papamora@tin.it
web	www.cascinapapamora.it

Agriturismo

Map 6 Entry 10

Il Gioco dell'Oca
via Crosia 46, 12060 Barolo

Raffaella spent much of her childhood here – the farm was her grandparents'. She is happy to be back, looks after her guests beautifully, feeds them well, and has tampered with the pretty, 18th-century farmhouse as little as possible. The well-worn, welcoming kitchen, much as it must have been 50 years ago, is for you to use as and when you like – the warm hub of a sociable house. Next door is a breakfast room set with little tables, but if it's fine you'll prefer to breakfast in the garden, which is big enough for everyone to find their own secluded corner. The bedrooms are simple and cosy, with family furniture and wooden beds that look as though they've been there forever. Bathrooms are bright and new. One bedroom has a hob, sink and fridge – a bonus if you have little ones with you. The farm, up in the hills near Barolo – a wonderful area for cheeses and wines – produces wine, fruit and hazelnuts. A pity the road is so close but you'll forgive that for the pleasure of staying at such a relaxed, welcoming and thoroughly Italian agriturismo.

rooms	7: 6 doubles/twins, 1 triple.
price	€60-€70. Triple €65-€75.
meals	Restaurant 500m.
closed	January.
directions	From Asti (east) exit autostrada TO-PC. Follow sign for Alba & Barolo. Left 2km before village, 50m on right sign for house.

	Raffaella Pittatore
tel/fax	+39 0173 56206
mobile	+39 338 5999426
email	gioco-delloca@piemonte.com
web	www.gioco-delloca.it

Agriturismo

Map 6 Entry 11

Auberge de la Maison
fraz. Entrèves, 11013 Courmayeur

Mont Blanc, the Grandes Jorasses and the Courmayeur valley – what a setting!
You're in the old part of the village of Val Fenet, three kilometres from
Courmayeur. The Auberge is surrounded by gentle terraces, gardens and meadows
and has a quietly elegant and exclusive feel. Yet it's not in the least intimidating,
thanks to the cheerful (and efficient) staff and friendly feel. Bedrooms are
uncluttered, stylish and comfortable, with mellow colours and lots of space. Many
have a third bed disguised as a sofa; nearly all have a balcony, and views that range
from good to superb. A Tuscan influence is detectable in the décor (the owner is
from Florence); his impressive collection of pictures and prints of Valle d'Aosta,
from old promotional posters to oil paintings, makes a fascinating display on the
walls, while an old, reassembled wooden mountain house is an unusual feature in
the reception/sitting area. The inn has a small fitness centre, too, with a sauna and
hydromassage. Depending on the season, you can fish for trout or play a round of
golf, ski right to the ski lift or don crampons for a winter ascent.

rooms	33: 27 doubles, 3 family rooms, 3 suites.
price	€130-€190. Half-board €185-€240.
meals	Dinner €30.
closed	40 days after end of ski season.
directions	From Courmayeur for Traforo del Monte Bianco, past garage & Entrèves, keep right, signed.

	Leo Garin
tel	+39 0165 869811
fax	+39 0165 869759
email	info@aubergemaison.it
web	www.aubergemaison.it

Les Écureuils

fraz. Homené Dessus 8, 11010 Saint Pierre

No designer chic here, but a hard-working farm, specialising in – and known for – goat's cheese. Going back to the 14th century, the building was a half-way house between the valley and the high alpine pastures. The bedrooms are simple and homely. There are patterned walls and knotted pine, old linen window-hangings and photos showing the farm in different seasons. The dining room, just off the kitchen, is bistro-like; crochet-trimmed shelves carry books and ornaments. Excellent food is presented in a stylish, rustic fashion – everything, apart from the local bread and wine, is home-grown or homemade. (There's a little farm shop, too, where you can stock up on goat's cheese if you haven't overdosed already.) Outside, the garden is steep but the odd chair or bench on the small terraces makes a great place to sit and absorb the glorious views across the Valle d'Aosta. Three generations of the family live here. They are quiet, friendly and immensely committed to what they do. Given time, they'll talk to you about their way of life.

rooms	5: 3 doubles, 1 triple, 1 single.
price	€44-€50.
meals	Dinner €13-€20.
closed	December-January.
directions	From Aosta SS26 for M. Biano. At Sarre right up hill to Ville-sur-Sarre; left signed to Les Écureuils.

	Famiglia Gontier-Ballauri-Moniotto
tel	+39 0165 903831
fax	+39 0165 909849
email	lesecureuils@libero.it
web	www.lesecureuils.it

B&B

Map 1 Entry 13

Photo Albergo Milano, entry 18

lombardy

Villa Simplicitas & Solferino
22028 San Fedele d'Intelvi

The presiding genius behind this quaint, wonderful place is Ulla. Everything about her 19th-century villa is a reflection of her human approach; she's serene, imaginative, unconventional. Bedrooms, in the villa or annexe, are decorated with murals, soft browns and wrought-iron or brass beds; all draw in the grand old sweet-chestnut trees that survey the garden and seem to be a part of the rooms. There's a warm sense of fun glowing in every corner, whether from a dotty old lamp stand – balefully ugly – or from the antique piano and the billiard table that's as old as the house. The food (four courses, no choice), served with understated elegance in the handsome conservatory or on the candlelit terrace, is superb. Above all, there is an abiding impression of deep rural tranquillity; it's worth sacrificing a couple of days of sun-baking on the lake shores to stay here. Strike out from the door on wonderful walks, reach Como in 15 minutes by car. The lakes, with the mountains, are irresistible – and due to the high altitude, you never get too hot at night.

rooms	10 doubles.
price	€94-€140.
meals	Half-board €60-€90 p.p. Full-board €70-€100 p.p.
closed	10 October-April.
directions	From Como, north for Argegno; left thro' San Fedele. After 1st bus station bear left; follow winding road for 2km. Invest in a good map!

Signora Ulla Wagner
tel	+39 031 831132
fax	+39 031 830455
email	info@villasimplicitas.it
web	www.villasimplicitas.it

Hotel

Map 2 Entry 14

Villetta Il Ghiro & Villetta La Vigna
via al Forno 5, Cardano, 22010 Grandola ed Uniti

Wisteria was growing *through* the old convent when Ann and her husband fell in love with it. The roof had fallen in too but, undeterred, they went ahead and turned it into the lovely place it is today. Though you can't see the lake from here, you do get a glimpse of the championship golf course Ann's father-in-law once part-owned – the second oldest in Italy. The apartments are old-fashioned, comfortable, homely and quiet, with large, airy rooms and outside stairs. Il Ghiro is on the first floor of a former hay barn; La Vigna, above the garages, has a second bedroom opening off the first and a little balcony to catch the afternoon sun. Children are welcome but must be supervised in the immaculate lawned gardens because of the pool (which is fenced). There's tennis too. Birdsong is all you hear, vistas all you see, yet you are a short drive from the tourist bustle of Menaggio and Como. The position is wonderful, on the isthmus between Lakes Lugano and Como, on the edge of a cobbled village, encircled by mountains, meadows, hamlets and winding country lanes. *Minimum stay one week.*

rooms	2 apartments: 1 for 2, 1 for 4-8.
price	Apartment for 2, €428-€852. Apartment for 4-8, €857-€2,314. Prices per week.
meals	Self-catering. Restaurants 5-minute walk.
closed	October-April.
directions	From Menaggio N340 for Porlezza to Grandola, towards Porlezza & Lugano. Right at bakery; immediately right for Cardano. Right into via al Forno.

	Mrs Ann Dexter
tel	+39 0344 32740
fax	+39 0344 30206
email	ann.dexter@libero.it

Alberghetto La Marianna

via Regina 57, 22011 Cadenabbia di Griante

Paola understands the needs of the modestly-heeled traveller like no other: she and her family ran one of Italy's most popular youth hostels for 20 years. Now they've bought this lakeside villa and set it up for B&B. It has been simply modernised and redecorated and has a relaxing feel. Bedrooms are fresh and functional, with cheerfully tiled shower rooms and lakeside views. Some have balconies, one has its own little terrace; a road runs between you and the busy lake; if you're a light sleeper, it might be worth giving up those watery views for a room at the back, at least in summer. Paola is a delight and, in her own words, treats guests as friends. Breakfasts include homemade bread, cakes and jams; she's also a good cook and a "mistress of desserts" – try them out in the restaurant for dinner (run by husband Ty and chef Antonio). You won't be short of advice here on things to do: visits to gardens and villas, boat tours to Isola Comacina, day trips to St Moritz and the Engadine. Or simply dream away the hours on the terrace that juts onto the shimmering lake.

rooms	8: 7 doubles, 1 single.
price	€77-€83. Single €58-€64.
meals	Dinner with wine €30.
closed	Mid-November-mid-March. Open 26 December-6 January.
directions	From Como on west lakeside road to Cadenabbia 30km, 300m after ferry port.

Paola Cioccarelli

tel	+39 0344 43095
fax	+39 0344 43095
email	inn@la-marianna.com
web	www.la-marianna.com

B&B

Map 2 Entry 16

Albergo Olivedo
Piazza Martiri 4, 23829 Varenna

Laura's 'Liberty' style hotel, soft orange-hued, with balconies and Art Nouveau lamps, has a jaunty, independent air. A friendly little reception with burr maple counter and speckled floor would grace a French pension. A chess board waits on the small landing sitting area. Polished parquet floors, grandmother's furniture with starched cotton cloths, firm upright beds and wonderful views over the lake are redolent of an early 19th-century grand tour. But the excellent shower rooms are strictly modern. A few steps away, the family's latest acquisition, the classic, 19th-century Villa Toretta, sits above the harbour. Here, frescoes, decorative iron staircase and lofty ceilings have been carefully restored. Traditional tiles, handsome beds and fine old furniture give these lakeside rooms a distinctive, elegant air. Stroll to the Olivedo for meals – Laura's brother is the chef. Fresh, local food is served on the hotel pavement or in the dining room overlooking the lively harbour and the breezy little Como ferry. The halcyon days of 'afternoon tea' may be gone, but the welcome is warm and timeless.

rooms	14 doubles.
	Villa Torretta: 5 doubles.
price	€100–€130.
meals	Half-board €150–€180 for two.
closed	2 November–20 December.
directions	From the north, SP72 from Colico to Varenna.

	Laura Colombo
tel	+39 0341 830115
fax	+39 0341 830115
email	olivedo@aruba.it
web	www.olivedo.it

Hotel

Map 2 Entry 17

Albergo Milano
via XX Settembre 29, 23829 Varenna

Colourwashed houses cluster round the church on a little, rocky promontory. The lake laps gently on three sides; on the fourth, tree-covered mountain slopes rear steeply upwards. Wander along a cobbled street, catching glimpses of the lake down every side alley, and you come to Albergo Milano, smack on the waterfront. It's pretty, traditional, disarmingly small, and Bettina and Egidio are engaging hosts, thrilled to be running their own little hotel. Everywhere is freshly and stylishly furnished, with dashes of colour to add warmth and some lovely country furniture. Each bedroom is different, each with a balcony or terrace and a lake view. The dining room has been sympathetically re-tiled, and its big new windows open onto a wonderful wide terrace, where you eat out on fine days, the lake stirring beside you. A step away, in the old part of town, are a charming new suite with great views and an apartment with kitchenette and living room. Bettina is a mine of information about this area – so near Lake Como – and there's a regular train service into Bergamo and Milan. A little gem.

rooms	9 + 1: 8 doubles, 1 suite for 4. 1 apartment for 4.
price	€115-€145. Apartment €100-€110 for 2.
meals	Dinner €25.
closed	December-February.
directions	From Lecco SS36 for Sondrio; 1st exit for Abbadia Lariana. After 15km, before tunnel, left for Varenna.

	Bettina & Egidio Mallone
tel	+39 0341 830298
fax	+39 0341 830061
email	hotelmilano@varenna.net
web	www.varenna.net

Hotel & Self-catering

Map 2 Entry 18

Il Torchio

via Ghislanzoni 24, loc. Vescogna, 23885 Calco

Marcella's happy personality fills the house with good cheer. She and Franco are artists – she an animator, he a painter; if you like the bohemian life you will like it here. Franco also has an antiquarian bookshop in Milan, which explains all the books in the sitting room. Their home began life in 1600 as the stables of the noble Calchi family; you enter through a fine stone archway into a courtyard. Franco's bold paintings adorn the walls and every corner is crammed with curios that Marcella has picked up on her flea market forays. Bedrooms are endearingly old-fashioned – no frills but good, comfortable beds. The big, private suite is entered via French windows, and has green views down to Calco. There's a huge, comfortable bed, family photos on the walls, and a cabinet filled with children's old toys. The bathrooms are basic with lovely hand-painted tiles. The whole family is a delight, including the cats, and Marcella's cooking is superb. Canoe or ski (a one-hour drive), or visit Verona, Lake Como and the chic shops of Milan.

rooms	3: 1 suite with bath; 2 doubles sharing bath.
price	€52. Suite €67.
meals	Dinner €15, on request.
closed	Rarely.
directions	From Calco right at lights after garage for Corso Italia. Right via Ghislanzoni. At top, drive on right of right-hand turn; 100m, 2nd left (signed Vescogna). On left.

	Signora Marcella Pisacane
tel	+39 039 9274294
fax	+39 039 508724
email	il_torchio@hotmail.com

B&B

Map 2 Entry 19

Casa Clelia
via Corna 1/3, 24039 Sotto il Monte Giovanni XXIII

The hotel has been sculpted out of the 11th-century convent, using the principles of eco-bio architecture. Cows peer from sheds as you arrive, chickens, geese and sheep bustle – this is a working farm. The main house stands proud against wooded hills and beyond are convent, outhouses, orchards and barns. Rosanna is a dear and looks after you as well as she looks after her young family. She is a talented cook and one of her treats is her taster menu – your chance to sample, guilt-free, several delicacies all at once. The bedrooms, a good size, are stunning and warmly original, all wood, stone and bold colours; bathrooms are modern, lighting subtle. Heat comes from a woodburner integrated with solar panels; cork and coconut ensure the sound-proofing of walls. There are three resident children, so your own will be welcome, free to run wild in the gardens, orchards and eight hectares of woods. Hard to imagine a more wonderful place for families… or for a get-away-from-it-all weekend. There's horse riding nearby, too.

rooms	10: 8 doubles, 2 triples.
price	€85–€100.
meals	Lunch or dinner, with wine €15–€29. Restaurant closed Monday.
closed	Rarely.
directions	Exit A4 at Capriate to Sotto il Monte. Follow yellow signs to Casa Clelia.

Signora Rosanna Minonzio

tel	+39 035 799133
fax	+39 035 791788
email	info@casaclelia.com
web	www.casaclelia.com

Agriturismo

Map 2 Entry 20

La Dolce Vite

via Cola di Rienzo 39, 20144 Milan

Enrica welcomes you with a big wide smile to her handsome 1920s villa
(a rare sight on this well-heeled street of apartment buildings), hands you a
key and dashes out to her yellow Smart Car – just ahead of the traffic warden.
The housekeeper steps in and your heart lifts as you enter the hall, then the big
sitting rooms, with views to the rose-spilled terrace and trees in the back garden.
Light floods the stairwell from a glass dome above, bouncing off the ochre
polished plaster walls and stone stairs. And up to Japanese-styled bedrooms
on the top floor, tucked under the sloping roof (warm in summer). Though not
big, these rooms, and their smart shower rooms recently designed by an architect,
have a restful simplicity. Downstairs, loaded bookcases, walls hung with 20th-
century paintings and big, inviting, cotton-covered sofas to rest in. Breakfast, as an
Italian, on good coffee, sweet bread and *marmellata*. Business people, artists,
designers and travellers would love it here. And if you really want to feel at home,
Enrica's gentle shaggy dog is always ready for a run! *Metro 12-minute walk.*

rooms	3 doubles.
price	€110–€120. Singles €75.
meals	Lots of restaurants nearby.
closed	August.
directions	Via Cola di Rienzo is east of Piazza Napoli in the Solari Zona.

	Enrica Weiss
tel/fax	+39 02 48952808
mobile	+39 347 3773044
email	info@ladolcevite.net
web	www.ladolcevite.net

B&B

Map 2 Entry 21

B&B Milan

via Vetta d'Italia 14, Zona Fiera, 20144 Milan

Swapping the joys of agriturismo in Liguria for the metropolitan pleasures of her native Milan, Donata recently opened her new terraced house as a B&B. Young Milanese have converted these flat-fronted houses, with their painted façades and tiny front gardens, into elegantly simple homes. Number 14 feels friendly and quiet and behind it, a patchwork oasis of small gardens gives a sense of neighbourly intimacy. Strong clear colours, high ceilings, parquet floors and modern-classic furniture make for fresh, cheerful and arty bedrooms. Zippy yellow and purple rubber flooring, good lighting and powerful showers start the day. Then it's down to the simply chic kitchen and Donata`s fresh cakes, breads and steaming coffee served in the bamboo-planted courtyard. Catch a bus and head to Piazza del Duomo or to the haute couture of Via della Spiga; window shopping and people gazing... such are the joys of high-fashion Milan. If not planning a night at La Scala, then enjoy a glass of wine with your vivacious and kind hostess in the lovely brick-vaulted sitting room before heading off for dinner.

rooms	3 doubles.
price	€110–€140. Singles €75.
meals	Resturants nearby.
closed	August.
directions	From San Agostino station Metro MM2; walk through Parco Solari; follow via Dezza until Piazza Versuvio and onto via Vetta d'Italia (10-15 min walk).

	Donata Giovannetti
tel/fax	+39 02468267
mobile	+39 333 8396441
email	info@bedandbread.it
web	www.bedandbread.it

B&B

Map 2 Entry 22

Antica Locanda dei Mercanti

via San Tomaso 6, 20123 Milan

Entering the gloomy, cavernous courtyard, you wouldn't imagine the lightness and charm of this small, discreet boutique hotel on the second floor of an 18th-century building in the heart of Milan. Heavy glass doors slide open to a simple reception where chic Italians and visitors mingle; young staff whisk you off to rooms whose individuality and style promise country-house comfort rather than the spartan modernity associated with this energetic city. This is an enterprise run by real people with passion. From the smallest room with its elegant Milanese fabrics and wicker chair with cherry striped and piped cushions to the largest, airy room with its muslin-hung four-poster, terrace, olive tree and scented climbers, each space surprises. Fine linen, deep mattresses, dramatic murals, fresh posies, stacks of magazines, small, gleaming shower rooms – and, soon, ceiling fans giving way to air conditioning: each room bears the distinctive hallmark of Paola, the engaging and energetic owner. No communal space, so breakfast is delivered to your room. Chic simplicity, and La Scala a heart beat away.

rooms	14: 13 doubles, 1 suite.
price	€129-€165. Suite €275.
meals	Breakfast €10. Lovely restaurants nearby.
closed	Rarely.
directions	Via S. Tomaso is a small street off via Dante, halfway between the Duomo and Piazza Castello. No sign, just a brass plate.

tel	+39 02 8054080
fax	+39 02 8054090
email	locanda@locanda.it
web	www.locanda.it

Hotel

Map 2 Entry 23

Hotel du Lac

via Colletta 21, 25084 Villa di Gargnano

The hotel oozes old-fashioned charm. A 1900s townhouse, it shares the same street as the villa from where D H Lawrence eulogised about the "milky lake" – Lake Garda. The ox-blood façade with white relief and green shutters is as striking as the view from the patio that overhangs the water; you can swim from here. Valerio's grandparents lived in the house until 1959 and much of their furniture remains. The family is charming and could not be more helpful. Roomy bedrooms are wonderfully old-fashioned with big beds and wardrobes, Thirties' lights and polished terrazzo floors; beds are deeply comfortable and dressed in crisp cotton. Six rooms look onto the lake and have small balconies; others have terraces. The dining room, around a central courtyard with a palm that disappears into the clouds, looks directly onto the water. You can also dine upstairs on the open terrace, where metal tables and chairs are shaded by an arbour of kiwi – a magical spot at night, the water lapping below, the lights twinkling in the distance. There's even a small music room with a piano to play – guests sometimes do.

rooms	12 doubles.
price	€90–€120.
meals	Restaurant à la carte, from €35.
closed	November–mid March. Out of season call +39 0365 71269.
directions	In Riva del Garda, SS '45 bis' for Limone-Gargnano; 400m after Erg petrol station, slip road to lake & left into via Colletta. Parking 100m from hotel, left at the 'Comunale' car park.

Signor Valerio Arosio

tel	+39 0365 71107
fax	+39 0365 71055
email	info@hotel-dulac.it
web	www.hotel-dulac.it

Hotel

Map 3 Entry 24

Hotel Gardenia al Lago
via Colletta 53, 25084 Villa di Gargnano

Jasmine-scented gardens and green lawns reach to Lake Garda's edge; an immaculate terrace makes the most of the views. The hotel stands, a feast of colour and design, against the steep, wooded foothills of Mount Baldo. It was bought by the Arosio family as a summer home in 1925. They were piano-makers from Lodi – note the original piano in the music room – and in the 1950s turned the house into a guesthouse. Today it is a small, restful, civilised hotel. The bedrooms have been renovated – some frescoes being uncovered in the process – and are beautiful, with distinctive Empire antiques, exquisite floor tiles and muslin billowing at French windows. Many have balconies or terraces; bathrooms are Edwardian-style and superior. The dining room has a more Sixties flavour and in summer you eat under the trees, by candlelight. The entire family – parents and sons – are delightful, and many guests return. Lemon and olive trees surround you – they produce wonderful olive oil – and a grassed garden hugs the lakeside. Take a dip off the small beach further along: the water is the purest in Italy.

rooms	25 doubles.
price	€100-€206. Singles €70-€123.
meals	Dinner €30.
closed	First week of November-week before Easter. Out of season call +39 0365 71269
directions	In Riva del Garda, SS '45 bis' for Limone-Gargnano; 400m after Erg petrol station, slip road to lake & left into via Colletta. Parking 100m from hotel, left at the 'Comunale' car park.

	Giorgio & Andrea Arosio
tel	+39 0365 71195
fax	+39 0365 72594
email	info@hotel-gardenia.it
web	www.hotel-gardenia.it

Hotel

Map 3 Entry 25

Dimora Bolsone

via Panoramica 23, 25083 Gardone Riviera

Film-like, the lake glitters between the cypress trees – an expanse of blue far below. Enjoy it as Catia, Raffaele and Rocky the spaniel settle you on the terrace with an elderflower cordial. She is slight and thoughtful, he is an importer of Amazonian fish, economist, lecturer, sailor, antique collector, big game hunter and green aficionado – and relishes showing you around the 46 acres of remarkable terraced garden. The 15th-century house reposes gracefully among its stone steps, flower-covered loggias and lemon trees; step inside to a cool, ordered calm. Big, dark, immaculate bedrooms have light polished wooden floors, soft washed walls and delicious linen. All are different – gilt cornices and flirty, feminine rococo in one, sober masculinity and a high 15th-century bed in another. Start the day feasting on almond cookies, tortes, local cheeses, cold meats and… homemade ice cream. Later retire to a sitting room/library with green leather armchairs and vast stone fireplace. An essay in perfection and a feast for the senses: the creation of exceptional owners. *Children over 12 welcome. Minimum stay two nights.*

rooms	5 doubles.
price	€190. Singles €160.
meals	Restaurants nearby.
closed	30 November–28 February.
directions	A4 exit Desenzano del Garda or Brescia Est. Take 45 Bis for Gardone Riviera. Left at Il Vittoriale, signed San Michaele; 2km, on left.

	Raffaele & Catia Bonaspetti
tel	+39 0365 21022
fax	+39 0365 293042
email	info@dimorabolsone.it
web	www.dimorabolsone.it

B&B

Map 3 Entry 26

Villa San Pietro
via San Pietro 25, 25018 Montichiari

A splendid 17th-century home. Annamaria, warm, vivacious, multi-lingual, is married to Jacques, French and charming; they have a young child, and Anna's parents live in self-contained splendour at the far end. A rather grand name for a house that is one of a terrace, but once inside you realise why we have included it here. It is an immaculate home and no expense has been spared. There are oak beams, ancient brick floors, fine family antiques, floral fabrics, not a speck of dust. Guests have their own sitting room with a frescoed ceiling, and the bedrooms are delightful. Another exceptional thing about the house is the large garden and terrace, and there is also a pretty ground-floor loggia for memorable meals (Annamaria's dinners are sophisticated regional affairs, we are told.) You are close to the town centre yet in a quiet road, and Montichiari is perfectly sited for forays into Garda, Brescia, Verona and Venice. Your hosts, who own a cosmetic company, can even arrange massages and facials. *Minimum stay two nights.*

rooms	5 doubles.
price	€95-€100. Singles €80. Extra bed €20.
meals	Dinner with wine, 5 courses, €25-€30.
closed	Rarely.
directions	From Milan motorway A4 exit Brescia east towards Montichiari, city centre & Duomo. Via S. Pietro leads off corner of central piazza.

Jacques & Annamaria Ducroz

tel	+39 030 961232
fax	+39 030 9981098
email	villasanpietro@hotmail.com
web	www.abedandbreakfastinitaly.com

B&B

Map 3 Entry 27

Tenuta Le Sorgive - Le Volpi
via Piridello 6, 46040 Solferino

Although one cannot deny the beauty of Lake Garda, it's a relief to escape to the open and unpopulated land of Lombardy. This 19th-century *cascina* with ochre-washed façade and green shutters has been in the Serenelli family for two generations. The exterior, crowned with pierced dovecote and flanked by a carriage house and stables with wide open arches, remains impressive, even if the breakfast area is unexciting and some character has been lost during restoration. Le Sorgive is still a working 28-hectare family farm with vines, cereal crops and livestock; the big rooms, with wooden rafters, are a mix of old and new. Some have attractive, metalwork beds, others a balcony; two have a mezzanine with beds for the children. All are crisp and clean. This is a great place for families to visit as there's so much to do: horse riding and mountain biking from the farm, go-karting and archery nearby, watersports at Garda. There's also a large gym and a pool. Vittorio's sister has a *cascina* down the road where you can sample gnocchi, Mantovan sausages and mouthwatering fruit tarts.

rooms	8 + 2: 8 twins/doubles. 2 apartments for 4.
price	€85–€105. Apartments €516–€845 per week.
meals	Dinner with wine €15–€23. Restaurant closed January & Monday-Tuesday.
closed	Rarely.
directions	Exit A4 Milano-Venezia at Desenzano for Castiglione & then Mantova. Solferino signed to left. House on left before town.

Signor Vittorio Serenelli

tel	+39 0376 854252
fax	+39 0376 855256
email	info@lesorgive.it
web	www.lesorgive.it

B&B & Self-catering

Map 3 Entry 28

Trebisonda

via Tononi 100, loc. Trebisonda, 46040 Monzambano

Enrico and Valeria have exchanged the rat race for the country life amid olive and peach groves and three hectares of prairie. They are full of enthusiasm for this place and keen to share its beauty. The farmhouse, which dates back to the 15th century, has been renovated and decorated with understated good taste. Apartments on the first-floor of the stables (horses sometimes stabled below) are accessible directly from the garden. Big and light, they have white walls and the original tiled floors. Fabrics and towels are cream and white, the furniture a mix of antique, Conran and flea-market finds. Shower rooms are gorgeous, old railway sleepers set against white walls make for a perfect ascent to beds upstairs, kitchens are simple but well-equipped. Enrico and Valeria breed horses, and will take you to meet the foals. Breakfast is an array of organic honeys and homemade jams, served in the main house. Cycle along the Mincio river, visit Lake Garda, Mantova or Venice, play golf… or stay here and glory in the views. *Minimum stay two nights.*

rooms	3 apartments: 2 for 2 + 2; 1 for 4.
price	€75 for 2. €95 for 3. €120 for 4.
meals	Trattoria nearby.
closed	Rarely.
directions	From autostrada Milano-Venezia exit Peschiera del Garda & Valeggio. Cross old bridge in Borghetto, direction Solferino. Signed, after 3km.

	Signora Valeria Moretti
tel/fax	+39 0376 809381
mobile	+39 335 647 7885
email	trebisonda@libero.it
web	www.trebisonda.com

B&B & Self-catering

Map 3 Entry 29

Photo Ploerr, entry 31

trentino-alto-adige

Relais & Châteaux Hotel Castel Fragsburg

via Fragsburger Strasse 3, 39012 Merano

Stay in May and you'll see and smell the glory of the wisteria that drapes itself the length of the loggia where meals are served. The Fragsburg, built as a shooting lodge for the local gentry, perches on the side of a wooded hill with a crystal-clear view across the valley – mountains and valley unfurl. Perhaps the most magnificent spot from which to enjoy the view is the pool. Sun yourself on the screened deck on a hot day, then wander the grounds, beautiful with sub-tropical trees, surrounded by vineyards. Big bedrooms and huge suites have been redecorated and the combination of rugs, wood and some antique painted headboards softens any newness. Beds are deeply inviting with piles of pillows; white bathrooms are stunning. And then there's the wellness centre, studded with treatments, purifying products, aromatic smells and white robes. The whole feel of the place is Tyrolean, from the staff costumes to the delicious teatime strüdel. The fairytale castles and scenery of this northern region are not to be missed, and the Ortner family ensure you get the most out of your stay. Truly delightful.

rooms	20: 6 doubles, 14 suites.
price	€200-€309.
	Half-board €120-€160 p.p.
meals	Dinner à la carte, from €40.
closed	9 November-25 March.
directions	Exit A22 Bolzano Sud; Merano Sud. Right to Merano; 1.5km; right at Shell station to Scenna. 2.5km on, bridge on right, signed Labers; over and 5km on.

Signor Alexander Ortner

tel	+39 0473 244071
fax	+39 0473 244493
email	info@fragsburg.com
web	www.fragsburg.com

Hotel

Map 3 Entry 30

Ploerr

Oberinn 45, 39050 Renon

Heidi country – and if gentle walks with heavenly views, fresh home cooking and a pack of cards for entertainment are what make your holiday perfect, then you'll love it here. The Vigl family run the guest house and nine-hectare farm with quiet efficiency. Franz milks the cows, sitting on a one-legged stool, Maria Luisa cooks for the trattoria, son Herbert looks after the guests – beautifully. Rooms are simple with spotless white duvets on new pine beds and all but one have a balcony and a view. Shower rooms are spotless – but take a big fluffy towel if you can't live without one! For breakfast there are their own cheese and eggs, served outside in the fresh mountain air; this is also a popular lunch stop for walkers. Pretty alpine tables and cushioned benches are yours for the evening. Children love it here, with the endless fields, the cows with their bells, the two wooden swings in the garden. Gentle Franz was anxious to emphasise that the family still think of themselves as farmers, and they open their house to guests in the best tradition of hospitality. *Minimum stay three nights*.

rooms	11: 10 doubles, 1 single.
price	€48. Half-board €35 p.p.
meals	Breakfast €9.
	Lunch or dinner, 3 courses, €13.
closed	10 January–20 February.
directions	Exit A22 at Bolzano Nord; to Renon. At Colalbo left before petrol station & left to Anna di Sopra. After 4km, signed.

Signor Herbert Vigl

tel	+39 0471 602118
fax	+39 0471 602251
email	berggasthof@ploerr.com
web	www.ploerr.com

Hotel

Map 4 Entry 31

Hotel Cavallino D'Oro

Piazza Kraus 1, 39040 Castelrotto

The village is postcard Tyrolean, and the Little Gold Horse has been welcoming travellers for 680 years. The market still runs every Friday in summer: farmers set up their stalls at the foot of the 18th-century bell tower (that still chimes through the night!). This was Austria not so very long ago: the local customs are still alive, and regular concerts take place at the inn over dinner. Bedrooms are mostly delightful, though a few have roof lights only. Others look onto the medieval square, the best have balconies with incredible views. There's a fascinating mix of antique country beds – some hand-decorated, some four-poster, some both. Many of the doors are painted, as are the beams in the green and peach sitting room; room 9 has the original ceiling. Dine in the sparkling dining room; breakfast in the rustic *stübe*, a wood-panelled room with geraniums at the window and check tablecloths. Susanna and Stefan are as friendly as they are efficient. Go swimming, walking and biking in summer, sleigh riding and skiing in winter, and you can take the free shuttle to the new cable car and Alpe di Siusi.

rooms	18: 5 doubles, 2 twins, 4 triples, 4 singles, 3 suites.
price	€80. Suites €100. Singles €50. Half-board €50-€75 p.p.
meals	Lunch €12. Dinner €22.
closed	November.
directions	A22 motorway, exit Bolzano Nord. Castelrotto signed at exit. Hotel in market square in town centre.

	Susanna & Stefan Urthaler
tel	+39 0471 706337
fax	+39 0471 707172
email	cavallino@cavallino.it
web	www.cavallino.it

Hotel

Map 4 Entry 32

Schwarz Adler Turm Hotel

Kirchgasse 2, 39040 Kurtatsch/Cortaccia

All around are the soaring, craggy Dolomites – nothing like them to give a sobering perspective on man's place in nature's scheme. If you do feel overawed, you'll be soothed on arrival – Manfred, Sonja and their staff are so delighted to see you, so eager to do all they can to please. Though the hotel is young, it is a faithful reproduction of a 16th-century manor house and blends in well with the village. Its roomy, light bedrooms are carpeted and hotel-comfortable, and have glorious alpine views. Each has a loggia, balcony or direct access to the garden. The pretty village of Cortaccia (known as 'Kurtasch' by the locals) stands at 300 metres and looks down over a wide valley floor studded with orchards. This was Austria (the area turned Italian in 1919) and the hotel's cuisine reflects this – a tour de force of gourmet Italian and South Tyrolen dishes. You could complete the soothing process by a visit to the Verona Opera Festival; the town is just an hour's drive away and the hotel will arrange tickets – and a bus to get you there.

rooms	24 doubles.
price	€120–€160.
meals	Half-board €138–€178.
closed	22-27 December; 2 weeks January.
directions	From A22 exit Egna/Ora. On for 8km for Termeno; left for Cortaccia; signed.

	Famiglia Pomella
tel	+39 0471 880600
fax	+39 0471 880601
email	info@turmhotel.it
web	www.turmhotel.it

Hotel

Map 3 Entry 33

Hotel Berghofer
Bampi Zeno, Oberradein 54, 39040 Radein

At the end of the meandering track: birdsong and fir trees, cowbells and meadows, the scent of larch and pine. The tranquillity continues: there are shelves of books and magazines beside the fire, light modern furniture, an abundance of flowers, a cuckoo clock to tick away the hours. Bedrooms, named after the peaks you can see from large windows, have glazed doors leading to a private balcony each, and breathtaking Dolomites views. Rugs are scattered, pale pine floors and light walls are offset with painted wardrobes and stencilled borders. Some rooms have an extra store room, a few can be linked – ideal for a family; all have a separate seating area and a large bathroom. Dine in the charming 1450 *stübe*, purchased from a local farmer and painstakingly moved, timber by timber, up the hill. The restaurant displays a wonderful 18th-century *stufa* (stove); the food is regional and stylish. Ski in winter, hike among the alpine flowers in summer, return to a massage or hay-sauna, catch the sun set over the mountain.

rooms	13: 12 suites for 2, 1 chalet for 4.
price	Half-board €184–€216 for two.
meals	Half-board only. Restaurant closed Tuesdays.
closed	Certain weeks in February, May & November.
directions	A22 exit Neumarkt/Auer; SS48 to Kaltenbrunn; 200m after garage, left for Radein; on to Oberradein; hotel signed.

	Markus Waldthaler
tel	+39 0471 887150
fax	+39 0471 887069
email	info@berghofer.it
web	www.berghofer.it

Hotel

Map 4 Entry 34

Bio-Hotel Hermitage

via Castelletto Inferiore 69, 38084 Madonna di Campiglio

It's not often that a bio-hotel comes with such a splash of luxury. Built a century ago, the old Hermitage has been entirely refashioned — with a modern 'eco' eye and a flourish of decorative turret. A wooden floor spans the reception area; behind is a vast and comfortable living room. A Tyrolean-tiled woodburner dominates the centre; windows open onto a balcony with the best views in the Alps. You eat at red-clothed tables on Trentino dishes and homemade pasta in the *stübe*, with its lovely panelled ceiling of old, recycled wood. The main restaurant is larger but as beautiful. Bedrooms are serene, some are under the eaves, most have a balcony and the suites are huge. Wooden floors are softened by Persian rugs or pale carpets from Argentina, curtains and bedspreads are prettily checked. There's a superb wellness centre and an indoor pool with a ceiling that sparkles. Bars and chic boutiques are a ten-minute walk, and the hotel has its own bus that shuttles you to the slopes. Santa tips up at Christmas distributing presents for the children from a little cabin at the end of the garden.

rooms	25: 18 doubles/twins, 7 suites for 3-4.
price	Half-board €70-€170 p.p.
meals	Half-board only.
closed	May & October-November.
directions	Exit A22 St Mich & Mezz for Madonna di Campiglio for 75km; Madonna bypass through mountain; take next exit. Hotel signed on left.

	Famiglia Maffei
tel	+39 0465 441558
fax	+39 0465 441618
email	info@biohotelhermitage.it
web	www.biohotelhermitage.it

Hotel

Map 3 Entry 35

Photo Hotel Villa Alberti, entry 46

veneto
fruili-venezia
giulia

All'Eremo Relais

strada delle Rocca 2, loc. Casetta, 37011 Bardolino

Far from the madding crowds, you are ensconced in an Italian family's solid, 1970s farmhouse overlooking Lake Garda. In true Italian style, Mamma and daughter are in the kitchen baking brioche for breakfast; Papa snoozes in the chair. The downstairs, open-plan room is the heart of the house, all chunky beams, wall paintings and agrarian artefacts. Pleasingly cluttered, somewhat chaotic, this is where you are welcomed by young, enthusiastic Emma, her parents and the family's cats. Bedrooms are a good size and clean, the slightly smaller one trumpeting the best view. Some are a touch 'retro' with green fabric wallpapers and the odd white plastic mirror, but all have stripped floors, shutters and comfortable, crisp-cottoned beds. The parents sleep on the same level as the guests; Emma is above. One double is en suite, the others share a shower room. Take breakfast on the terrace, forget the plastic chairs and absorb the unfolding landscape that reaches from the vineyards to the hazy hills beyond. Slip off to the lake, dine on fabulous fish, sample the opera in Verona, come and go as you please.

rooms	3: 1 double; 2 twins/doubles sharing shower room.
price	€70–€100.
meals	Restaurants 1km.
closed	Rarely.
directions	A22 exit Affi; lake road north to Garda for 3.5 km; at lights in Albare, left towards Bardolino; after 3 km, 'Corteline'; 500m on right, take minor road Sem e Pigno until end; follow dirt track on left to house.

Elena Corsini Piffer

tel	+39 045 7211391
fax	+39 045 8679756
email	info@eremorelais.com
web	www.eremorelais.com

B&B

Map 3 Entry 36

La Foresteria Serego Alighieri

via Stazione 2, 37020 Gargagnago di Valpolicella

Bought by Dante's son in 1353, the estate has been in the family every since. It is vast and magnificent, and it lies in the very heart of Valpolicella, so wine is the thing. Apartments are named after local grapes and the wine shop is open six days a week. They also produce olive oil, balsamic vinegar, grappa, honey and jam and if you're serious about cooking you can do a course – pre-arranged, for a minimum of 12. Learn how the ingredients are grown, how the locals would prepare and eat them, and with which wine; then have a go in the professionally equipped kitchen. The apartments are roomy, with an elegant green, white and soft-yellow décor and are in a separate, carefully restored wing. 'Oseleta', for two, is on three floors of an old tower, with rooms linked by a narrow spiral stair. All of them have kitchens, though it's hard to imagine guests here lugging plastic bags from the car to self-cater; nor is there anything so brash as a swimming pool! The gardens and orchards are dreamy, and the all-pervading peace a balm – even the staff, Italian and delightful, speak in soft voices.

rooms	8 apartments: 4 for 2, 2 for 3, 2 for 4.
price	Apartment €127-€194 for 2. €183-€257 for 3. €205-€313 for 4.
meals	Breakfast included. Restaurants 5km.
closed	January.
directions	A22 exit Verona Nord for Valpolicella/Trento. At end left for S. Ambrogio for La Foresteria.

tel	+39 045 7703622
fax	+39 045 7703523
email	serego@seregoalighieri.it
web	www.seregoalighieri.it

Self-catering

Map 3 Entry 37

Villa Spinosa - Azienda Agricola
Jago 12, 37024 Negrar in Valpolicella

Wake to views over vineyards, raise a glass to the sunset from the terrace, sleep near the maturing casks. Only bathing in wine would ensure a more intimate encounter with the juice of the grape. The Spinosa family have owned these vineyards, in the heart of Valpolicella Classica country, since the 1800s. Tucked behind their 19th-century villa are the original workers' quarters that pre-date the house; now a three-storey, self-catering apartment. With high beamed ceilings, thick walls and richly stained floorboards it retains its rustic feel – matched by simple, solid and comfortable wooden furniture. The large kitchen has a lovely old fireplace and handsome family dining table, while a steep wooden staircase leads to the sitting room, and up again to airy attic bedrooms. Rugs and bedspreads add warmth and colour to a neat décor. It's a short walk to Negrar for restaurants while Verona is 15 minutes by car and Lake Garda not much further. Enrico is efficient, on hand to help, and delighted to give you a tasting tour of the winery. And there's a delightfully elegant, traditional Italian garden to enjoy.

rooms	1 apartment for 6-8.
price	€90.
meals	Enoteca 1km.
closed	Rarely.
directions	SP34 to via Valle di Pruviniano; 2km; at Valgatara, right to via Chiesa for Negrar; right after church, left at x-road to Negrar; straight on at x-road; right after 25m into courtyard.

Enrico Cascella Spinosa

tel/fax	+39 045 750 00 93
mobile	+39 340 3060480
email	villaspinosa@valpolicella.it
web	www.villaspinosa.it

Self-catering

Map 3 Entry 38

Cà del Rocolo
via Gaspari 3, loc. Quinto, 37034 Verona

Such an undemanding, delightful place to be and such a warm, enthusiastic young family to be with. Maurizio ran a restaurant in Verona, Ilaria was a journalist and has three cookbooks to her name… they gave it all up for a better life for their children. Their 1800s farmhouse is on the side of a hill overlooking forested hills and the vast Lessinia National Park. Maurizio has done much of the renovation himself and the result is authentic and attractive. Simple cotton rugs cover stripped bedroom floors, rough plaster walls are whitewashed, the rooms are big and airy, with solid country furniture, excellent beds and bathrooms, and there's a shared kitchen. Breakfasts are at the long farmhouse table or out on the terrace, making the most of the views. Delicious organic food, seasonal cakes with home-grown fruits, happy conversation. Dinner, mostly vegetarian, is an occasional affair. It's a seven-hectare organic farm, with olives and fruit trees, hens and horses; there are nature trails galore, a saltwater pool in the offing, and always something going on.

rooms	3: 2 doubles, 1 family.
price	€63-€70; €390-€450 per week.
meals	Restaurant 4km.
closed	Rarely.
directions	Detailed directions will be sent by email or fax.

Ilaria & Maurizio Corazza

tel	+39 045 8700879
fax	+39 045 8700879
email	info@cadelrocolo.com
web	www.cadelrocolo.com

Agriturismo

Map 3 Entry 39

Villa Bogoni
via Veneto 19/a, 37060 Sorgà

Faded knights, long-dead courtiers, nymphs and satyrs, exquisite scrollwork ... the frescoes here are said to be the work of Giulio Romano, Raffaello's protégé. Lara's mother, Adriana, discovered them in 1980, uncovering more and more as she restored. If you rent the whole place you may stay in a room in which you can gaze on them from your ornately gilded bed. Wander past more frescoes to the main villa (note the holes – they're part of a special technique to get the plaster to stick to the walls), where bedrooms are traditional and full of family antiques: mirrors from 18th-century Venice, rich bedspreads, beautifully carved beds. The three attic bedrooms lie beneath chunky beams; another room has a little private terrace. Adriana cooks local dishes for dinner: perhaps risotto with beetroot; sausages, stuffed tomatoes and courgette flowers; chocolate mousse. Breakfast on brioche, jams, honey, cheese and ham on the terrace, before sweeping views over flat grassland. The area is pleasantly undiscovered – and elegant, softly-spoken Lara is full of information and happy to chat.

rooms	7 doubles.
price	€105-€120.
	Whole villa €3,500-€4,500 per
	week, with buffet breakfast.
meals	Dinner €22.
closed	Rarely.
directions	A22 Modena-Brennero, exit
	Nogarole-Rocca for Erbè-Sorgà;
	15km. In village, villa on right.

	Simone Udovini
tel	+39 045 7370129
fax	+39 045 7370129
email	info@villabogoni.it
web	www.villabogoni.it

B&B & Self-catering

Map 3 Entry 40

Agriturismo Tenuta La Pila

via Pila 42, 37040 Spinimbecco di Villa Bartolomea

Raimonda and Alberto will soon have you chatting over a welcome drink in the kitchen; he speaks a clutch of languages, she's bubbly. Each B&B room is named after a fruit and smartly decorated: cream walls and exposed brick, crisp bed linen and starched towels, antique furniture to add a homely touch and sofabeds are large and comfortable. The apartments, on two floors of a separate building once used for drying tobacco, have immensely high beams and are decorated in a similar style. You get a table, chairs and sofabed in the large central living area, and neat corner kitchens. Cheerful bedrooms have flower prints and check bedspreads, and there's a large room for yoga retreats or seminars. Breakfast is a spread of home produce: kiwi jam, eggs, fruit, bread, yogurt. The farm is surrounded by fertile fields, trees and kiwi vines meandering across the plains, yet Verona, Venice, Lake Garda and Mantova are an easy drive. Then return to a peaceful patio-garden, a game of tennis, a dip in the pool, and skittles or boules beside the huge magnolia. *Minimum stay two nights.*

rooms	5 + 2: 5 rooms for 2-3. 2 apartments for 4-6.
price	€70. Apartments €819 per week.
meals	Dinner €15. Restaurants 2km.
closed	Rarely.
directions	From SS 434 Verona-Rovigo exit Carpi for Spinimbecco. At village, left at 'Stop', after 500m left onto Strada dell'Argine Vecchio della Valle & onto Via Gorgo da Bagno. After 1km along asphalt road left into farm.

	Raimonda & Alberto Sartori
tel	+39 0442 659289
fax	+39 0442 658707
email	post@tenutalapila.it
web	www.tenutalapila.it

Agriturismo & Self-catering

Map 8 Entry 41

Il Castello

via Castello 6, 36021 Barbarano Vicentino

A narrow, winding road leads up to the *castello* at the foot of the Berici hills. Also known as the Villa Godi-Marinoni, the castle was built by Count Godi in the 15th century, on the ruins of an old feudal castle. Massive hewn walls enclose the compound of terraced vines, orchard and Italian garden; you enter via an arched entrance, ancient cobbles beneath your feet. The villa itself is still lived in by the family: Signora Marinoni and her son, courteous and attentive, run this vast estate together. Guest apartments (one with a kitchen on the far side of a courtyard) are in an outbuilding with curious gothic details in the plastered façade; furnishings are a mix of dark antique and contemporary. Hidden below the castle walls is the garden with fish pond; in spring, hundreds of lemon trees are wheeled out to stand grandly on pedestals. The climate is mild and the hillside a mass of olive groves. Olive oil, honey and five DOC wines are produced on the ten-hectare estate – there's a wine cellar in the bowels of the castle, and a *cantina* where you can buy. *Minimum stay one week.*

rooms	4 apartments for 2-4.
price	€52-€58.
meals	Self-catering. Restaurants nearby.
closed	Rarely.
directions	A4 exit Vicenza Est; at r'bout follow signs to Riviera Berica for 15km. In Ponte di Barbarano, at traffic lights right towards Barbarano. At main square, left to Villaga; villa 500m on left.

Signora Elda Marinoni

tel	+39 0444 886055
fax	+39 0444 777140
email	castellomarinoni@tin.it
web	www.castellomarinoni.it

Self-catering

Map 4 Entry 42

Casa Belmonte

via Belmonte 2, 36030 Sarcedo

From the moment the gates swing open you are in for a treat. Motor up the long, statuette-lined drive, step onto the gravel and your luggage is whisked up to your room. Bedrooms have elegance, seduction and style: soft colours, rich fabrics, antiques, monogrammed sheets and towels; bathrooms are big and mosaic-tiled. Once her children had flown the nest Mariarosa turned her full attention to creating these six gorgeous retreats. She is the most delightful hostess and genuinely loves having people to stay. The house sits on the top of Belmonte hill overlooking the small town of Sarcedo in seven hectares of vineyards, olive groves and manicured gardens – come for the azaleas in May, and the pool. Views are panoramic, and delicious breakfasts of yogurt, fruit, cheese and ham are served in the summer house. Roberto is proud of his small wine cellar, and selects some of the best wines from Italy for his most important guests. Casa Belmonte is an easy launch pad for forays to Venice, Padua, Verona and Piacenza, and, considering that luxury doesn't come much better than this, is good value.

rooms	6: 2 doubles, 1 twin, 2 suites, 1 single.
price	€129–€181. Singles €103–€129. Suites €181–€258.
meals	Breakfast €15–€23. Restaurants 2km-7km (Michelin starred).
closed	Rarely.
directions	A31 exit for Dueville. Left & left again for Bassano. After 2km left for Sarcedo. There, entrance 600m after lights to right of junction. Bell on gate.

Signora Mariarosa Arcaro

tel	+39 0445 884833
fax	+39 0445 884134
email	info@casabelmonte.com
web	www.casabelmonte.com

B&B

Map 4 Entry 43

Villa Rizzi Albarea

via Albarea 53, 30030 Pianiga di Venezia

Hidden behind the house is the loveliest wild garden. Exciting pathways thread their way past statues and trees; there are bridges of Murano glass and a romantic lake with an island and swans. To the front, a lawn next to the old, art-filled chapel, roses in the cloisters, pines, palms, peonies and ancient magnolias. The house is intriguing, too: the oldest Palladian villa between Venice and Padua. Once a convent for the Giudecca nuns, its origins go back ten centuries. Though wars and fire have meant much restoration, it's a beautiful place, deep in the country but not isolated, barely touched by the nearby motorway. The bedrooms are a fresh mix of traditional and flounced, with delectable antiques and comfortable beds, some with old frescoes, others with stunning rafters. Shower rooms sparkle, Persian rugs glow on stone or wooden floors. Be charmed by birdsong and roses in summer; in winter, by Vivaldi and a big fire. In spite of breakfasts served by gloved butlers – and sauna, gym and two pools – the atmosphere is personal, thanks to these generous hosts. *Minimum stay two nights.*

rooms	7 + 1: 7 suites. 1 apartment for 2-4.
price	€180-€280. Apt €200-€280.
meals	Restaurants nearby.
closed	Rarely.
directions	A4 Milano-Venezia exit Dolo, over lights, 1.5km; right at Albarea sign, 1km; signed.

Aida & Pierluigi Rizzi

tel	+39 041 5100933
fax	+39 041 5132562
email	info@villa-albarea.com
web	www.villa-albarea.com

B&B & Self-catering

Map 4 Entry 44

Villa Colloredo
Brusaura 24, 30030 Sambruson di Dolo

Handsomely ranged around a courtyard, these 18th-century Venetian buildings – all peachy stone and olive green shutters – hold a cool surprise. Bold paintings, modern sculptures and colourful collages dot the interiors: part of the private collection of the Meneghelli family. Architecturally, the converted stables and grain stores behind the family villa fuse modern styling and original features. Beamed ceilings, wooden or tiled floors and family antiques contrast with white walls, streamlined kitchens, simple rustic furniture and colourful artworks. Spaces have been imaginatively used – a shower, perhaps, in a glass-topped cube – to maximise the open, airy feel. Upper floors have lovely low windows, with views to fields, orchards or courtyard. Two of the larger apartments can be joined together – great for families. You can breakfast in the arched portico, lined with shrubs and fruit trees, and there's a statue-strewn garden behind the villa. Drop in on Padua; borrow a bike and cycle to Venice along the Brenta river. Family-run with a welcoming, homely feel. *Minimum stay three nights.*

rooms	2 + 4: 2 doubles.
	4 apartments for 4.
price	€60-€80. Apartments €80-€110.
meals	Restaurant 200m.
closed	Never.
directions	From A4, exit Dolo & follow to Sambruson; turn right opposite church.

	Andrea Meneghelli
tel	+39 041 411 755
mobile	+39 348 2102337
email	andrea@villacolloredo.com
web	www.villacolloredo.com

B&B & Self-catering

Map 4 Entry 45

Hotel Villa Alberti

via E Tito 90, 30031 Dolo

Pluck fruit from the orchard, wash it in the fountain, pick a quiet spot in the walled garden; you could get used to the aristocratic life. This 17th-century villa, once the summer residence of Venetian nobility, has been restored by the Vio family to combine grand features with a warm and unstuffy mood. A family of architects, the Vios have rescued original shutters and flooring, Murano glass lights and chandeliers, decorative ironwork lamps and balconies. Father is proud of the Italian garden with its box hedge lined paths, statues and century-old trees. The reception hall – a sweep of dark polished wood, rich rugs and deep sofas – leads to three floors of bedrooms furnished in a simple but refined style: wooden or stone floors, a few antiques, silky bedspreads. Ask for one overlooking the garden rather than the road. The rooms in the *barchessa* (the workers' house) are more rustic with beams and terracotta floors. Feast on polenta dishes and risottos on the terrace in the summer. A delightful, knowledgeable family and a refreshing alternative to Venice, 15km away.

rooms	20 doubles.
price	€90–€130.
meals	Dinner €20.
closed	Rarely.
directions	A4 exit Dolo-Mirano. At traffic lights in Dolo, left, direction Venice. 2km along river, over bridge & cont. in same direction along opp. bank for 1.5km. Hotel on right.

	Anna Vio
tel	+39 041 4266512
fax	+39 041 5608898
email	info@villalberti.it
web	www.villalberti.it

Hotel

Map 4 Entry 46

Locanda ai Santi Apostoli
strada Nova 4391, 30131 Venice

You could walk straight past without even noticing that there is a hotel within this palazzo – and miss the nicest surprise. The Locanda is on the third floor of the Bianchi Michiel, known locally as the Palazzo Michiel Brusà on account of its having burnt down three centuries ago. Nor does the courtyard, through which you pass, give any clue as to what is in store. The next minute, you're in a Henry James novel… a Venetian palace close to the Rialto on the Grand Canal. Public rooms, opening off a central salon, are still hung with the fabrics and papers of grander days; each room has been furnished differently with all the comforts, atmosphere and hospitality are of an elegant Venetian home. Ask for a room with a view: the two at the front, looking across the Grand Canal to the fish markets, are wonderful. Ludovica is delightful, keen to update the 15th-century palazzo that her family has owned since it was built. The private dock, a minute away, allows direct access to water taxis and gondolas. There is some noise, but this is Venice. A marvellous little find.

rooms	10: 9 doubles, 1 family room for 4.
price	€140-€300.
	Family room €320-€420.
	Singles €120-€150.
meals	Restaurants 3-minute walk.
closed	January; 2nd & 3rd weeks of August.
directions	Water bus stop: Ca'd'Oro (line 1). Private dock for water taxis.

	Ludovica Bianchi-Michiel
tel	+39 041 5212612
fax	+39 041 5212611
email	aisantia@tin.it
web	www.locandasantiapostoli.com

Hotel

Map 4 Entry 47

Residenza Goldoni
San Marco 5234, 30124 Venice

Cross the uneven paving stones and enter the tall narrow building on the as-narrow street. This is the 11-bedroom Goldoni, endearingly Italian and fabulously well placed – two minutes from the Rialto. No room for taxi or car: you get here by foot. Ascend the stairs, of which there are a few, and pass little landings on which the weary may rest. Staff are friendly and kind, quite used to helping guests with their bags. The rooms in the attic are the best: characterfully beamed and with amazing views – pink rooftops, baskets of geraniums, washing lines dancing in the breeze. But don't expect sofas and space. Rooms are neat and clean, colours beige and cream, bed linen crisp and white. Antiques are polished and tables protected by glass, bathrooms squeeze in tiny baths but some lack space for doors, most rooms have minibars and a few have terraces – small ones. Simple breakfast is served in your room whenever you want. You are surrounded by tiny streets and bridges, restaurants and bars, churches and shops, chiming church bells and tourist bustle.

rooms	11: 10 twins/doubles, 1 suite for 4.
price	€100–€200. Suite €150–€250.
meals	Restaurants nearby.
closed	Never.
directions	Water bus 1 or 82 to Rialto bridge; walk up Calle Larga Mazzine, which narrows to Mercerie S Salvador; 1st left into Calle Stagneri; Goldoni on right.

Andrea Spellanzon

tel	+39 041 2410086
fax	+39 041 2774728
email	info@residenzagoldoni.com
web	www.residenzagoldoni.com

Hotel

Map 4 Entry 48

Hotel Locanda Fiorita & Ca' Morosini

Campiello Nuovo, San Marco 3457/A, 30124 Venice

A low-budget option for those who have neither boundless wealth nor the inclination to spend their time lounging around a grand Venetian hotel. Tucked away behind the Campo Santo Stefano, close to the Accademia Bridge, this is a sweet, peaceful place, and a convenient base (near the vaparetto) from which you may head off in all directions. It is a faded russet palazzo hung with vines, in a tiny square which somehow contrives to look green in an area without gardens. The terrace at the front is a charmingly ramshackle affair, from which people spill out onto the *piazzetta* for cappuccini and newspapers. Bedrooms vary in size and have pleasantly faded Venetian-style tables and chests and some antique mirrors. Annexe rooms are on two floors in a separate building, newly decorated in bold colours and with slightly bigger showers. No restaurant, but there are plenty of places to eat nearby, and an internet café round the corner. Cross the Accademia Bridge and dive into the network of alleyways on the far side, trailing a thread like Ariadne so that you can find your way back again.

rooms	Locanda Fiorita: 10: 4 doubles; 6 twins/doubles. Ca' Morosini: 6 + 1: 4 twins/doubles, 2 triples + 1 apartment.
price	€60–€145. Singles €45-90–€120. Ca' Morosini: €120–€210.
meals	Restaurants nearby.
closed	Never.
directions	Directions on booking.

	Renato Colombera
tel	+39 041 5234754
fax	+39 041 5228043
email	info@locandafiorita.com
web	www.locandafiorita.com

Locanda Casa alla Fenice

Rio Terrà degli Assassini 3701, San Marco, 30124 Venice

A great little spot, just off the beaten track. Hire a water taxi from the station and you will be ferried almost to the door. Elizabetta, with a history of hospitality behind her, has taken on where the Battistini family left off, and the attention to detail is exceptional: chocolates for your birthday, fresh flowers. Your rooms are on the first floor of this small townhouse in what was a red light district in the 1700s… now utterly quiet, apart from the evening serenade of the gondolier. High-ceilinged, light, airy and romantic – blessed with air con – bedrooms have mottled marble floors and individual touches: a decorated door, a chandelier, an ornate mirror. White curtains billow at windows that open to alley views. Bedheads are newly gilded, fabrics are fancy and some rooms carry a beautiful mural of a 17th-century Venetian scene painted by a young local artist. Shower rooms are well-lit. Packeted breakfasts are brought to your room – but it may be more fun to visit the local bar. With your own keys you can come and go as you please. *Minimum stay two nights.*

rooms	5: 3 twins/doubles, 2 singles.
price	€55-€230. Singles €50-€185.
meals	Restaurant 50m.
closed	Never.
directions	5-minute walk from San Marco or water taxi to Rio Terrà degli Assassini.

Elisabetta Cuomo
tel	+39 041 5280105
fax	+39 041 5220896
email	info@casaallafenice.com
web	www.casaallafenice.com

B&B

Map 4 Entry 50

Pensione La Calcina
Fondamenta Zattere ai Gesuati, Dorsoduro 780, 30123 Venice

Catch the sea breezes of early evening from the terrace butting out over the water as you watch the beautiful people stroll the Zattere. Or gaze across the lagoon to the Rendentore. Ruskin stayed here in 1876, and for many people this corner of town, facing the Guidecca and with old Venice just behind you, beats the crowds of San Marco any day. The hotel has been discretely modernised by its charming owners; comfortable bedrooms have air con, antiques and parquet floors. Those at the front, with views, are dearer; the best are the corner rooms, with windows on two sides. A small top terrace can be booked for romantic evenings and you can breakfast, lunch or dinner at the delightful floating restaurant, open to all – simple dishes are available all day and the fruit juices and milkshakes are delicious. Pause for a moment and remember Ruskin's words on the city he loved: "a ghost upon the sands of the sea, so weak, so quiet, so bereft of all but her loveliness, that we might well doubt, as we watched her faint reflection on the mirage of the lagoon, which was the City and which the shadow."

rooms	29: 20 doubles, 7 singles.
price	€99–€186. Singles €96–€106.
meals	Lunch or dinner €10–€40.
closed	Rarely.
directions	Water bus line 51 or 61 from Piazzale Roma or railway station; line 82 from Tronchetto.

	Signor Alessandro Szemere
tel	+39 041 5206466
fax	+39 041 5227045
email	la.calcina@libero.it
web	www.lacalcina.com

Hotel

Map 4 Entry 51

Pensione La Calcina - Apartments

Fondamenta Zattere ai Gesuati, Dorsoduro 780, 30123 Venice

A two-minute stroll from the hotel of the same name, a clutch of beautiful apartments on the fashionable Zattere. Though they vary in size and in feel, each has a sitting room, a double bedroom and a bathroom; three have kitchens, all are named after flowers. 'Giglio' is large and lovely, with a white-walled sitting room, exposed beams in a vaulted ceiling and a view onto a garden. 'Rosa' is deliciously rustic, with lovely old pieces of furniture and colourful rugs, and a fabulous kitchen. Marble-floored 'Viola' feels Venetian, with its white drapes, fragments of Istrian stone and glimpse of church and small square; 'Iris' looks onto an elegant well with a little fountain and has a modern air. 'Dalia', the smallest, is designed by the Italian architect Scarpa. Inspired by views that sail over the boat-busy lagoon he has created a nautical den – wooden panelling, padded seating, latticed windows, a boatish door; views skim the water and the sunlight dances on the ceiling. All have fridges, and you breakfast at the hotel (see above). Deep comfort in one of the greenest, quietest corners of Venice.

rooms	2 + 3: 1 suite for 2, 1 suite for 4. 3 apartments for 3.
price	€136-€239.
meals	Lunch or dinner €10-€40.
closed	Rarely.
directions	Water bus line 51 or 61 from Piazzale Roma or railway station. Line 82 from Tronchetto.

Signor Alessandro Szemere

tel	+39 041 5206466
fax	+39 041 5227045
email	la.calcina@libero.it
web	www.lacalcina.com

B&B & Self-catering

Map 4 Entry 52

Fujiyama Bed & Breakfast

Calle Lunga San Barnaba 2727A, Sestiere Dorsoduro, 30123 Venice

Jasmine, wisteria, shady trees – hard to believe this pool of tranquillity is minutes from the hurly-burly of Venice's streets and the grandeur of the Rialto and St Mark's Square. Even more unusual – for this city – to step through an oriental tea room to reach your bedroom. The four rooms are on the upper two floors of this tall, narrow 18th-century townhouse and continue the gentle Japanese theme. Carlo worked in Japan for eight years – also Algeria, Egypt, Holland – and his love of the Far East is evident throughout the house. Rooms, with views over the garden or Venetian rooftops, exude a light, airy and ordered calm with polished dark wood floors, cream walls, Japanese prints and simple oriental furnishings. Shower rooms are small but neat and spotless. Breakfast on the terrace in summer or in the tea room in winter. A charming and warm host, full of stories and happy to chat, Carlo will recommend good local restaurants – especially those specialising in fish. Retreat here after a busy day exploring this magical city and sip a cup of jasmine tea on the shady terrace.

rooms	4 doubles.
price	€80–€130.
meals	Restaurants next door.
closed	20 July–10 August.
directions	From station, take water bus line 1. Get off at stop Cà Rezzonico & walk to end of Calle Lunga San Barnaba.

Carlo Errani

tel	+39 041 7241042
fax	+39 041 2771969
email	info@bedandbreakfast-fujiyama.it
web	www.bedandbreakfast-fujiyama.it

BftB

Map 4 Entry 53

B&B Ca' Bernardi

San Polo 1321, 30125 Venice

Pass down a narrow alleyway, through the large and lovely courtyard, tall walls towering above, and enter the 15th-century palazzo. The apartment is on the ground floor, the B&B on the first. Catch your breath inside – such a calm, eclectic décor touched with Persian rugs, silk curtains, fresh flowers and influences from Bali and Morocco. Amelia is a Californian artist and her paintings hang on every wall. She and her mother Deborah live nearby, so there's no need to tiptoe around your hosts. Most guests are English speaking and the bedrooms have been designed to meet American expectations: superb linen, mattresses, showers; hand-crafted beds; the internet. An ecological awareness permeates this serene place. One room looks onto the canal – the other two onto the courtyard. In the apartment downstairs the style is uncluttered, the whitewashed walls making the most of the light. Breakfast is a pretty basket of brioche and bread in the courtyard. The little vaporetto is five minutes away – no bridges! – the local shop across the square and the Rialto, markets and Accademia not much further.

rooms	3 + 1: 2 family rooms for 2-3, 1 family room for 2-4. 1 apt for 4.
price	€125-€165 for 2; €150-€180 for 3; €175-€220 for 4. Apartment €125-€220.
meals	Restaurants nearby.
closed	Last 2 weeks in August. 2 weeks in December-January.
directions	From Piazzale Roma, water bus towards Lido; exit San Silvestro; walk towards Campo San' Aponal; 3rd left; 3rd right.

Amelia Bonvini

tel	+39 041 5224923
fax	+39 041 0997849
email	info@cabernardi.com
web	www.cabernardi.com

B&B & Self-catering

Map 4 Entry 54

Casa San Boldo - Grimani & Loredan
San Polo 2281, 30125 Venice

Your own tennis court – in Venice. Enjoy a game or settle with a picnic beneath the jasmine-covered bandstand in the garden. Francesca's parents live on the ground floor and share the court and garden. These very well-restored apartments are smart yet cosy: family antiques, fresh flowers, new sofas, Persian rugs on parquet floors. There are intriguing quirks too: an original window and its glass preserved as a piece of art, a 1756 dowry chest from Alto Adige. And you're never far from a window with bustling canal views. The smaller apartment on the first floor has a sweet double/twin tucked away beneath the rafters, and a larger double room downstairs with modern paintings by a local artist. The little kitchen is beautifully equipped, the dining room has high ceilings and a Venetian marble floor. 'Grimani' has a bedroom on the ground floor with garden views and another up, with iron-framed beds and a lovely old desk. Multi-lingual Francesca who lives nearby is kind, friendly and runs cookery courses that include buying the produce from the Rialto market, just around the corner.

rooms	2 apartments: 1 for 4-6, 1 for 4.
price	Grimani €1,550-€1,950. Loredan €1,150-€1,550. Prices per week.
meals	Restaurants 5-minute walk.
closed	Rarely.
directions	Park at Piazzale Roma nearby. Details on booking.

	Francesca Pasti
tel	+39 041 5241070
fax	+39 178 2208 993
email	venezia@adriabella.com
web	www.adriabella.com

Madonna

Campiello Piave, Cannaregio, Venice

Bliss to escape the Venetian crowds and return to a friendly little ground-floor apartment with an entrancing walled garden in this peaceful and pretty part of town. Passionflowers climb the warm brick walls; there are chairs and a table, roses and hydrangeas. Close by is the Madonna dell' Orte Church (known as Tintoretto's church) and the area is pretty and quiet, with – for Venice – a rare feeling of space. Susan is an American and comes to Italy whenever she can but lets her apartment at other times. It has all the attraction of a real home. Though the rooms aren't large, they are furnished with style and individuality; interesting pictures hang on white walls, terracotta floor tiles are dotted with rugs. The bedroom is cool and airy with muslin curtains; the living room has two large sofas that turn into single beds. A big gilt mirror, a stereo, cushions and plenty of books make this a charming and restful room. At one end is a long, galley-style kitchen, equipped with hob, microwave and fridge (no oven but loads of restaurants nearby) and a door opening into that lovely garden.

rooms	Apartment for 2-4.
price	£500 per week.
meals	Self-catering.
closed	Rarely.
directions	Nearest water bus stop: Madonna dell'Orta line 42 or 52.

Susan Schiavon

tel	+44 (0)20 7348 3800
fax	+44 (0)870 134 2820
email	susan.venice@iol.it

Self-catering

Map 4 Entry 56

Club Cristal

Calle Zanardi 4133, Cannaregio, 30100 Venice

The concept of the wrong 'location' has little meaning in Venice: every area is a discovery. Near the Campo dei Gesuiti, on the northern edge, this is wonderfully quiet and as beautiful as anywhere. A canal skirts one side of the house, a large garden much of its length. Via a fine marble stair you enter a huge living room, cluttered yet welcoming with its books, magazines and two friendly dogs. The floors are of marble, there are two columns, some landscapes on the walls, vast potted plants, a piano and big doors onto a roof terrace. The green, silk-hung dining room is equally unexpected; bedrooms, too. One has a pink, extremely comfortable queen-size bed, a 17th-century fireplace, hand-painted double doors, an endearingly old-fashioned bathroom and views to garden and canal; another double is very small. Note, the canal bustle gets going around 7.30am. Much charm and character here, thanks to Susan, a fascinating lady who is passionate about Venice and its ongoing restoration. *Children over 12 welcome. Daylight arrival recommended.*

rooms	5 twins/doubles.
price	£80–£130. Single £50–£85.
meals	Dinner with wine £25–£30.
closed	Rarely.
directions	Bus to Piazzale Roma, line 1 to Ca'd'Oro.

Susan Schiavon

tel	+44 (0)20 7722 5060
fax	+44 (0)20 7586 3004
email	info@club-cristal-venice.com
web	www.club-cristal-venice.com

B&B

Map 4 Entry 57

Casa Martini

Rio Terà San Leonardo 1314, Cannaregio, 30121 Venice

An old Venetian townhouse and stylish B&B – you'd never guess such a fabulous place existed, tucked as it is down a side alley off a bustling, untouristy street. Smiling Orietta loves Venice and the house in which her husband grew up; these owners will make your stay a joy. During the winter months she brings you breakfast in the elegant little *salotto* with its balcony overlooking the Ponte di Guglie; in summer, you start the day on the terrace under the huge parasol, surrounded by flowers and overlooking the colourful façades. Peaceful, comfortable, air-conditioned bedrooms over three storeys (no lift) are furnished in 18th-century Venetian style, with damask wallpaper and ornate bedheads; lovely bathrooms have walk-in showers and fluffy white towels. Discover the open-air markets, restaurants, bars and shops that jostle outside the door, take a tour of the Ghetto, walk to St Mark's Square (15 minutes) or hop on the vaporetto. Outside are signs of the gate that used to close the entrance at night, and a long list of the rules for the inhabitants, inscribed in stone in 1541.

rooms	9: 6 doubles, 2 family, 1 single.
price	€80–€160. Family €180. Singles €60–€90.
meals	Restaurants walking distance.
closed	Rarely.
directions	A few minutes' walk from Ponte delle Guglie, & short walk from S. Lucia railway station. Water bus line 52 (stop: Guglie) & line 82 (stop: S. Marcuola).

Orietta & Luigi Martini
tel	+39 041 717512
fax	+39 041 2758329
email	locandamartini@libero.it
web	www.casamartini.it

B&B

Map 4 Entry 58

Martinengo Apartment

Calle Martinengo dalle Palle, Castello, Venice

Recline languorously on one of many lovely rugs, bring your own CDs, revel in the sensation of staying in a 17th-century Venetian home: this first-floor apartment is as far from a 'serviced apartment' as you can get. The furniture is deliciously antique, the walls drip with paintings ancient and modern, there are stacks of records and books, intriguing wooden statues and carvings abound, rooms stretch on and on. The double bedroom has high ceilings, terrazzo floors, stunning mirrors, a four-poster, a Venetian chandelier: almost outrageously luxurious, with a bathroom to match. The little study (which doubles as a single room) invites idleness or scholarship, the street is so narrow you could exchange cooking ingredients with your neighbour, and there is a delightful little terrace with a long view down the narrow side canal. The kitchen — slightly old-fashioned — is bright and pretty, with great marble slabs and everything you need (and a small supermarket next door). An unusual and wonderfully central Venetian retreat, worth every penny. *Maid service mid-week. Ask about prices in low season.*

rooms	1 apartment for 4-5.
price	£1,250 per week.
meals	Self-catering.
closed	Never.
directions	Water bus stop: Line 82: Rialto - San Marco.

	Susan Schiavon
tel	+44 (0)20 7348 3800
fax	+44 (0)870 134 2820
email	susan.venice@iol.it
web	www.apartments-venice.com

Self-catering

Map 4 Entry 59

Locanda al Leon

Campo Santi Filippo e Giacamo 4270, Castello, 30122 Venice

Such friendly people, such a perfect spot: three minutes' walk from the Basilica end of St Mark's Square, and the same from the airport bus and the vaporetto stops. This small, unpretentious, family-run hotel, its characterful old entrance down a tiny alley, is an excellent choice if you're visiting Venice on a tightish budget but want to be at the centre of it all. It's been modestly modernised: all is spotless, everything works, and there's heating for winter stays. Clean, carpeted bedrooms (the biggest on the corner of the building, looking onto the Campo San Filippo e Giacome and the Calle degli Albanesi) have Venetian-style bedheads with scrolled edges and floral motifs; there are matching striped counterpanes and curtains, modern Murano chandeliers and neat shower rooms. Breakfast is taken at little tables on the big, first-floor landing (no lift) buffet-style: breads and croissants, yogurts and fruit juice – what you'd expect for the price. And there's no shortage of advice – one or two members of the delightful Dall' Agnola family are always around.

rooms	11: 8 doubles, 1 triple, 2 singles.
price	€80–€160. Triple €100–€180. Singles €60–€130.
meals	Restaurants 150m.
closed	Rarely.
directions	Water bus line 1 or 82 to San Zaccaria. Follow Calle degli Albanesi until last door on left; signed.

	Marcella & Giuliano Dall' Agnola
tel	+39 041 2770393
fax	+39 041 5210348
email	leon@hotelalleon.com
web	www.hotelalleon.com

Hotel

Map 4 Entry 60

Castello di Roncade
via Roma 14, 31056 Roncade

An imposing entrance, a garden full of statues and roses and a grand 16th-century villa do not mean impossible prices. Three beautiful double rooms, furnished with antiques, are available in the house itself and – ideal for families – three vast and simply furnished apartments in the corner towers, the largest with a very good kitchen. All have big wardrobes and dark wooden floors, central heating in winter, air con in summer, thick walls keep you cool. Surrounding the castle and the village are the estate vineyards which produce some excellent wines; try the Villa Giustinian Rosso della Casa or the Pinot Grigio and you'll be sorely tempted to take a case home. Or sample them at dinner in the villa, an occasional rather than a regular event but a fabulous experience, with everyone seated at one table in a magnificent family dining room. The owners and their son Giorgio are helpful hosts who love meeting people and are proud of their wines. Don't take the car to Venice; instead catch the bus to Treviso – an ancient place of cloisters and canals, frescoes and churches – and then the train.

rooms	3 + 3: 2 doubles, 1 triple.
	3 apartments: 2 for 2-4; 1 for 4-6.
price	€83-€93.
	Apartments €31-€36 p.p.
meals	Occasional dinner available.
	Self-catering in apartments.
closed	Rarely.
directions	Exit A4 for Trieste at Quarto d'Altino towards Altino & then Roncade. Castello 7km from A4 exit.

	Barone Vincenzo Ciani Bassetti
tel	+39 0422 708736
fax	+39 0422 840964
email	vcianib@tin.it
web	www.castellodironcade.com

B&B & Self-catering

Map 4 Entry 61

Maso di Villa

via Col di Guarda 15, 31058 Collalto di Susegana

Under an hour from Venice, high up on a hill, Maso di Villa is a world away from the usual Italian agriturismo set-up. Chiara Lucchetta, the owner, has renovated this glorious old farmhouse with breathtaking attention to detail. Everything, from the beautifully restored Veneto furniture and the stripped wooden beams to the light switches – in the original style, salvaged from antique shops – has been put in place to produce a quiet symphony of rural Italy. Although grand and imposing on the outside, the house couldn't be more homely and cosy within. The bedrooms are comfortable and painted in warm colours, some with stunning ornate headboards designed by Chiara's father and carved locally. Knotted old wooden pillars shore up the ceiling in the sitting room, which is scattered with armchairs and bathed in sunlight. And everywhere in the house there are astonishing views; on one side, the Dolomites, on the other, the unbroken expanse of vineyards and woodland that is the Prosecco wine region. Enjoy abundant breakfast on the terrace, wander in the gardens: this is a magical place.

rooms	6: 4 doubles, 2 twins.
price	€120-€150. Singles €105.
meals	Trattoria 300m (closed Mon/Tues).
closed	Rarely.
directions	A4 Venice-Trieste; dual c'way 10km; A27 for Belluno; past Treviso Sud; exit Treviso Nord; right for Treviso-Conegliano, SS13 Pontebbana; 18km; in Susegana left at lights for Collalto, 5km; on left, entrance in Morgante II Street, green gate.

	Chiara Lucchetta
tel	+39 0438 841414
fax	+39 0438 981742
email	info@masodivilla.it
web	www.masodivilla.it

B&B

Map 4 Entry 62

Arte Culinaria

via dall'Oglio 10, 31030 Cison di Valmarino

Learn to cook delectably – and stay in a charming farmhouse while you do so. Antonella's a chef and an inspired teacher, Philip's a banker from Arran who will keep your glass topped with Prosecco as you cook, and nine-year-old Giovanni will request his favourite puds, sticky toffee and tiramisu… Guests from outside may arrive to tuck in, too. Philip and Antonella bought the house in 1990 and set about the mammoth task of restoring it. It's 19th century with a newer wing (the original farmer had to accommodate his 11 children somewhere) and the guest rooms in the old part. Rugs on gleaming wooden floors, some delightful antique English and Italian furniture, comfortable beds and splashes of bright colour create a warmly characterful air. Breakfast is outside under the portico in summer, or upstairs beside the lovely Aga in winter. The big, low-beamed sitting room has some fine paintings, including a 16th-century Madonna and child, and a grand piano. Out in the pretty garden are a well and an 18th-century bread oven; glance upwards and you'll see the castle and wooded hills.

rooms	2 + 1: 1 twin/double, 1 family suite. 1 self-catering double.
price	€90.
meals	Dinner €35.
closed	Rarely.
directions	A27 exit Vittorio Veneto Nord. Right after toll to Vittorio Veneto; right to Tarzo, Revine Lago. Left after petrol station (12km); through Mura, then right into Cison de Valmarino. Yellow house after small bridge, on left.

	Signora Antonella Tagliapietra
tel/fax	+39 0438 975510
mobile	+39 347 2734063
email	arteculinaria@tiscali.it
web	www.arteculinaria.it

Il Giardino Segreto

Piazza della Vittoria 22, 31020 Cison di Valmarino

For years it was Janine's dream to do up a farmhouse. She found one, and a partner to share the dream. She is Belgian, Angelo is Italian and the house is in a hamlet surrounded by mountains, its little garden hidden behind green gates. A great deal of work has gone into restoring the place and keeping as much of the 18th-century feel as possible; the stairs creak charmingly, the chestnut floorboards show the cracks of age and you get a delightful living room/kitchen all to yourselves with big French windows and an open fire. Right next door in the *cantina*, where grappa was once made, is a bedroom upstairs and a living room (all yours) down. In Casa Vecchia there are two twins upstairs and a cheery dining room/kitchenette down: go B&B or self-cater. Furniture includes country antiques, colours are pleasing; no TV, hundreds of books. Janine lives near by, and breakfasts and dinners are delicious. The village is a great starting point for walks and mountain bike rides; the Passo San Boldo with its 18 hairpin bends is a bit of a challenge. *New townhouse B&B in Vittorio Veneto.*

rooms	2 + 2: Casa Vecchia 2 twins. Main house + annexe for 4-5.
price	B&B €60–€75. Casa Vecchia €750 per week. Main house + annexe €1,120 per week.
meals	Dinner with wine €15–€20. Osteria (lunch) next door.
closed	Rarely.
directions	A27 exit Vittorio Veneto Nord for centre, right for Cison, 10km. Green gate set back from main square by side of Locanda Bar Al Bàkarò.

Janine Raedts & Angelo Vettorello

tel	+39 0438 85953
mobile	+39 320 0525289
email	giardinosegreto@tiscali.it
web	www.giardino-segreto.it

B&B & Self-catering

Map 4 Entry 64

B&B Casa Ciriani

via Guazzi 1, 35031 Abano Terme

Set back from the road, the gated villa looks cool and inviting: shaded by trees, shuttered against the sun. Mariantionetta and her husband built it in 1974; now she and daughter Silvana live here and run the B&B with informal charm. You feel you are staying in a peaceful family home. Enter the huge hall with a traditional mosaic underfoot; it sweeps into the drawing room and was designed, and laid (in parts!) by Mariantionetta. Upstairs, the family room has some wonderful antique pieces and paintings by nieces and nephews. In the twin, a beautiful old yellow chest catches the eye – and a private suntrap terrace for a sundowner. The double room is more informal and countrified, with a wicker-framed bed and amply-stocked bookshelf. Spotless bathrooms are a good size. Breakfast on the cool portico in summer: a delightful spot, with wrought-iron furniture, earthenware jars, garden views and Mariantonietta's jams. The owners are passionate gardeners and a stroll after breakfast is rewarding. Venture out to a local museum or Palladian villa, plan a night at the magical opera in Verona.

rooms	4: 2 doubles, 1 twin, 1 family.
price	€65–€80. Singles €40–€50.
meals	Good choice nearby.
closed	Christmas & New Year.
directions	Firenze-Venezia, exit Padova Sud after toll for Padova; 1st lights, main road left for Rovigo; 3km; 2nd lights, right for Abano; 1km; 3rd lights, right via S.Maria d'Abano; 700m, left into via Guazzi; 200m.

	Silvana & Mariantonietta Ciriani
mobile	+39 368 377 9226
fax	+39 049 715272
email	bb.casaciriani@libero.it
web	www.casaciriani.com

B&B

Map 4 Entry 65

Villa Selvatico

via Selvatico 1, 35010 Codiverno di Vigonza

Live like a Venetian noble, gazing over your parkland with distant views of spires, tree-lined avenues and the vineyards of the Veneto plains. This 15th-century patrician's summer villa has been in the Da Porto family for generations. The Da Portos are kind and gracious and offer three apartments in the main house, separate from the family. (Ask to be shown round their bit: wonderful paintings, wonderful history.) Rooms are airy and traditionally furnished – often family antiques – with tiled or stripped wood floors. Portraits of the Da Portos add a personal touch. The largest, 'Le Magnolie', includes a grand Venetian carved bed and elegant sitting room scattered with Persian rugs. 'Il Fogher' has dark beamed ceilings and country style furniture while 'Il Portico', accessed from the garden, is full of light. 'La Serra', the summer house by the river, has glorious views and an outside eating area. Apart from Le Magnolie's kitchen, cooking areas are tucked into living rooms. Help yourself to fruit and vegetables from the garden. There are shady garden spots, walks along the river and, of course, Padua.

rooms	4 apartments: 2 for 2-4, 1 for 4-6, 1 for 4-8.
price	Apts €70-€80 for 2. €90-€110 for 4. €190-€230 for 8.
meals	Restaurants 1-8km.
closed	Never.
directions	A4 exit Padova Est. After lights into SR308 to Castelfranco Veneto; 4th exit, Reschigliano; left at r'bout to Sant'Andrea; right at T-junc.; 200m after church right into via Selvatico; 2nd gate at end on right.

Antonio & Vittoriana Da Porto

tel	+39 049 646092
fax	+39 049 646092
email	villaselvatico@tiscali.it
web	www.villaselvatico.com

Self-catering

Map 4 Entry 66

Gargan L'Agriturismo
via Marco Polo 2, 35017 Levada di Piombino Dese

Such a surprise: behind the austere façade lies a sophisticated interior and some very good food. Elegant rooms, delightful antiques, pale-painted beams, tables laid with linen and silver… such are the rewards for those who cross the uneventful landscape of the Veneto to get here. Bedrooms are old-fashioned and pretty, with iron bedheads and cotton quilts, mellow brick floors and Persian rugs, fine pieces of family furniture (Grandma was from Tuscany, Grandfather from Veneto) and armchairs to sink into. The several rooms on the ground floor given over to dining, one with a fine old chimney-piece, indicate the importance attached to food. Tables are immaculate and the food well-presented; it is gentle Signora's passion, and she is aided by a team of chefs. Children will enjoy the park-like gardens and resident donkey and dogs. Venice, Padua, Vicenza and Treviso are an easy drive so this would be a good base for those planning to explore, then retreat to the countryside and the agriturismo's delights.

rooms	6: 4 doubles, 2 suites.
price	€65. Suite €85.
meals	Lunch or dinner €20, on request.
closed	January; 15-31 August.
directions	A4 exit Padova Est, SS515 for Treviso. After Noale & level crossing for Badoere, Montebelluna. After S. Ambrogio left at lights. In Levada di Piombino, right at church; farm 100m.

Signor Alessandro Calzavara

tel	+39 049 9350308
fax	+39 049 9350016
email	gargan@gargan.it
web	www.gargan.it

Agriturismo

Map 4 Entry 67

Hotel Villa Luppis
via San Martino 34, 33080 Rivarotta di Pasiano

Still the grand country mansion it became in the early 1800s, when Napoleon secularised the monastery that had been here for centuries; the present owner's ancestors later made it a base for diplomatic activities. Geographically, it feels in limbo, too – on the border between Veneto and Friuli and surrounded by acres of flat farmland. The hotel, all creamy peeling stucco and terracotta roof tiles, is reached via an imposing gateway. Twelve acres of grounds include lawns and venerable trees, gravel paths and a fountain. Inside, the various formal reception and dining areas are graced with antiques and presided over by dignified staff. Bedrooms are elegantly old-fashioned, with comfortable beds and excellent bathrooms. You can go for walks along the river bank but really this place works best as a centre for day excursions. There's a daily shuttle into Venice and the staff will organise trips to other towns and cities, as well as to the Venetian and Palladian villas along the river Brenta. Cookery courses are on offer – and wine-tastings in what was once the monks' ice-cellar.

rooms	39: 31 doubles, 2 singles, 6 suites.
price	€205–€245.
	Singles €100–€112.
	Suite €260–€300.
meals	Dinner from €50.
closed	Rarely.
directions	From Oderzo towards Pordenone. Right at Mansue, signed. From A4, exit Cessalto (12km) for Motta di Livenza & Meduna di Livenza.

Signor Giorgio Ricci Luppis

tel	+39 0434 626969
fax	+39 0434 626228
email	hotel@villaluppis.it
web	www.villaluppis.it

Hotel

Map 4 Entry 68

Agriturismo Tenuta Regina
Casali Tenuta Regina 8, 33056 Palazzolo dello Stella

Views stretch to Croatia on a clear day. Great for a family holiday: an hour to Venice, Treviso, Trieste and Austria, 30 minutes to the sea, and a pool with snazzy loungers and a big garden with volleyball. The owners have children themselves, are wonderfully easy-going and proud of their new restoration; the breakfast room was completed in 2005. Now grandfather's farmhouse and grain store look spanking new outside and in, but the lovely old ceiling rafters remain. The most homely apartment is the largest, on the western end of the farmhouse: two storeys of laminated-wood floors and gleaming doors, a pristine white kitchen, four immaculately dressed beds and a sprinkling of attractive family pieces. Perhaps even a bunch of fresh roses – Giorgio's passion. The other apartments, three in front of the pool, two just over the road, feel more functional. Comfortable and open-plan, they come with new mattresses, spotless showers, dishwashers and safes; two are wheelchair-friendly. *Minimum stay two nights; July-August one week.*

rooms	8 apartments for 2-7.
price	€75-€100 for two.
meals	Restaurants 1.5km.
closed	Rarely.
directions	A4 Venezia-Trieste, exit Latisana; signs for Trieste. At Palazzolo, right at 1st lights for Piancada; continue for 7km.

	Alessandra Pasti
tel	+39 0431 587941
fax	+39 0431 587941
email	tenutaregina@adriabella.com
web	www.adriabella.com

Agriturismo & Self-catering

Map 5 Entry 69

Villa Corèn

via Cividale 1, 33040 Siacco di Povoletto

Dottor Cecioni loves his wines and his *sigaretti*, speaks fluent English and has your best interests at heart. His beautiful old villa lies in the vine-rich foothills of the Dolomites; he runs B&B in the house, and apartments in the restored cellars and barn. The sheer size of the place may overwhelm you on arrival, but it soon feels like home. Past the family portraits and the sitting rooms, the old frescoes, the wonderful wooden doors and the fine family furniture and up to two rooms let to one party. Windows are huge, the shower room is basic and the twin is large and quite lavish. Over the way are the apartments, nicely private with their own entrances and gardens. Beautiful terracotta, old beams, huge ceilings, open fireplaces, and a welcome pack of olive oil, coffee and three bottles of estate wine. Up to bedrooms simply decorated, nothing fancy – floral bedcovers, a rug here and there, the odd antique. No feminine touches but somehow it feels like home. Free bikes, a jacuzzi and sauna, a trattoria over the road, Slovenia a short drive. Perfect! *Apartments minimum stay one week July-August.*

rooms	2 + 6: 1 double, 1 twin, sharing bath, let to same party only. 6 apartments: 2 for 2, 4 for 4.
price	€77. Apartments €60 for 2, €85 for 4.
meals	Dinner with wine €20. Restaurants nearby.
closed	October-May.
directions	From the Tangenziale (ring road), exit Povoletto for Siacco.

Daniele Cecioni

tel	+39 0432 679 078
fax	+39 0432 679 078
email	info@villacoren.com
web	www.villacoren.com

Agriturismo La Faula
via Faula 5, Ravosa di Povoletto, 33040 Udine

An exuberant miscellany of dogs, donkeys and peacocks on a modern, working farm where rural laissez-faire and modern commerce happily mingle. La Faula has been in Luca's family for years; he and Paul, young and dynamic, abandoned the city to find themselves working harder than ever. Yet they put as much thought and energy into their guests as into the wine business and farm. The house stands in gentle countryside at the base of the Julian Alps – a big, comfortable home, and each bedroom delightful. Furniture is old, bathrooms new. There is a bistro-style restaurant where wonderful home-reared produce is served (free-range veal, beef, chicken, lamb, just-picked vegetables and fruits); on summer nights there may be a barbecue. An enormous old pergola provides dappled shade during the day; sit and dream awhile with a glass of estate wine or acquavita. Or wander round the vineyard and *cantina*, watch the wine-making in progress, cool off in the river – and visit the beaches of the Adriatic. *Discounts for longer stays. No meals during grape harvest. Minimum stay three nights.*

rooms	9 + 4: 9 twins/doubles. 4 mini-apartments for 2-4.
price	€40. Half-board €55–€65. Apartments from €60.
meals	Breakfast €5–€7. Dinner €15–€18.
closed	Rarely.
directions	A23 exit Udine Nord. SS13 to Tarvisio/Austria, follow signs to Pavoletto/Attimis.

	Paul Mackay & Luca Colautti
tel	+39 0432 666394
fax	+39 0432 647828
email	Send emails via web site.
web	www.faula.com

Agriturismo & Self-catering

Map 5 Entry 71

Casa del Grivò
Borgo Canal del Ferro 19, 33040 Faédis

This is the house that Toni built – or, rather, lovingly revived from ruin. The smallholding sits in a hamlet on the edge of a plain; behind, wonderful, high-wooded hills extend to the Slovenian border, sometimes crossed to gather wild berries. Your lovely hosts have three young children. Simplicity, rusticity and a 'green' approach are the keynotes here; so you'll sample traditional wool-and-vegetable-fibre-filled mattresses. Beds are comfy and blanketed, some with wonderful quilts. Your children will adore all the open spaces, the animals and the little pool that's been created by diverting a stream. Adults can relax with a book on a bedroom balcony, or in a distant corner of the garden. Maps are laid out at breakfast, and there are heaps of books on the region; the walking is wonderful, there's a castle to visit and a river to picnic by. Paola cooks fine dinners using old recipes and their own organic produce. There's a lovely open fire for cooking, and you dine by candlelight, sometimes to the gentle accompaniment of country songs: Paula was once a singer. *Minimum stay two nights, five in summer.*

rooms	4: 1 double, 2 family rooms sharing 2 bathrooms; 1 family room with separate bathroom.
price	€55. Half-board €45 p.p.
meals	Dinner from €25. Lunch in summer only. Picnic on request.
closed	December.
directions	From Faédis, via dei Castelli for Canébola. After 1.5km right, over bridge; 2nd house on left.

	Toni & Paola Costalunga
tel	+39 0432 728638
fax	+39 0432 728638
web	www.grivo.has.it

Agriturismo

Map 5 Entry 72

Golf Hotel Castello Formentini

via Oslavia 2, 34070 San Floriano del Collio

A wild boar prances on a weathervane above a creeper-covered tower. The medieval, hilltop castle near the Slovenian border, surrounded by rolling hills and vineyards, is a very comfortable, very stylish place to stay – whether your room is in the castle itself (ask if that's what you'd prefer) or in the mellow, friendly little inn across the way. The Formentini have been here since 1520 and the wild boar motif, in triplicate on the family coat of arms, recurs throughout – on fine porcelain, damask linen, white sheets. Amoretti biscuits, candles, a bottle of Prosecco and a note from the Contessa welcome you to a pleasant and generous bedroom. Enjoy a candlelit bath in a delicious bathroom and sleep deeply – you won't oversleep: the church clock begins its routine at 7am and continues until ten at night. Breakfast is on a stone terrace looking down over the village rooftops – a lavish affair that should fuel you through the most energetic day. The hotel has a couple of tennis courts, a pool and a nine-hole golf course – and you have discounts for four more in the area.

rooms	15: 6 doubles, 6 twins, 2 singles, 1 suite.
price	€225. Singles €135–€175. Suite €325.
meals	Restaurants 1km. Cold buffet free to guests, with wine.
closed	Mid-November–March
directions	From Goriza signs for hotel, 6km.

	Contessa Isabella Formentini
tel	+39 0481 884051
fax	+39 0481 884052
email	isabellaformentini@tiscalinet.it
web	www.golfhotelformentini.com

B&B

Map 5 Entry 73

Photo La Fenice, entry 79

emilia-romagna

Antica Torre

Case Bussandri 197, loc. Cangelasio, 43039 Salsomaggiore Terme

Two golden labradors ambling across the pristine gravel paths in the lee of the 14th-century tower and enormous colonnaded barn, covered in vines, exude a peaceful contentment – which belies the energy that the family pour into this enterprise. From sweeping flagstones at dawn to the final flourish of a delicious bottle at dinner, this family is devoted to agriturismo. Don't expect to stumble across farm machinery or be set upon by winsome lambs: Antica Torre, with its many buildings, has the air of a model farm. The big rooms in the *casa rustica*, with their ancient polished brick and tile floors, have strange and wondrous rustic furniture, and curly metal bed heads inject a light-hearted air. Otherwise, expect simple bathrooms, immaculate housekeeping and an honest rurality. With its huge fireplace and long tables covered in red gingham, the barn, where generous breakfasts are served, has a distinctly alpine air. In the evening, deep in the ancient Cistercian cellar, to the strains of plain chant and Puccini, feast with locals and guests on Vanda's astonishingly good cooking.

rooms	9: 8 twins/doubles, 1 suite for 4.
price	€100. Half-board €70 p.p.
meals	Dinner with wine €25.
closed	December-February.
directions	From Salsomaggiore centre, SP27 for Cangelasio & Piacenza. Fork left (signed Cangelasio); 1.5km; left for Antica Torre. Driveway left after 1.5km.

	Signor Francesco Pavesi
tel	+39 0524 575425
fax	+39 0524 575425
email	info@anticatorre.it
web	www.anticatorre.it

Agriturismo

Map 8 Entry 74

Villa Bellaria

via dei Gasperini, 29010 Cortina di Alseno

Off the track, but not isolated, tucked under a softly green hillside, this cream-painted *casa di collina*, with its wide hammock'd veranda and well-established garden, has been a retreat from summer heat since 1900. Having moved here 15 years ago, Marina, warm and kind, herself a keen traveller, decided to throw open its doors and share her enthusiasm for this lovely, little-known area with its medieval villages, castles and thermal cures. On the stairs, etchings of The East India Company recall the Raj. A much-loved, ornately carved mirror, made by her cabinetmaker father at his renowned atelier in Milan, graces a wall. Immaculate bedrooms are a happy mix of wrought-iron bedsteads, delicately embroidered blinds, tile floors and contemporary art. After breakfast alfresco – and delectable homemade tart – head off through leafy lanes to the walled hill town Castel Arquato, or Piacenza and Parma. After a hard day exploring or being sporty, contemplate the area's gastronomic delights: nothing sums up Emilia-Romagna so well as its food. This is a comfortable, civilised bolthole – and great value.

rooms	3 doubles.
price	€55-€62. Singles €35-€42.
meals	Restaurants nearby.
closed	Rarely.
directions	At traffic lights in Alseno head for Vernasca. On for 5km, right into small street for Cortina; house 2km with green gate on left.

	Sig.ra Marina Cazzaniga Calderoni
tel	+39 0523 947537
mobile	+39 338 6925674
email	info@villabellariabb.it
web	www.villabellariabb.it

B&B

Map 8 Entry 75

Villa Gaidello

via Gaidello 18, 41013 Castelfranco Emilia

A neat, pretty pattern of vineyards and fields edged with cypresses, two infant canals and a lake with swans: an unexpected find just off the main Modena-Bologna road. Paola's restaurant in a stone barn serves the most wonderful organic dishes and looks like an old oil painting – a long table bright with flowers, expectant rows of chairs, shadowy, arched ceilings, shelves of gleaming jars… There are three old farmhouses to stay in on the estate. The first, the *casa patronale*, is Gaidello, overlooking the garden and the lake. Further along the winding, tree-lined road are green-shuttered Gaianello and San Giacomo. The apartments range from old, thick-walled rooms with dark, period furniture to slightly more modern spaces with lighter furnishing and pale floor tiles. Bathrooms and kitchens are basic and functional. San Giacomo also has two independent double rooms with wrought-iron beds, fresh colours, matching friezes and wooden stable doors. Paola is the hard-working genius behind this peaceful place, a relaxed and friendly hostess. *Ask about gastronomic visits and courses.*

rooms	2 + 7: 2 doubles. 7 apartments for 1-6.
price	€93-€126. Apartments €86-€228.
meals	Dinner €45. Restaurant closed Mondays & Sunday evenings.
closed	August.
directions	From Modena, via Emilia to Castelfranco Emilia. Left at hospital lights for Nonantola. Under bridge, immed. right; 3rd left onto via Gaidello, 500m; signed.

	Signora Paola Bini
tel	+39 059 926 806
fax	+39 059 926 620
email	info@gaidello.com
web	www.gaidello.com

Agriturismo & Self-catering

Map 8 Entry 76

Azienda Agrituristica Tizzano

via Lamizze no. 1197, 41050 Monteombraro

Animals everywhere. Ducks pick their way through scattered straw across the yard, goats and ponies wander free, a tabby cat basks on ancient stone steps. Tizzano is a proper, organic farm, which Stefano hopes to make self-sufficient one day. His mother, Leonilde, uses the home-grown produce – meat and cheeses from the rare, white Modenese cow, chestnuts and cherries – in her cooking. But there are other reasons for coming here, especially if you seek an authentic taste of rural life. The farmhouse is medieval, set among fields on a hillside (not the easiest place to find!). Roses and vines climb its rough, peeling walls, small, shuttered windows keep the inside cool and an old archway leads to the kitchen, bright with postcards. The simple dining room serving simple food is reminiscent of a village school 50 years ago. Big, clean, camping-style bedrooms (two in the old barn, with kitchenettes planned) have lovely views. Their furniture dates back to the time of Stefano's grandparents. Stefano knows the area inside out and can tell you all about walks and places to visit. Good value.

rooms	8: 2 doubles, 2 triples, 2 family rooms for 4. Barn: 1 family for 3, 1 family for 5.
price	€44. Family room €70-€90. Half-board €35 p.p.
meals	Dinner €20.
closed	Rarely.
directions	A1 Modena-Bologna exit Spilamberto; left for Bazzano, right for Monteombraro. Before village, right on via Lamizze for 3km; left at no. 1197.

	Stefano & Leonilde Fogacci
tel	+39 059 989581
fax	+39 059 989581
email	agriturismo.tizzano@libero.it
web	www.agritizzano.it

Agriturismo

Map 8 Entry 77

La Piana dei Castagni
via Lusignano 11, 40040 Rocca di Roffeno

Write, paint, read or potter: here, deep in the woods, there's nothing to distract you. This is a secret little Hansel and Gretel house with demure shutters and lace-trimmed curtains. It stands isolated among chestnut trees, reached via a long, wriggling track; below are bucolic meadows, falling to a farm or two, and a further distant descent along the yawning valley. An old stone farmhouse converted and adapted for B&B, La Piana is a modest place to stay. The bedrooms, named after local berries, are a good size and painted in clean, pastel colours; tiny pictures hang above beds and little windows set in thick walls look out over the glorious valley. The shower rooms – one of them a restyled chicken shed! – are simply tiled. Valeria lives ten minutes away at La Civetta. She is gentle, kind, spoiling; even the breakfast *torti di noce* are homemade. She will also help organise everything, from trekking to truffle hunting. Rocca di Roffeno is a pretty village with 14th-century buildings and towers, a smattering of Roman ruins and lots of restaurants with Bolognese delicacies to try.

rooms	5: 2 doubles, 2 triples, 1 single.
price	€60-€80. Triple €80-€100. Singles €35.
meals	Dinner €17, set menu.
closed	December-March.
directions	From Tolè, follow signs for S. Lucia & Bocca Ravari; after 'Torre Jussi' follow signs.

Signora Valeria Vitali

tel	+39 051 912985
fax	+39 051 912985
email	info@pianadeicastagni.it
web	www.pianadeicastagni.it

Agriturismo

Map 8 Entry 78

La Fenice

via S. Lucia 29, Ca' de Gatti, 40040 Rocca di Roffeno

A spectacular spot – such views – and a great place for all the family. Remo and
Paolo are brothers and farmers (the farm has been in the family for five
generations) and are constantly restoring and renovating their beloved Fenice – in
true Romagna style. Guest bedrooms in the old house have a hotchpotch of
furniture that hangs together well, and lovely big rafters, some very low. Rooms
are darkish, windows small; most have their own entrances, some have fireplaces
and logs on the house; it's super-cosy in winter. More low rafters in the recently
renovated, cloister-like building next door where five new bedrooms lie. Active
teenagers will be happy here: there are mountains bikes, quad bikes, archery and a
pool, and horse riding is a five-mile drive. La Fenice's restaurant is another reason
to stay; the food is locally sourced, reasonably priced and truly delicious. You are
800m above sea level – all that fresh air and outdoor living will build up an
appetite. Visit the stones of Rocca Malatina, the waterfalls of Labante, the
restaurants of hilltop Zocca. *Half-board minimum stay three nights.*

rooms	14: 9 doubles, 1 twin/double, 2 triples, 2 family.
price	€80. Half-board €120 for two.
meals	Dinner from €25.
closed	7 January-6 February.
directions	From Bologna SS64 south 30km, right to Tole, then towards Cereglio. After 1.5km, right. La Fenice 5km from Tole on right.

Remo & Paolo Giarandoni

tel	+39 051 919272
fax	+39 051 919024
email	lafenice@lafeniceagritur.it
web	www.lafeniceagritur.it

B&B

Map 8 Entry 79

B&B a Bologna
via Cairoli 3, 40121 Bologna

Before it became a B&B, nuns lived here – but don't expect cloisters. This is a modern Italian city apartment block with a central lift and a winding stair. Davide offers a pleasant, peaceful, no-frills place to stay in the centre of the city. A long, narrow, white-painted corridor, enlivened with the occasional picture, leads to clean, light bedrooms, cool with tiled floors and blinds. The furniture is fairly plain but comfortable, beds are floral and there's lots of space. Two of the bedrooms share a huge bathroom and a washing machine – ideal for a family. Breakfast is in your room or in the dining area but, if you prefer it earlier or later than the norm, Davide will give you vouchers for the bar round the corner. It's all very flexible and friendly, you have your own keys so you may come and go as you please, there are plenty of good restaurants to choose from, the Piazza Maggiore is only a ten-minute walk and a bi-weekly market a short stroll. Davide also runs a hilltop agriturismo a 15-minute drive outside the city with amazing views.

rooms	4: 1 double, 1 triple; 2 doubles, sharing bath.
price	€65–€110. Triple €95–€120.
meals	Restaurants nearby.
closed	January.
directions	Right out of train station; 1st left onto via Amendola; 2nd right onto via Milazzo; 100m, left onto via Cairoli. On 2nd floor; ring bell.

	Davide de Lucca
tel/fax	+39 051 4210897
mobile	+39 328 3161357
email	takakina@hotmail.com
web	www.traveleurope.it/bolognabb

B&B

Map 8 Entry 80

Art Hotel Novecento
Piazza Galileo 3/4, 40123 Bologna

Another Art Hotel, another lovely old townhouse in the centre of Bologna. But this one has been refitted in a style that has echoes of 1930s Viennese Secession. Bedrooms are black, white and beige, smart and minimalist, with low-slung beds, Asian-inspired furniture, sparkling marble bathrooms and expensive linen. A central staircase with wrought-iron railings climbs past the different floors to the very top; here presides a grand suite with an arched triple window and a balcony overlooking the peaceful street below. The place runs on perfectly oiled wheels, the staff are helpful, the bikes are free and you can ask for breakfast in bed. Like Art Hotel Orologio round the corner, this fabulous hotel is in a very central position, with the town hall, the Palazzo Communale, right behind. If you crave something lush and splendid after the Novecento's cutting-edge art and clean lines, drop by. Two 16th-century doorways are attributed to Alessi and a fine collection of miniatures and paintings from the Bolognese School await your discovery.

rooms	25: 15 doubles, 9 singles, 1 suite.
price	€191–€326.
	Singles €135–€211.
	Suite €278–€434.
meals	Restaurants nearby.
closed	August.
directions	In *centro storico*, 300m from Piazza Maggiore. Garage.

Signor Mauro Orsi

tel	+39 051 7457311
fax	+39 051 7457322
email	arthotel.novecento@inbo.it
web	www.bolognarthotels.it

Hotel

Map 8 Entry 81

Art Hotel Orologio
via IV Novembre 10, 40123 Bologna

Just off the Piazza Maggiore – one of Italy's most beautiful medieval squares – is the Orologio, a tall, narrow slice of building wedged between a bank and a bookshop. It would be easy to miss, its glass and brass entrance guarded by small shrubs is so discreet. Immediately above the door, plants trail through a pretty, latticed railing in front of a green-shuttered window. Step into a reception hall, hung with clocks and big mirrors, and make your first acquaintance with the kind, friendly, multi-national staff. Above are the tranquil sitting and breakfast rooms (breakfast is an excellent spread), then the well-decorated bedrooms with their padded headboards, soft carpets and papered walls. Bathrooms are immaculate, generous suites come with sitting areas, sofabeds and statues, and well-dressed windows look over an intriguing maze of terracotta rooftops or across to the piazza and the Duomo. You are wonderfully central yet this intimate hotel is fabulously quiet. Outside the entrance is seating so you can watch the comings and goings of the square before joining the glorious fray.

rooms	34 doubles.
price	€173-€326.
	Suite €260-€434.
meals	Restaurants nearby.
closed	Rarely.
directions	From station, buses 25 or 37 stop in Piazza Maggiore, 70m from hotel. Parking.

	Signora Cristina Orsi
tel	+39 051 7457411
fax	+39 051 7457422
email	arthotel.orologio@inbo.it
web	www.bolognarthotels.it

Art Hotel Commercianti
via dei Pignattari 11, 40124 Bologna

The Basilica of San Petronio, one of the greatest churches of the Catholic world, is on the other side of the street; opposite its west front is the Piazza Maggiore, Bologna's great square. You are in the heart of it, and yet there is little noise and barely any traffic. The Commercianti is, astonishingly, a restored 12th-century building whose conversion has managed to avoid the errors of many. Bedrooms are magnificent, many with their massive old (and low!) beams exposed and six with little terraces overlooking the gothic Basilica. The suites are particularly impressive, with lovely sloping beamed ceilings. One room has the exposed remnants of an early fresco but all have a slightly medieval feel, with white, rough-plaster walls, some wrought-iron furniture, wooden floors and Persian rugs. The marble, blue-carpeted staircase leads down past a fine marble bust to the breakfast room, where the first meal of the day does full justice to its impressive setting. Magnificently central, and if you don't wish to walk, take a bike instead: they're free for guests.

rooms	34: 22 doubles, 7 singles, 3 suites for 3, 2 suites for 4.
price	€196-€214. Singles €139. Suites €284-€258.
meals	Restaurants nearby.
closed	Rarely.
directions	Hotel in *centro storico*, in pedestrianised area. Garage.

	Signor Mauro Orsi
tel	+39 051 7457511
fax	+39 051 7457522
email	arthotel.commercianti@inbo.it
web	www.bolognarthotels.it

Hotel

Map 8 Entry 83

Hotel Corona d'Oro 1890
via Oberdan 12, 40126 Bologna

The palazzo, with its glorious 14th-century wooden portico, is full of history. And the Liberty-style interiors are spectacular. A lavish plastered frieze runs round the glass-roofed central hall; two columns tower above the patterned wall-seats. Old-fashioned gold-striped sofas and armchairs, slightly formal, are entirely fitting. Huge potted plants stand on a marble floor, there are Venetian wall lights and Art Nouveau glass; the effect is opulent and makes the Corono d'Oro special. Just off the hall is a charming little bar/breakfast room, a mirror reflecting light off the whole of one wall. Bedrooms are not large but solidly comfortable, in a rather traditional 'hotel' style, with brass-edged sockets and light fittings, heavy curtains and built-in desks. Some have tiny terraces or balconies overlooking the glass roof of the central hall; bathrooms are impeccable. Breakfast is a huge treat, the staff are charming and you are as central as it gets, just off a pedestrian street 200 metres from Bologna's two leaning towers.

rooms	40: 30 doubles, 8 singles, 2 suites.
price	€191–€326.
	Singles €135–€211.
	Suite €278–€434.
meals	Restaurant next door.
closed	August.
directions	In *centro storico*, in little street off via Rizzoli. Parking.

	Signor Mauro Orsi
tel	+39 051 7457611
fax	+39 051 7457622
email	arthotel.corona@inbo.it
web	www.bolognarthotels.it

Azienda Vitivinicola e Agrituristica Trerè

via Casale 19, 48018 Faenza

Braided vineyards stretch as far as the eye can see. In the middle of this flat, green patchwork: a compact grouping of rosy buildings and a clump of tall trees in one corner. The entertainingly angular farmhouse is surrounded by converted barns and stables – now apartments and a conference room. This is a wine-producing estate; around the house are certificates and awards, a shop and a fabulous little rose-and-gold wine museum. Despite all this, there's a family feel; toys are scattered about and the atmosphere is easy. The bedrooms in the house have a light and pretty elegance, with beamed ceilings, pastel walls, lovely old family furniture and memorable touches – the deep lace trim of a white sheet folded over a jade bedcover, a wall full of books. The apartments, in the old stables, are attractive but more modern and functional. Each has French windows opening onto a private patio, and a mezzanine with an extra bed tucked under a skylight – fun for kids. The restaurant is only open on weekend evenings, but there are other places to eat nearby. *Air conditioning in apartments.*

rooms	7 + 4: 3 doubles, 2 twins, 1 triple, 1 suite for 2-5. 4 apts: 3 for 4, 1 for 6.
price	€62-€70. Singles €42-€52. Suite €135-€150. Apt €86-€77 for 4. €135-€150 for 6.
meals	Breakfast €5. Dinner €20 (closed January-February & Mon-Thurs). Restaurants 2km.
closed	Rarely.
directions	From Faenza via Emilia SS9 for Imola/Bologna; 3km left after Volvo garage on via Casale; signed.

	Morena Trerè & Massimiliano Fabbri
tel	+39 0546 47034
fax	+39 0546 47012
email	trere@trere.com
web	www.trere.com

Agriturismo & Self-catering

Map 9 Entry 85

Torre Pratesi

via Cavina 11, Cavina, 48013 Brisighella

The invention of gun powder rendered this beautiful, squat and angular 16th-century tower defunct. It was later roofed and turned into a hunting lodge; a farmhouse was added in 1800; now it is a small hotel. The two buildings are an impressive sight, the renovation a sensitive one. The décor is a gentle mix of antique and contemporary, with wrought-iron furniture, red leather armchairs, kilim rugs and, usefully, a coffee machine in every room. Each floor of tower – reached via a lift or spiral stair – has one big tiled room with small windows and gorgeous great rafters. The suites in the old farmhouse have small sitting areas, some with an open fireplace. Torre Pratesi is still a working farm and you may be encouraged to purchase some of the olive oil, cheese or wine. All are put to good use in the kitchen by Nerio. A path leads down from the well-kept orchard and garden to the pool and outdoor jacuzzi. This is great walking country, with marked trails stretching away from the ridge behind the house, and the mountain views are very fine.

rooms	9: 3 doubles, 6 suites.
price	€129-€155.
	Suites €155-€181.
meals	Dinner €39-€44.
closed	10-25 January.
directions	From Brisighella through Fognano. Right just after village. On SP63, 3km to Torre Pratesi.

	Nerio & Letty Raccagni
tel	+39 0546 84545
fax	+39 0546 84558
email	torrep@tin.it
web	www.torrepratesi.it

Relais Varnello
via Rontana 34, 48013 Brisighella

Just above the pretty town of Brisighella, but you'll need the car – it's quite a hike! In young gardens, the brick buildings stand sparklingly clean and tickety-boo. Nicely-furnished rooms have views across the valley or garden; the suites are in a separate building, with a sauna. The farm produces Sangiovese DOC wine and olive oil, which you can buy along with Faenza pottery showing the family crest. Giovanni has been producing oil and wine all his life and you won't leave here without a bottle or two – its delicious. If you speak a little Italian, pick his brains, he has a vast knowledge of Italian grapes (over 1,000 varieties) and will happily tell you about some of the best wines available. Spend your days lounging by the pool: there are wide views over the Padana and to the Adriatic, and there's a private wild park – Giovanni's pride and joy – just a stroll away: a lovely place for a picnic and a book. Higher up the hill is the Pacro Carné, with Club Alpino Italiano (CAI) walking trails. *Minimum stay two nights.*

rooms	6: 4 twins/doubles, 2 suites.
price	€130. Suites €180.
meals	Dinner from €20. Restaurant 400m.
closed	January-15 March.
directions	From Brisighella on SP23 Montecino & Limisano road, signed to Riolo Terme. After 3km, left after Ristorante È Manicômi, signed to Rontana. Relais 1st building on right.

Signor Giovanni Liverzani

tel	+39 0546 85493
fax	+39 0546 83124
email	info@varnello.it
web	www.varnello.it

Agriturismo

Map 9 Entry 87

B&B Valferrara

via Valferrara 14, Pantano, 42033 Carpineti

Along an ancient road, now a footpath, between Canossa and Carpineti, this 17th-century travellers' lodge sits in the silent hamlet of Valferrara. Weary merchants would rest their heads in peace – and absorb the calm and protection of the surrounding forested hills and distant castle of Carpineti. Ruined when Giuliano and Cosetta discovered it in 1994, the *casa di scale* ('tiered house'), complete with flat-roofed Emilian tower – where a clutch of apartments are almost ready – has been completely and masterfully restored with local materials, and the parquet flooring fashioned from recycled beams of oak. Cosetta restores local antique furniture and the house is full of it; crisp cotton envelops large, beautifully framed beds and an eye-catching walnut writing desk stands elegantly near one of her several finely polished wardrobes. Expect a warm welcome and a delicious breakfast – under the cool portico, in the walled garden or in the dining room: a fabulous conversion of the old stables. Fresh parmesan can be sampled locally and smiling Cosetta, also a great cook, provides dinner on request.

rooms	3: 1 double;
	2 doubles sharing bathroom.
price	€76–€90.
meals	Restaurants 1km–4km.
	Dinner on request.
closed	Rarely.
directions	From A1 Bologna-Milano exit Modena Nord. Follow SS via Emilia to Reggio Emilia exit Scandiano to Viano; to Carpineti; At Cigarello right to Pantano. After 4km right to Valferrara. On left at end of road.

	Cosetta Mordacci & Giuliano Beghi
mobile	+39 340 1561417
email	info@bb-valferrara.it
web	www.bb-valferrara.it

Photo Monte Pù, entry 96

liguria

Villa Elisa
via Romana 70, 18012 Bordighera

The climate is kind: visit at any time of the year. The hotel was built in the 20s when Bordighera, a pretty town with sloping tree-lined roads and pastel houses, became a winter retreat. Maurizio's father, who ran it for years, was a painter and had artists to stay – bedroom walls are still hung with the works they left him. Some still come, following in the steps of Monet. Your hosts are the nicest you could wish to meet. Maurizio takes groups off into the Maritime Alps in his minibus and guides them back on three-hour walks, Rita likes to spoil – she has even provided a playroom for children, and special activities for summer. Bedrooms have parquet floors and are dressed in blue; bathrooms are white-tiled with floral friezes and heated towel rails; larger rooms have terraces with views to the hills. There's a courtyard garden scented with oranges and lemons, and a wonderful pool area with plenty of quiet corners. The pebbled beach is a ten-minute dash down the hill and the restaurant is charming; fresh fish is on the menu and the wine list is long. *Air conditioning extra charge.*

rooms	34 + 1: 30 doubles, 3 singles, 1 suite. 1 apartment for 4.
price	€116-€176. Singles €78-€108. Suite €196-€246. Apt €204-€264. Half or full-board option for weekly stays.
meals	Lunch or dinner from €40.
closed	5 November-22 December.
directions	Via Romana parallel to main road through town (via Aurelia), reachable by any crossroad that links the two. Villa at western end.

	Signora Francesca Oggero
tel	+39 0184 261313
fax	+39 0184 261942
email	info@villaelisa.com
web	www.villaelisa.com

Hotel & Self-catering

Map 6 Entry 89

Casa Forcheri

via Scala Santa 6, 18010 Diano Castello

You're greeted in the entrance *salotto* by framed daguerreotypes of Uncle Raffaele and Aunt Santina... having passed the arms of the Bishop of Turin on the stairs. This big, gracious apartment is part of a townhouse which once belonged to Maura's forebears. High, beautifully frescoed ceilings, ornate floor tiles and lovingly maintained family antiques lend a charmingly dynastic air and the two-bedroom apartment is characterised by coolness and space – a pleasant antidote to the heat outside. The dining room leads to a large, modern, glazed terrace-drawing room which can be opened right up to bring in the evening breeze. Recline on a sofa and browse through Maura's collection of books on the region. Though the big kitchen with its antique dresser has a pre-war feel, it is well equipped with all mod cons. You are right in the middle of Diano Castello, where styles veer delightfully from medieval and baroque to Genoese-Romanesque. Either side, the views are wonderful – in one direction, the ancient hilltop village; in the other, hills, olive groves and sea. *Minimum stay one week.*

rooms	Apartment for 4.
price	€650-€750 per week.
meals	Restaurant in village.
closed	Rarely.
directions	Exit motorway at San Bartolomeo Al Mare towards Diano Marina & then to Diano Castello; park in car park near church.

Maura Muratorio

tel/fax	+39 0183 498226
mobile	+39 335 45 66 17
email	mauram@libero.it
web	www.casaforcheri.it

Self-catering

Map 6 Entry 90

Villa della Pergola

via privata Montagù 9/1, 17021 Alassio

Above the pretty town of Alassio hang vast, spellbindingly lovely gardens. It's nearly 20 years since the last Hanbury left but the family's legacy remains. Hidden among the glorious trees and shrubs planted by Sir Daniel is this lovely, 19th-century house. Built in Italian colonial style, with colonnades, balustrades and loggias, Villa della Pergola is a chance to see how the English aristocracy once lived on the Riviera. Supreme elegance *all'inglese* combines with the best Italy has to offer: wonderful marble, the yellow, blue and ochre tones of Liguria, columns, Moorish fountains, astonishing views. Though Marcella's family bought the house in 1985, they have kept its English country-house flavour. Luxurious bedrooms in soft, restful colours are each named after a member of the Hanbury family – Daniel, Ruth, Cecile; they still feel part of a long-cherished family home and you almost expect Sir Daniel to knock on your door and invite you down to breakfast when you're ready. Indeed, the breakfast will include marmalade made to the recipe of a former Hanbury family cook. *Minimum stay two nights.*

rooms	6: 3 doubles, 1 triple, 1 suite for 2-3, 1 family.
price	€190-€250.
meals	Restaurants within walking distance.
closed	Rarely.
directions	Highway A10 Genova-Ventimiglia, exit Albenga 5km, exit Andora 10km.

	Marcella de Martini
mobile	+39 3332 789305
fax	+39 0182 554969
email	info@villadellapergola.it
web	www.villadellapergola.it

Casa Cambi
via Roma 42, 17034 Castelcecchio di Rocca Barbena

You can hardly believe that such a village has survived unspoilt into the 21st century. It's a fairytale tangle of winding cobbled streets and medieval stone houses on a green and rocky hilltop. All around are dramatic mountains and stupendous views. A square, uncompromising castle dominates the hill; immediately below is Anna's entrancing house. A tiny front door (the house is 700 years old, after all) takes you straight into a delightful, vaulted room – a soothing mix of creams and whites, ochres and umbers. Pale walls contrast with a gleaming wooden floor and old polished furniture; its subtle, restrained country charm sets the tone for the rest of the house. All the rooms are a delight, all full of unexpected touches – jugs of fresh wild flowers, hessian curtains on wrought-iron poles, a rack of old black kitchen implements stark against a white wall... Anna adores her house and has lavished huge care on it. She's bubbly and friendly and loves cooking; her kitchen is a joy to be in. Breakfast out in the pretty terraced garden among olive and fig trees and revel in those mountain views.

rooms	4: 2 doubles, 1 twin, 1 family.
price	€90.
meals	Dinner from €25.
closed	5 November-March.
	Out of season fax: +39 010812613.
directions	A10 exit Albenga. S582 for Garessio for Castelvecchio do Rocca Barbena, 12km. Free car park outside pedestrianised Borgo, 5-min walk.

Anna Bozano

tel	+39 0182 78009
fax	+39 0182 78009
email	casacambi@casacambi.it
web	www.casacambi.it

B&B

Map 6 Entry 92

Palazzo Fieschi

Piazza della Chiesa 14, 16010 Savignone

The name of this elegant townhouse near Genoa commemorates former owners, the distinguished Fieschi family, once a power in the land. Now it belongs to Simonetta and Aldo Caprile, who left the world of commerce for a life of hotel-keeping. They have carefully renovated the old palazzo, and added every modern comfort to its *cinquecento* grandeur. The oldest working hotel in Liguria, it overlooks a square and is a short walk to the centre; there's also a shuttle service for guests. The surrounding countryside is steep and wooded, away from the autostradas and with walking nearby. Bedrooms are white-walled and spotless, many with fabulous carved or painted bedheads. The rooms vary, but those on the mezzanine floor in the oldest section of the house have the most character: beautiful tiles, grand doorways, low ceilings. The dining room, with its chandeliers and sweeping red drapes, is popular for weddings. The Capriles are courteous hosts, and you may encounter the odd musical evening in winter. *Minimum stay two nights.*

rooms	24: 13 doubles, 2 triples, 1 family, 8 singles.
price	€118-€130. Triples €135-€162. Family room €150-€170. Singles €73-€98.
meals	Lunch or dinner €26-€41.
closed	25 December-February.
directions	From A7 exit to Busalla. In Busalla for Casella; 3.5km, left for Savignone. Hotel in village centre.

Aldo & Simonetta Caprile

tel	+39 010 9360063
fax	+39 010 936821
email	fieschi@split.it
web	www.palazzofieschi.it

Villa Gnocchi

via Romana 53, San Lorenzo della Costa, 16038 Santa Margherita Ligure

Why bother with Portofino after a visit to Roberto's villa? It is an idyllic spot, yet close to the action. Roberto, a farmer, trained at Pisa University and inherited the house from his grandfather in a run-down state – what you now see is the result of years of hard work. They love farming here, deep in the country but within sight of the sea; sip a glass of chilled wine from the terrace and gaze down the coast. Bedrooms are individual: some white, some ochre, all simple and charming. Grandfather's old furniture graces parquet floors; muslin curtains flutter at open windows. The check-clothed dining room, too, is friendly and inviting. The only sound to break the peace is birdsong – and the faint hoot from the train and the traffic below. Santa Margherita – a 15-minute walk downhill, a bumpy taxi ride up – is a charming little town: a beach, fishing boats, good shops, lively bars. Old framed prints on the walls, delicious meals on the table, paths to most of the villages and buses from the gate: a wonderful spot, and your hosts couldn't be more generous and friendly.

rooms	9: 5 doubles, 2 twins, 2 family.
price	€100.
meals	Half-board €70 p.p.
closed	Mid-October-Easter.
directions	From Santa Margherita for S. Lorenzo, 4km. Pass big sign 'Genova & S. Lorenzo' on left, Rapallo & A12 on right, 50m ahead, left down narrow road. At red & white barrier ring bell.

	Signor Roberto Gnocchi
tel/fax	+39 0185 283431
mobile	+39 333 6191898
email	roberto.gnocchi@tin.it

Agriturismo

Map 7 Entry 94

Hotel Villa Edera
via Venino 12, 16030 Moneglia

The villa, perched above the village of Moneglia, is reached through five low narrow tunnels: thrilling for some, daunting for others… Regulars sometimes come by train and walk, but staff will gladly fetch you. This is the best sort of family-run hotel. Orietta, the elder daughter, is manageress – businesslike yet approachable, she sings in the local choir and loves meeting people who share her interest in music. Her husband and her sister's husband are waiters; mother Ida is a brilliant cook, preparing Ligurian dishes, some vegetarian, with the freshest organic produce, and fabulous breakfasts. Father Lino ensures that it all runs like clockwork. Orietta is a keen walker who may take guests out for some proper hikes – unless you prefer to catch a boat to Portofino and explore the Cinque Terre by sea. You are fairly close to the railway here (a significant part of the landscape, threading the Cinque Terre villages together) but you would never know. A fitness room, sauna, jacuzzi, lovely pool – and the beach a ten-minute walk. *Minimum stay two nights.*

rooms	27: 21 doubles, 2 family, 2 singles, 2 suites.
price	€120-€190. Singles €80-€120. Suites €160-€250. Half-board €65-€105 p.p.
meals	Lunch or dinner €25-€30.
closed	10 November-15 March.
directions	Exit A12 at Sestri Levante; signs for Moneglia tunnel. Immed. after 5th tunnel right (at sports field); signed. Free parking.

	Signora Orietta Schiaffino
tel	+39 0185 49291
fax	+39 0185 49470
email	info@villaedera.com
web	www.villaedera.com

Hotel

Map 7 Entry 95

Monte Pù

loc. Monte Pù, 16030 Castiglione Chiavarese

The farm stands, remote and blissfully silent, on the site of a ninth-century Benedictine monastery whose tiny chapel still survives; the cherry and pear orchards and trout ponds are surrounded by woods. Pù (from the Latin *purus*) means pure, referring to the quality of the air and natural spring water and harking back to the importance of purification in monastic life. Organic produce is served in the restaurant; rabbits, goats, hens, cows all contribute in their various ways. Aurora sometimes finds time to sit with guests on summer evenings – to gaze at the stars, the fireflies and the lights of fishing vessels on the sea far below. It is a very beautiful place. One of the bedrooms has an optional kitchen, well-equipped but, understandably, seldom used. Provided you can face negotiating the steep, rugged road, this makes a good base; if you prefer, a minibus to Genoa can be arranged, which can also call at Sestri Levante station. Archery, flower-arranging and cookery lessons are offered, and there's a huge sitting/recreation room. The chapel can even be used for weddings, provided the reception is held here too.

rooms	10 + 1: 5 doubles, 3 triples, 2 family. 1 apartment for 6.
price	€80. Half-board €58 p.p. Apartment €120.
meals	Dinner €20-€28.
closed	November-Easter.
directions	From Sestri Levante for Casarza. Approx. 1km beyond Casarza, left to Massasco & Campegli. Monte Pù on left just before Campegli, up 4km of private road.

	Signora Aurora Giani
tel	+39 0185 408027
fax	+39 0185 408027
email	montepu@libero.it
web	www.montepu.it

Hotel & Self-catering

Map 7 Entry 96

Agriturismo Giandriale
loc. Giandriale 5, 19010 Tavarone di Maissana

Once city dwellers in Milan, Giani and Lucia have made the restoration of what was a very run-down property their life's work. The position is isolated but the surroundings are heavenly: high pastures dotted with trees, dense woods beyond, alpine views. The Val di Vara is a completely protected environmental zone, where hunting is forbidden and only organic farming allowed. You may join in with the farm activities if you wish, or doze off with a book. Simple bedrooms (no hanging space) are in the house and outbuildings: thick stone walls, wooden furniture, colourful rugs, cane and bamboo. Traditional farm furniture, much of it chestnut, stands alongside the modern. Your hosts have young children and will be happy to meet yours – there's so much space to run around in, and Lucia will help children identify flowers, trees and wildlife. There's even an adventure park in the trees. Breakfasts are sociable affairs around the big table, a feast of home-grown produce. Beware the rough and narrow track: leave the low-slung Morgan behind! Tranquillity is your reward.

rooms	6 + 2: 3 doubles, 3 triples. 1 apartment for 4, 1 for 5.
price	€60. Apartment €37 p.p. with breakfast.
meals	Dinner €15.
closed	Rarely.
directions	From Sestri Levante N523 for Parma. On for 14km thro' tunnel & immed. right before 'Torza' for Tavarone then Giandriale. Steep, pot-holed track to top.

	Giani & Lucia Nereo
tel	+39 0187 840279
fax	+39 0187 840156
email	info@giandriale.it
web	www.giandriale.it

Agriturismo & Self-catering

Map 7 Entry 97

Agriturismo Ca' du Chittu
via Camporione 25, 19012 Carro

A white house stands out against the rounded shoulder of a wooded hill. Beehives colonise one slope; all around are orchards, vegetable plots and vines. It's rural, genuine, satisfying. The farm belongs to Ennio and Donatella, who work immensely hard and are proud of their 'five-daisy' award for organic produce, all of which can be sampled in Donatella's cooking. Wonderful smells emanate from the kitchen as you pass; meals are at long tables in the plain, uncluttered dining room. There's a lived-in, comfortable sitting room, too, full of games and books. You have plenty to do: explore the surrounding hills on horseback or mountain bike, book in for a cookery or painting course. Then retreat to a simple, immaculate, white-walled bedroom with old country furniture and wooden bedstead. The rooms on the first floor open onto a terracotta-tiled terrace with lovely views. All the bedrooms are named after someone who has worked for Ennio and Donatella over the last 20 years – Livia, Francesca, Orietta… It's a nice touch, typical of this couple's warmth and generosity.

rooms	7 doubles.
price	€58.
	Half-board €44 p.p.
meals	Dinner, 8 courses, €21.
closed	Rarely.
directions	From A12 exit Casello. At Carrodano direction Sesta Godano. On outskirts of Carro for Velva; after 1km left for Pavareto; 500m: 1st house on left.

	Donatella & Ennio Nardi
tel/fax	+39 0187 861205
mobile	+39 335 8037376
email	caduchittu@virgilio.it
web	www.caduchittu.it

Agriturismo

Map 7 Entry 98

La Carnea

via San Rocco 10, Carnea, 19020 Follo

Laura and Beppe are happy in their haven: an old stone farmhouse in the wooded hills overlooking the Ligurian coast. Young, relaxed, full of smiles, they do B&B for the love of it, glad to share the good life. On the terraces are vines and olives; vegetables and fruit are organically grown. The bedrooms, in converted outhouses, are simple and small and the bathrooms, some shared, are rudimentary, but you have your own entrance and an incomparable view. Laura cooks, Beppe plays guitar; join in a sing-song after supper. Delicious meals with a vegetarian slant are served in an IKEA-look dining room with views to the sea; breakfasts linger until 11am. La Carnea is a wonderful way to enjoy life's simple pleasures and if you do so to excess you can walk it off by taking the coastal route between the cliff towns along the Cinque Terre, or trek in the nearby woods. There are no signs indicating La Carnea so have faith in the directions; there is a hint along the route – *siete quasi arrivati!* ('you're almost there!') – to reassure you. *Not suitable for children. Minimum stay 2-7 nights depending on season.*

rooms	6: 4 doubles, 2 with sep. bathrooms; 2 doubles sharing bathroom.
price	€70-€76. Extra beds €10 p.p.
meals	Half-board €50-€53 p.p.
closed	Rarely.
directions	A12 exit La Spezia, Vezzano Ligure for Bottagna & Follo. Over bridge, immed. left; right for Carnea. At foot of village sharp left via S. Rocco. At chapel, right on dirt road, 1.5km.

Laura & Beppe Castiglioni

tel	+39 0187 947070
fax	+39 0187 947070
email	agriturismocarnea@hotmail.com
web	www.agriturismocarnea.it

Agriturismo

Map 7 Entry 99

Villa Margherita by the Sea B&B

via Trento e Trieste 31, 19015 Levanto

Federico, the young, understated owner of this family hotel, assures us that if you want to explore his native Cinque Terre, the train and a pair of walking boots are the answer. (Or hop on a boat.) He himself will shuttle you to the local station of this old-fashioned seaside town. Built in 1906, the villa once mingled with the smart set and played her part in the summer seasons between the wars, when Levanto was seriously fashionable. Fishermen still fish, children build sandcastles but the glitterati have moved on. Sensitively renovated in classic Liguria ochre and decorative fresco, the house sits in leafy, terraced gardens with tall palms. White walls, muslin-clad windows and deep armchairs welcome. Charm abounds – in each marble stair, graceful iron banister and decorative floor tile. Simply furnished, flowery bedrooms, family bathrooms and unfussy style imbue the house with the spirit of a well-loved, long-established pensione. And if you and your family stay in the comfortable garden flat, join the others for breakfast in the traditional blue and yellow breakfast room.

rooms	7 + 1: 7 doubles. 1 apartment for 4.
price	€85–€125.
	Apartment €400–€1,100 per week.
meals	Restaurants nearby.
closed	Never.
directions	From A12 exit Carrodano & Levanto; right after station; left onto main street; right Corsa Italia up hill; hotel on left; parking signed.

	Federico Campodonico
tel/fax	+39 0187 807212
mobile	+39 328 8426934
email	info@villamargherita.net
web	www.villamargherita.net

B&B & Self-catering

Map 7 Entry 100

Hotel Stella Maris

via Marconi 4, 19015 Levanto

A grand villa of 1870, oozing character and largesse. The frescoed ceiling in the entrance is a dream, a mere hint of what is to come. Bedrooms have frescoed or stuccoed ceilings, some of which depict the activities carried out in each when the place was a private villa. Every room is tall and splendid; antiques and chandeliers are de rigeur, décor is wine-red and cream. White bathrooms are perfectly proportioned and planned, with delicious linen; rooms in the annexe navy and modern. Ask on booking for one of the quieter rooms. Renza is adorable; she has an eye for comfort and has thought of everything, even a washing-machine for long-stay guests. She genuinely loves looking after people and does the cooking herself, including occasional dinners served alfresco with music. The restaurant is classically elegant and, though tables are separate; Renza is happiest when guests link up. Breakfast is simple buffet, coffee comes from a vending machine. The town is lovely, full of activity and character, and with a good beach. *Minimum stay two nights.*

rooms	8: 4 doubles, 1 single, 3 suites for 3-4.
price	Half-board: €200-€240; singles €120; suites €300.
meals	Half-board only.
closed	November.
directions	Via Marconi lane off via Jacopo da Levanto. Hotel above Banco Chiavari bank. Entrance around corner, use 1st-floor bell.

	Signora Renza Pagnini
tel	+39 0187 808258
fax	+39 0187 807351
email	renza@hotelstellamaris.it
web	www.hotelstellamaris.it

Hotel

Map 7 Entry 101

Agriturismo Villanova

loc. Villanova, 19015 Levanto

Villanova is where Barone Giancarlo Massola's ancestors spent their summers in the 18th century; it has barely changed since. The villa is a mile from Levanto, yet modern life feels far behind as you wend your way up the hills through olive groves. The red and cream villa stands in a small, sunny clearing. Giancarlo, quiet, charming, much-travelled, loves meeting new folk; his cat and golden retriever are friendly too. Guest bedrooms are in both the main house and in a small stone farmhouse behind; they have an elegant, country-house feel, and are large, airy and terracotta-tiled. Furniture is of wood and wrought iron, beautiful fabrics are yellow and blue. All have private entrances and terraces with pretty views. Two of the apartments are separate, a third is in the farmhouse. Giancarlo grows organic apricots, figs and vegetables and makes his own wine and olive oil; breakfasts are delicious. This is a great place to bring children: swings and table tennis in the garden, space to run around in, the coast nearby. There's internet access, too. *Minimum stay two nights; one week August.*

rooms	9 + 4: 4 doubles, 3 triples, 2 suites for 3. 4 apartments for 3-6.
price	€90–€110. Triples €120–€150. Suites €120–€170. Apartments €600–€1,000 per week.
meals	Restaurants 1.5km. Self-catering in apartments.
closed	November–February.
directions	Exit A12 at Carrodano Levanto towards Levanto. Signs from junction before town (direction Monterosso & Cinque Terre).

Barone Giancarlo Massola

tel	+39 0187 802517
fax	+39 0187 803519
email	info@agriturismovillanova.it
web	www.agriturismovillanova.it

Agriturismo & Self-catering

Map 7 Entry 102

Photo Azienda Agricola Podere Salicotto, entry 193

tuscany

Villa Mimosa
Corlaga Bagnone, 54021 Bagnone

These are the Apennines, steep chestnut-covered hills that rise to 6,000 feet, topped with snow in winter. Bagnone is a tiny medieval village of huge charm, in a wilder countryside than its southern counterpart Chianti. This handsome, well-proportioned house – once a flour mill – is a warm and open-hearted retreat run by people for whom hospitality is second nature. The flagged dining room is cool and inviting, the reading room stuffed with good books, the first-floor sitting room a joy: light and airy, with old pattern-tiled floors, pretty vaulted ceiling, big cotton-covered sofas, a grand piano for those musical evenings, views over the richly wooded hills. Comforting bedrooms come English-style, with wash basins in the corner, bath and shower rooms with pink towels. Jennie and Alan are well-rooted here, will be hugely helpful and their food is worth climbing the hills for. (Occasional Aga cookery courses, too.) In the garden is an above-ground pool, sandy beaches are a half-hour drive, Lerici has a castle and a lovely bay, Parma, Lucca and Pisa are an hour away. Charming, hospitable, well-sited.

rooms	4: 3 doubles, 1 family room for 4.
price	€90–€110. Singles €60.
meals	Dinner with wine, 4 courses, €43.
closed	November–mid-February. Open Christmas & New Year by arrangement.
directions	Exit A15 at Aulla/Pontremoli. SS62 for Villafranca. Through archway, left into V. Niccolo Quatiere (signed Carabinieri). Left at 1st fork. At r'bout to Corlaga. Park behind church; walk back 50m. 2nd on left.

Jennie & Alan Pratt

tel	+39 0187 427022
fax	+39 0187 427022
email	mimosa@col.it
web	www.villamimosa-tuscany.com

B&B

Map 8 Entry 103

B&B Dimora Olimpia

Borghetto 27, 54017 Licciana Nardi

When they came here it was a ruin; eight years on, Olimpia and Gaetano's 16th-century farm house is an exquisitely restored home. For the full force of its charm, approach via the cobbled back street where chickens potter and an archway leads to a neighbouring farmer's house. This is a verdant, very unspoilt part of Tuscany – country roads, tiny villages, good walks, fine wines. Passionate lovers of old things, your hosts are also fluent guides to the region; there are uninterrupted views of fields, woods and rumpled hills from elegant terrace and pool. Gorgeousness abounds: bare beams and exposed brickwork have been lovingly preserved, there are old wall hangings, very fine, early country furniture and, in the snug bedroom, original shutters at tiny windows. The apartments are small, simple and charming, peaceful and cool, their beds aligned with the Earth's magnetic field to ensure perfect sleep. Shower rooms are first-class, kitchens are tiny, pillow cases are lined with lace. You will dine well in nearby restaurants and are most welcome to join B&B guests round the antique Indian table. Special.

rooms	2 + 1: 1 double, 1 suite. 1 apartment for 4.
price	€70-€75. Apartment €350-€450 per week.
meals	Restaurants 4km.
closed	Never.
directions	From Aulla SS62 to SS665, then Monti & Amola. Right for Dimora Olimpia in middle of village; on right.

Olimpia De Caro & Gaetano Azzolina

tel	+39 0187 471580
fax	+39 0187 472977
email	info@dimoraolimpia.com
web	www.dimoraolimpia.com

Fosdinovo Bed & Breakfast
via Montecarboli 12, 54035 Fosdinovo

You really are on top of the hill here and the views are wonderful. From the terrace you look over Castle Fosdinovo (one of over 100 castles in the area, flood-lit at night) to the Bocca di Magra estuary and Monte Marcello. On a clear day you can see Elba and Corsica – but don't count on it! The house was built in the early 1960s and is open plan. Slate steps lead up to a pleasant sitting area, with a teak-deck floor (from an old boat), a rough-cut stone fireplace and comfy leather sofas with views. Videos and books provide entertainment should you get snowed in. The bedrooms are white-walled, comfortable, practical and super-clean; new beds have embroidered linen sheets which belonged to Lidia's mother. Lidia and Andreas are friendly, enthusiastic and speak excellent English, and give you your own key so you can come and go as you please. There's a wonderful restaurant a five-minute drive away but you're welcome to bring your own drinks and snacks to eat on the terrace in the evening; you're also encouraged to help yourself to fruit from the orchard in front of the house. Breakfasts are a surprise every day.

rooms	2: 1 double, 1 twin.
price	€75.
meals	Good restaurant 5-minute drive.
closed	November.
directions	From A12 exit Sarzana; SS1 for 3km for Carrara-Massa; left SS446 for Fosdinovo. Pass village & castle. Right at x-roads for Carrara. 150m on, left on V. Montecarboli. After 400m track right. On left.

	Lidia & Andrea Fabbretti
tel/fax	+39 0187 68465
mobile	+39 3475971923
email	info@fosdinovo-bb.com
web	www.fosdinovo-bb.com

B&B

Map 8 Entry 105

La Cerreta
Castelnuovo di Garfagnana

Be different and head for the hills. The chestnut-covered slopes of northern Tuscany are resplendent in autumn when the smell of wood smoke hangs in the air, lush in spring and summer and perfect in winter – after a decent snowfall – for a day's skiing or sledging nearby. Dip down through the vines to La Cerreta, standing sentinel over the valley. Many views are described as breathtaking and here's another – across to the ancient walled town of Castiglione, encircled by snowy peaks. Inside are whitewashed walls, old beams, open fireplaces, two double rooms, sofabeds and a cot – but it's outside where the little house comes into its own. Imagine a sunny terrace and secret, shady corners for a languid afternoon. Then set off for the local restaurant where Mauro and his family will spoil you rotten. And if all gets too relaxing, you can always pop down the road to the six-hole golf course with its dinky clubhouse, or pack a picnic and walk in any direction. Jazz and opera fans can head for arty Barga – an irresistibly cobbled, medieval hilltop town where there's always a festival in the offing.

rooms	House for 4-6.
price	€500-€1,200 per week.
meals	Restaurants 2-3km.
closed	Rarely.
directions	Directions on booking.

Sarah Bolton
tel   +44 (0)117 926 0867
email   info@lacerreta.co.uk
web   www.lacerreta.co.uk

Peralta
Pieve di Camaiore, 55043 Camaiore

Peralta is precariously perched on the foothills of Mount Prana. The sculptress Fiore de Henriquez took it on 30 years ago, a labyrinth of ancient dwellings connected by steep steps and sun-dappled terraces. Lemon trees, jasmine and bougainvillea romp on every corner, a sculpture peeps from every cranny, the chestnut-groved valley swoops to the sea. The whole place hums with creativity. Rooms are properly rustic and full of charm, some light, some less so; all have vibrant walls, breathtaking views, perhaps an old red sofa, a simple bed covered in a striped cover, a rag rug on a terracotta floor. Four of the apartments have dishwashers, a rare concession to modernity. Australian Dinah and her helpers draw you together like one big family: there's a panoramic terrace where guests gather to swap stories, a light-filled studio for courses (art, writing, Tuscan cookery), a log-fuelled sitting room, a dining table for 14, a small pool. It is an adventure to get here – the approach road will thrill – and an adventure to stay. *Leave car at bottom of track; they will collect you. Children over 10 welcome.*

rooms	6 + 6: 4 doubles, 1 twin, 1 family. 6 apartments: for 2, 4, 5, 7 or 8.
price	€60-€110. Apartments €200-€2,120 per week.
meals	Breakfast €6 for self-caterers. Dinner with wine €25.
closed	Dec-Feb. (Self-catering never.)
directions	From A12 Livorno/Genoa, exit Camaiore. Left after Camaiore for Pieve, uphill, signs for Peralta. Left at fork for Peralta, pass blue sign & onto Agliano. Unsigned.

	Kate Simova & Dinah Voisin
tel	+39 0584 951230
fax	+39 0584 951230
email	peraltusc@tiscali.it
web	www.peraltatuscany.com

B&B & Self-catering

Map 8 Entry 107

Casa Gialla - La Bergenia
via di Contra No.38, 55041 Camaiore

Laura describes the style here as 'allegro': light, breezy, full of zing. She's a prestigious sculptress, and her artistic touches are everywhere. Take the open-plan sitting room: dried lavender and colourful pictures, wicker chairs elbow-deep in cushions, exposed brickwork around columns and archways. All three bedrooms link you to the lovely gardens; look out on lemon trees from the citrus-themed room, inhale the scent of roses from the rose room. All are serene in cream with one or two splashes of colour – a sprig of purple flowers on a wardrobe, an old print hand-tinted by Laura's grandmother. Immaculate white bathrooms have big showers. Breakfasts are an array of homemade cakes and breads, cheese, ham, eggs, most of it from a friend's organic *orto*; on fine days you eat on the rose-strewn pergola to a panorama of the Apennines, the hills sprinkled with villages down to the sea. Hidden up a private lane, five minutes from Camaiore, the peace is delicious. Later, join your charming hostess for an aperitif or a glass of fresh, cold peach juice. Handy for the Puccini festival. *Minimum stay two nights.*

rooms	3 doubles.
price	€130.
meals	Dinner on request.
closed	Rarely.
directions	Exit motorway at Camaiore and phone owner.

Laura Frigerio
tel	+39 0584 984035
mobile	+39 335 6180878
email	info@labergenia.it
web	www.labergenia.it

B&B

Map 8 Entry 108

Hotel Villa Volpi
via di Gugliano 47, 55029 Mastiano

You could be in an E M Forster novel. A ribbon of road twists its way up from Lucca (not for nervous drivers!) to this glorious, isolated place. A cluster of old, gravely beautiful buildings stands surrounded by olive groves and gentle hills, terraced fields and vines; perched on the hill opposite is a tiny church. (The hotel pool and gardens are wisely positioned to make the most of the stunning panorama.) Follow the gravelled drive to a mellow, arched doorway to be greeted by friendly, solicitous staff. Rooms in this villa-hotel are an appealing mix of understated elegance and farmhouse rusticity. Downstairs are two cream and ochre sitting rooms, one with, one without TV; upstairs is a cool library, dark with mahogany furniture. In the bedrooms, pale stone walls contrast with beam-and-brick ceilings and terracotta floors; beds wear green, red or yellow quilts; bathrooms are gorgeous. The windows are generously sized, framing the stunning outlook: rooms with a view, indeed. There's an excellent and stylish restaurant, too, popular with non-residents and guests.

rooms	16: 10 twins/doubles, 6 singles.
price	€130. Half board €20 p.p. extra.
meals	Dinner €20 (not Tues). Restaurants 4km.
closed	Last three weeks January.
directions	SS12 for Abetone Bagni di Lucca until Ponte a Moriano, 5km. Left at village square; left across bridge; right, then 1st left; signed.

Sig. Gianmaria Barbieri

tel	+39 0583 406137
fax	+39 0583 405007
email	info@hotelvillavolpi.com
web	www.hotelvillavolpi.com

Hotel

Map 8 Entry 109

Hotel Albergo Villa Marta
Ponte Guasperini 873, San Lorenzo a Vaccoli, Lucca

The huge table in reception, fashioned from an Indonesian bed, sets the mood. This is a youthful, unstuffy yet elegant place. Originally a hunting lodge, the 19th-century villa-hotel is the young creation of a husband and wife team who have their feet firmly on the ground and their heads full of plans... for Tuscan Christmasses, wine and chocolate tours, horse riding in the hills. The house rests in sweeping lawns enfolded by the Monti Pisani (from whose verdant hills you can spot Pisa's leaning tower). The whole feel is wonderfully intimate and yet there's masses of space. Bedrooms ooze subtlety and comfort: fabrics with flowers and stripes, peach and grey walls, one or two frescoed ceilings, lots of modern art. Bed linen is delicious, walk-in showers luxurious, views bucolic. A stress-free shuttle ferries you into Lucca; return to a cocktail in the Renaissance garden and a plunge in the pool. In winter you breakfast by an open fire – on freshly laid eggs and home-baked brioches. Fancy getting married here? You can – there's an enchanting private chapel on the hillside.

rooms	15: 13 doubles, 2 suites for 2.
price	€119-€170. Singles €90-€130.
meals	Lunch €20-€40.
closed	Rarely.
directions	A12 Firenze-Mare; exit Lucca Ovest; signs for Pisa onto SS12; signs to Villa Marta; in village, after 750m, left into via del Ponte Guasperini; entrance 500m on left. Can be tricky, ask for detailed directions on booking.

	Andrea Martinelli
tel	+39 0583 955774
fax	+39 0583 379999
email	info@albergovillamarta.it
web	www.albergovillamarta.it

Hotel

Map 8 Entry 110

Villa Alessandra

via Arsina 1100b, 55100 Lucca

They ask that you stay for at least three nights, so do – it is worth every penny. You will be a privileged guest in a beautiful country house close to one of Italy's most perfect towns. Despite a touch of formality you will find that you can treat the place as home; take your own picnic into one of the gardens, cool off in the pool, come and go as you please. The road to the house is a country lane, the countryside gentle and very lovely, the house within distant sight of Lucca. The two sitting rooms are stylish and welcoming with big floral sofas, *terre cuite* floors, beautiful murals and attractive little touches. All but one of the bedrooms has a view, all are appealing: white walls and open stonework, wicker armchairs, generous fabrics, splendid bathrooms. One has a four-poster. There are three bikes for you to borrow, walks into the hills, medieval Lucca to explore and the fashionable seaside resort of Forte dei Marmi to discover. Your hosts are very proud of their villa – rightly so – and breakfasts are quite a spread. *Minimum stay three nights.*

rooms	6: 5 doubles, 1 twin.
price	€125–€155.
	Whole villa €8,000 per week.
meals	Restaurants nearby.
closed	Christmas.
directions	From Lucca north on Camaiore road; cross River Serchio right to Monte S.Quirico; 1.5km right; left to Arsina (Via Billona) to via Arsina on right; after 1.1km drive on right.

	Signora Enrica Tosca
tel	+39 0583 395171
fax	+39 0583 395828
email	villa.ale@mailcity.com
web	www.villa-alessandra.it

B&B & Self-catering

Map 8 Entry 111

Albergo San Martino
via della Dogana 9, 55100 Lucca

There's a fresh-faced enthusiasm about the San Martino. Opened five years ago, it still shines: there's none of the tired cynicism that has overtaken so many central hotels in tourist towns. It is a pretty little three-storey building, painted yellow, a minute from the lovely Piazza Napoleone and a brief stroll from the mighty cathedral. There are no architectural flourishes, no rushes to the head – this is just a simple, comfortable little three-star in one of Italy's loveliest towns. The tiny lobby has a small sofa and armchair of soft blue leather, and original paintings above a Tuscan-style tiled marble floor. The staircase and landings (no lift) are brightly lit, the bedrooms have impeccably comfortable beds and furniture a touch more personal than that of a chain hotel; bathrooms are spot on. It is satisfying to throw open the shutters and gaze down on a quiet Tuscan street – you feel very much part of Lucca yet you are on a reasonably peaceful corner. Charming service; excellent breakfast on a sweet terrace; bikes to hire for jaunts around town. *Minimum stay two nights in high season.*

rooms	8: 7 doubles, 2 suites for 3-4.
price	€110. Suites €160.
meals	Breakfast €10. Restaurants nearby.
closed	Rarely.
directions	In the Old Town next to the cathedral. Ask for directions. Parking 400m: extra charge.

	Signor Andrea Marotti
tel	+39 0583 469181
fax	+39 0583 991940
email	info@albergosanmartino.it
web	www.albergosanmartino.it

Villa Michaela

via di Valle 8, 55060 Vorno

A lifetime's treat. Writers, celebrities and a First Lady have all stayed here, in the opulent Tuscan villa with its *House & Garden* interiors. You can even make it your own: indulge family and friends and get married in its chapel. You may have the best luck booking out of season. Come for a few days, join a Slow Food house party, sample local wines, listen to opera. An interior designer has worked his magic on every room, mingling fine English furniture with classic Italian style, while Puccini, Verdi and Dante lend their names to the grander bedrooms, awash with frescoed ceilings, lavish fabrics, king-size beds and double sinks. Also: a family kitchen, a formal dining room, a library and a room for TV, tennis and an outdoor pool. Dine alfresco, on culinary artist Luca's divine concoctions, and let your gaze drift over the floodlit gardens, heady with gardenias, to the 50 acres of pine forests and olive groves beyond. You are bathed in tranquillity yet it's a five-minute walk to the delightful village of Vorno, and unspoilt Lucca is a ten-minute drive. *Coach house for six occasionally available.*

rooms	10 doubles.
price	€200-€300.
	Entire villa on request.
meals	Dinner €50.
closed	Never.
directions	SS12 from Lucca to Guamo. Follow signs for Vorno. Villa behind church.

Vanessa Swarbreck

tel	+39 0583 971371
fax	+39 0583 971292
email	vanessaswarbreck@yahoo.co.uk
web	www.villamichaela.com

B&B & Self-catering

Map 8 Entry 113

Fattoria di Pietrabuona

via per Medicina 2, Pietrabuona, 51010 Péscia

Hide yourself away in the foothills of the Svizzera Pesciatina – Tuscany's 'Little Switzerland'. Home to a beguiling brood of ancient breed Cinta Senese pigs, this huge estate immersed in greenery is presided over by the elegant Signora – an unlikely pig farmer. The farm buildings have been cleverly divided into apartments that fit together like a puzzle; we liked the three oldest best, near the main villa and each very private. The rest – and the communal pool – are quite a drive up winding hills and some of the roads, though well-maintained, are precipitous in parts: not for the faint-hearted nor those worried about heavily-laden hire cars. All have gardens, outside seating and stupendous views. The exteriors are full of character, the interiors are simple and some of the newer apartments have steep stairs. Bring a Tuscan cookbook: the kitchens, some with old sinks but with new everything else, ask to be used, and there's a small shop next to the office selling estate produce. The views are amazing, particularly from the pool, and the villages are worth a good wander. *Minimum stay one week.*

rooms	14 apartments: 5 for 2, 5 for 4, 3 for 6, 1 for 8.
price	€400–€1,200 per week.
meals	Restaurants & pizzerias nearby.
closed	November–February, but open Christmas & New Year.
directions	Exit A11 at Chiesina Uzzanese towards Péscia, then Abetone & Pietrabuona. After P. left for Medicina; left again. After 500m road becomes an avenue of cypresses. Villa & Fattoria at end.

	Signora Maristella Galeotti Flori
tel	+39 0572 408115
fax	+39 0572 408150
email	info@pietrabuona.com
web	www.pietrabuona.com

Self-catering

Map 8 Entry 114

Poderino Lero

via in Campo 42, 51010 Massa e Cozzile

An old farmhouse up in the hills with beautiful views over olive groves and Montecatini – a perfect place to unwind. There's a homely atmosphere here, with family, cats, dogs – and Maria Luisa and Lucia, who love having people to stay. Built against a hill centuries ago, a lemon tree clambering up its front, the house is cool in summer and warm in winter. The bedroom in the main house has a stone floor, white walls and is furnished with country antiques; it's slightly dated but in a nice way, and has a relaxed feel. The other rooms to the side of the house have been done in a modern style, and have walk-in showers. There's good, homemade breakfast from Maria Luisa, while dinner, up in the hills, is a ten-minute drive. Downstairs is a large open room with fireplace and comfortable sofas which opens onto the garden – relax on sunloungers and drink in the views: you are surrounded by tumbling olive groves and vines. Chimes and mosaics in the garden, small pieces of Lucia's artwork inserted into the masonry, serene sculptures dotted around – a deeply relaxing place.

rooms	3 + 1: 2 doubles, 1 triple. 1 apartment for 2-4.
price	€68. Singles €45. Triple €90. Apartment €500 per week.
meals	Dinner €30-€35. Restaurants 3km.
closed	Rarely.
directions	A11 Firenze-Pisa exit Montecatini Terme, follow signs to Pescia. At Montecatini towards Massa e Cozzile. After 2 curves, follow street down to Poderino Lero, signed.

	Signora Maria Luisa Nesti
tel	+39 0572 60218
fax	+39 0572 60218
email	poderinolero@yahoo.it

B&B & Self-catering

Map 8 Entry 115

Antica Casa "Le Rondini"

via M Pierucci 21, Colle di Buggiano

Imagine a room above an archway in an ancient hilltop village, within ancient castle walls. You lean from the window and watch the swallows dart to and fro – and there are *rondini* inside the room too, captured in an enchanting 200-year-old fresco. The way through the arch – the Via del Vento ('where the wind blows') – and the front door to this captivating house wait just the other side. Step into a lovely room, a study in white – fresh lilies, pure-white walls and sofas – dotted with family antiques and paintings. Fulvia and Carlo are warm, interesting hosts who immediately make you feel at home. The delightfully different bedrooms have wrought-iron bedheads, big mirrors and some original stencilling. Several, like the Swallow Room, have pale frescoes; all have good views. The little apartment, too, is simple, charming, peaceful. Just across the cobbled street is a pretty garden with lemon trees and plenty of shade – an idyllic place for breakfast on sunny mornings. A short walk brings you to the square where village ladies sit playing cards, children scamper and the church bell rings every hour, on the hour.

rooms	5 + 1: 5 doubles.
	1 apartment for 2-4.
price	€75-€115. Apartment €65 for 2.
meals	Restaurant 200m.
closed	November-February.
directions	A11 Firenze-Pisa Nord. Exit Montecatini Terme. Follow signs to Pescia. Left after 2nd set of traffic lights. Right after petrol station. Follow sign "Malocchio-Colle-Buggiano". Up hill to parking area on right.

	Fulvia Musso
tel	+39 0572 33313
fax	+39 0572 905361
email	info@anticacasa.it
web	www.anticacasa.it

B&B & Self-catering

Map 8 Entry 116

Tenuta di Pieve a Celle
via di Pieve a Celle 158, 51030 Pistoia

Fiorenza welcomes you with coffee and homemade cake, Julie – the retriever –
escorts you round the garden, and there are freshly-laid eggs for breakfast. This is
pure, genuine hospitality. Off a country road and down a cypress-lined drive, the
shuttered, ochre-coloured *colonica* sits amid the family farm's olive groves and
vineyards. The Saccentis (three generations) live next door but this house feels
very much like home. Bedrooms (one downstairs) are furnished with well-loved
antiques, rugs on tiled floors and handsome wrought-iron or upholstered beds.
Cesare, Fiorenza's husband, designed the fabrics – pretty country motifs – and his
collection of African art is dotted around the rooms. Books, flowers, soft lighting
give a warm and restful feel. There's an elegant but cosy sitting room, with
fireplace, where you eat breakfast if it's too chilly on the patio, and dinner is by
request. Sometimes the Saccentis join you: a real family affair. Laze by the pool
with views to distant hills, walk in the woods, borrow bikes or visit nearby Lucca.

rooms	5 twins/doubles.
price	€120–€140.
meals	Dinner €30, on request.
closed	Rarely.
directions	A11 for Pisa Nord. Exit Pistoia; signs for Montagnana; 2km, Tenuta on right. Ring bell at gates.

Cesare & Fiorenza Saccenti

tel/fax	+39 0573 913087
mobile	+39 335 247839
email	info@tenutadipieveacelle.it
web	www.tenutadipieveacelle.it

Agriturismo

Map 8 Entry 117

Villa Anna Maria

SS dell'Abetone 146, 56010 Molina di Quosa

The wrought-iron gates swing open to reveal a tropical paradise. You feel protected here from the outside world, miles from the heat and bustle of Pisa. It is an intriguing place, with numerous secret rooms behind locked doors; some bedrooms seem almost untouched since the 17th century. They are all different, themed and with high ceilings, the most curious being the Persian and the Egyptian. The entrance hall is splendidly marble, graced with columns and chandelier; the library – a touch over the top for some – is perfectly in tune with the ornate house, and with its entertaining owner. Claudio collects anything and everything and rooms are crammed with antiques and silverware. A somewhat shambolic place – but your hosts care more about people than they do about money and there are no rules: treat this as your home. There's a game room with billiards and videos (3,000 of them!), table tennis, a huge dog, woodland paths, a pool with piped music among the bamboo, and a delightful barbecue area for those who choose to self-cater. *Minimum stay two nights.*

rooms	6 + 1: 6 doubles/triples (or 2 apartments for 2-8). 1 cottage for 2-3.
price	€120–€150. Singles €90. Apartments €800–€2,000 per week. Cottage €1,000 per week.
meals	Dinner €40.
closed	Rarely.
directions	From Pisa SS12 for Lucca. At S.Giuliano Terme, SS12 left down hill; after Rigoli to Molina di Quosa. On right opposite pharmacy.

Signor Claudio Zeppi

tel/fax	+39 050 850139
mobile	+39 328 2334450
email	zeppi@villaannamaria.com
web	www.villaannamaria.com

B&B & Self-catering

Map 8 Entry 118

Agriturismo Fattoria di Migliarino
viale dei Pini 289, 56010 Migliarino

On 3,000 farmed hectares fronting the sea is an agriturismo run on immaculate wheels. This is due to the charm and indefatigable energy of Martino and Giovanna, a young couple with four children who understand perfectly the needs of families. The B&B rooms are in the main house: Tuscan beds, soft wall lights and prints, mosquito-proofed windows, big arched sitting areas and a raftered dining room with two sociable tables. In the buildings beyond are 13 apartments of every shape and size. Most are two-storey, all have terraces divided by hedges of jasmine – you may be as private or as gregarious as you like. There's a family pool open from June to September, a new 'quiet' pool too, neatly gravelled pathways and lawned spaces with loungers, a well-being centre brimming with treatments, a farm shop for meat, wine and olive oil, football, tennis, ping-pong and sporting activities you can book yourselves into, including riding and sailing. It's five miles to Pisa, elegant Lucca is not much further and the sandy beaches are a bike ride away – you can hire a bike, too. *Dinner (min. 15) on request.*

rooms	10 + 13: 10 doubles. 13 apartments for 4-6.
price	€80–€140. Apartments €312–€1,370 per week.
meals	Breakfast €5 for self-caterers. Restaurants 1km.
closed	Never.
directions	Exit A11-A12 Pisa Nord, left for Pisa; 1st lights right under r'way bridge to viale dei Pini. Left after 800m; in via del Mare.

	Dott. Martino & Giovanna Salviati
mobile	+39 348 4435100
fax	+39 050 803170
email	info@fattoriadimigliarino.it
web	www.fattoriadimigliarino.it

B&B & Self-catering

Map 8 Entry 119

Antica Dimora Leones
via della Rocca 2, 56036 Palaia

A labyrinth of vaulted ceilings, stone fireplaces and original frescoes, this is that rarity: a hotel with an intimate feel. In the heart of the medieval borgo of Palaia, the palazzo was restored in the 1800s but goes way back to AD1000, when it formed part of the castle. Now it is an antique collector's paradise – which is no surprise: the owner's grandparents were antique dealers. It almost feels as though they are still here, wandering the historic corridors and rooms. Specialness is everywhere, from the high frescoed ceilings of the 'noble floor' to the bare beams and rooftop views of the characterful servants' quarters. Every floor has a wonderful sitting room or library, with books, comfy chairs and something precious in each corner. A tray of drinks awaits your arrival; the buffet breakfast (salami, cheeses, homemade cakes) is served in the beamed dining room or under wisteria in the pretty garden. So much history, yet there are some winning modern touches – notably the seven-person hydropool. Restorative, soothing, special – and don't miss the lovely Etruscan town of Volterra.

rooms	13: 12 doubles, 1 single.
price	€95–€120.
meals	Meals for small groups €25, on request. Restaurants 100m.
closed	Rarely.
directions	Superstrada Firenze-Pisa-Livorno, exit Pontedera, follow signs for Palaia centre. Just beyond clock tower on the corner.

	Andrea Soldani
tel	+39 0587 622024
fax	+39 02 4814736
email	info@leones-palaia.it
web	www.leones-palaia.it

B&B

Map 8 Entry 120

Venzano

Mazzolla, 56048 Volterra

A little secret garden, far from the madding crowd. This enchanting place was granted to the Augustinian order in the tenth century and remained in their hands for over 900 years. Venzano is now privately owned, and although the main thrust is still agricultural, gardening is the focus. For years Donald and friends have been creating a green enclave in a series of terraces moving outwards from a Roman spring. Their inspiration has been the legacy of the monks' love of plants, for their beauty and their usefulness... and you may help yourself to the results. There is a long tradition of Italian garden design, tempered here by a sense of humility when contemplating the beauty of the surroundings. Parts of the rambling building have been converted into big, lofty apartments; all have terraces, some with views of the rolling hills. Facilities are simple – bathrooms strictly functional, a washing machine to share, firewood and heating in cold weather – but the décor of the living spaces is as attractive as it is spare. Come for the perfectly simple life in a lesser-known corner of Tuscany. *Minimum stay one week.*

rooms	3 apartments: 2 for 2-3, 1 for 4.
price	€700–€1,120 per week.
meals	Self-catering. Trattoria 2km.
closed	November–March.
directions	From Volterra SS68 for Colle Val d'Elsa for 10km. Right for Mazzolla. After 3km right for Venzano.

	Donald Leevers
tel	+39 0588 39095
fax	+39 0588 39095
email	info@venzanogardens.com
web	www.venzanogardens.com

Self-catering

Map 8 Entry 121

 Hello

Villa Torricelli Ciamponi

viale Matteotti 40, 50038 Scarperia

A handsome palazzo surrounded by cypresses and pines – an oasis behind high walls. You sweep through the original gates and step into the hall, grand with fireplace and coat of arms, then up stone steps (or a lift for the weary). This was Signor Puccetti's grandmother's house, now converted into 11 fine flats; these three remain in the family. Some have beams, others tall ceilings, and the doors of the ground-floor spaces lead to private gardens. One apartment, roomy and inviting, was the wine cellar for the Torricelli Ciamponi farm where, two generations ago, Mugellan wine and Vin Santo were produced; another was the farm manager's office. Features include an old bread oven, generous dining tables, cream curtains, white walls, mod cons, no clutter. On the first floor is a cosy nest for two: Grandma's brass bed, a little round table and sofa, a new floor hand-crafted from the villa's wine barrels, a terrace overlooking the grounds. You are just half an hour by bus – or train – from Florence, two minutes from fine shops, delis and bars. A pine wood opposite promises fine walks. *Private parking.*

rooms	3 apartments: 2 for 4, 1 for 3.
price	€300-€800 per week.
meals	fRestaurants 2km.
closed	Rarely.
directions	A1 exit Barberino di Mugello for Scarperia; in Viale Matteotti, house with big gates & high wall.

Francesco Puccetti

mobile	+39 340 3578609
fax	+39 055 8431414
email	info@ilgiardinetto.com
web	www.ilgiardinetto.com

Self-catering

Map 8 Entry 122

Monsignor della Casa Country Resort
via di Mucciano 16, 50030 Borgo San Lorenzo

It could be a Giotto landscape: the view of Monte Senario has not changed for 500 years. But the old buildings in the hamlet where estate workers once lived have become an attractive 'resort', wonderful for all ages. Run by the charming Marzi family, the complex has a warm, inviting feel. Bay hedges and big terracotta pots of herbs scent the courtyards, there are cherry and olive trees everywhere, a playground and two safely fenced pools. The apartments, mostly on two floors, are stylish and uncluttered, with fireplaces, stonework, beams; all have little gardens; the villas have private pools. Airy bedrooms are painted in soft colours; some have four-posters with fine linen drapes, others wrought-iron beds. You can eat in the bar/restaurant where hams hang from the beams – the menu is Tuscan, the wine list long. Then burn off the calories in the Wellness Centre, splendid with sauna, jacuzzi and gym. Close by is the Renaissance villa where Monsignor Giovanni Della Casa, a descendant of the Medicis, was born in 1503.
Minimum stay 2-7 nights for B&B, depending on season.

rooms	16 apartments: for 2, 4, 6 or 8. 2 villas: 1 for 8-12, 1 for 12-16.
price	B&B: €145-€185. Apartments €600-€1,500 per week. Villas €1,550-€5,000 per week.
meals	Dinner €25-€40. Restaurants 5km.
closed	6 January-15 March.
directions	From m'way exit A1 Barberino di Mugello; signs to Borgo San Lorenzo; signs to Faenza; right after 2.7km , signs to Mucciano and Corniolo. After 1km left to villa.

	Alessio Marzi
tel	+39 055 840821
fax	+39 055 840840
email	booking@monsignore.com
web	www.monsignore.com

B&B & Self-catering

Map 8 Entry 123

Casa Palmira

via Faentina 4/1, loc. Feriolo, Polcanto, 50030 Borgo San Lorenzo

A medieval farm expertly restored by charming Assunta and Stefano who, being Italian, have a flair for this sort of thing. You are immersed in greenery yet half an hour from Florentine bustle. The views on the road to Fiesole are stunning; Stefano will take you round neighbouring villages in his mini-van, or you may hire a mountain bike, tucking one of Assunta's packed picnic baskets on the back. (They run cookery courses here, too.) The log-fired sitting room sets the tone: the *casa* has a warm, Tuscan feel, and bedrooms open off a landing with a brick-walled 'garden' in the centre – all Stefano's work. Most – but not all – are a good size and beautifully turned out with a clean, contemporary feel: beds dressed in Florentine fabric, polished wooden floors. You look onto gardens where Assunta grows herbs and vegetables, or onto vines and olive trees. You are 500m above sea level so... no need for air conditioning and no mosquitoes! Breakfast on apricots and home-produced yogurt; dine on Tuscan food. There is also an excellent restaurant up the road. *Check-in before 7pm. Minimum stay three nights.*

rooms	7 + 1: 4 twins/doubles, 1 twin, 1 triple, 1 family room. 1 apartment for 2-3.
price	€75-€95. Triple €115. Family €130. Apartment €500 per week.
meals	Dinner with wine €30. Restaurant 700m.
closed	10 January-10 March.
directions	From north, A1 exit Barberino del Mugello for Borgo S. Lorenzo. From Polcanto 17km; house on left.

	Assunta & Stefano Fiorini-Mattioli
tel	+39 055 8409749
fax	+39 055 8409749
email	info@casapalmira.it
web	www.casapalmira.it

Villa Campestri

via di Campestri 19/22, 50039 Vicchio di Mugello

High in the Tuscan hills, at the end of an avenue of cypresses, surrounded by parkland, olive groves and verdant lawns... a 13th-century dream. Pass the frescoes by a pupil of Giotto and the 14th-century chapel; observe the wooden ceilings and the time-worn terracotta tiles; contemplate the indoor well, the ultimate in medieval 'mod-cons'. Renaissance-style bedrooms come with antique furniture, rich fabrics and country views; the honeymoon suite has an unbelievably grand 18th-century canopied bed. On each floor is a welcoming sitting room, each with a massive stone fireplace and plump sofas. The light, Tuscan food has a serious local following, and the dining room, with its glittering Murano chandelier, 17th-century frescoes and Art Deco windows, is a spectacular setting for dining on homemade, home-grown delicacies. Try the olive oil menu (every course includes it) or visit the *oleoteca* in the cellar; you can attend courses, tastings and visit the mill. The peace here is a testament to Viola's gentleness and to her diligent, contented team.

rooms	25: 12 doubles, 2 triples, 1 single, 10 suites.
price	€144–€310.
meals	Dinner €36–€52.
closed	15 November–15 March.
directions	For Borgo San Lorenzo/Vicchio; through Sagginale; after 2 km, right for Cistio & Campestri; villa signed.

Viola Pasquali

tel	+39 055 8490107
fax	+39 055 8490108
email	villa.campestri@villacampestri.it
web	www.villacampestri.it

Hotel

Map 9 Entry 125

Locanda Senio

via Borgo dell'Ore 1, 50035 Palazuolo sul Senio

Food is king here: genuine home cooking from Roberta, and, in the restaurant, much gastronomic enthusiasm from Ercole. Echoing a growing movement to bring lost medieval traditions back to life, they are passionate about wild herbs and 'forgotton' fruits. The prosciutto from rare-breed *porcaro medievale* is particularly delicious. Breakfast is a feast of homemade breads, cakes, fruits and jams; dinner a leisurely treat served in the restaurant with nine tables and cosy log fire. The little inn occupies a stunning spot, in a quiet town in the Mugello valley surrounded by rolling hills… there are guided walks through the woods, gastronomic meanders through the valley and cookery courses from time to time. Bedrooms are comfortable and cosy, and it is worth paying extra for the suites – with open fireplaces – if you can; they're in the 17th-century building nearby. There's a new relaxation centre of which Roberta and Ercole are very proud – the jacuzzi, sauna and Turkish bath have a delicious aroma and a Swedish feel. Steps lead up to a pool with blue loungers; body and soul will be nutured.

rooms	8: 6 doubles/twins, 2 suites for 2-3.
price	€145–€170. Suites €165–€210 Half-board €105–€130 p.p.
meals	Dinner from €35.
closed	6 January–13 February.
directions	From Bologna A14, exit Imola for Rimini; 50m; for Palazuolo (40 mins). House in village, right of fountain & Oratorio dei Santi Carlo e Antonio.

Ercole & Roberta Lega

tel	+39 055 8046019
fax	+39 055 8043949
email	info@locandasenio.it
web	www.locandasenio.it

Hotel

Map 9 Entry 126

Albergotto Hotel

via de' Tornabuoni 13, 50123 Florence

You are an awfully long way from *The Mill on the Floss* but George Eliot once stayed here – as did Verdi and Donizetti. Peeking between two Gucci shops on one of Florence's swankiest streets (once described as 'the drawing room of Europe') the hotel still has an air of glamour though inside all is quiet; bustle quickly recedes behind the double glazing, the big fresh flowers and the old prints of Florence. Immaculate, traditional bedrooms have warm parquet floors, flowers, a military print or oil, the odd antique. There are good city views from large windows: rooms at the front overlook the beautiful Palazzo Strozzi; from the huge window in the fourth-floor suite you can see as far as Fiesole. Spotless bathrooms are mosaic-tiled with big white fulsome towels. There's a smart sitting room to return to, and the breakfast room is elegant: royal blue and gold curtains frame large windows, plates adorn walls, fresh flowers fill corners. Museums, galleries, restaurants and shops abound and you can walk to them all.

rooms	22: 18 doubles, 3 singles, 1 suite.
price	€160–€245. Suite €335.
meals	Restaurants nearby.
closed	Rarely.
directions	In Florence *centro storico*. Short walk from Santa Maria station. Secure parking €27 per day – ask on booking.

Carlo Martelli

tel	+39 055 2396464
fax	+39 055 2398108
email	info@albergotto.com
web	www.albergotto.com

Hotel

Map 8 Entry 127

Palazzo Niccolini al Duomo
via dei Servi 2, 50122 Florence

One minute you're battling with tourists in the Piazza del Duomo, the next you're standing inside this extraordinarily lovely palazzo. The *residenza* is on the second floor (with lift); two small trees, a brace of antique chairs and a brass plaque announce that you've arrived at friendly reception. Ever since it was first built by the Naldini family in the 16th century, on the site of the sculptor Donatello's workshop, the building's grandeur has been steadily added to. And the recent restoration hasn't detracted from its beauty, merely added some superb facilities. It's all you hope staying in such a place will be - fabulously elegant and luxurious, with 18th-century frescoes, trompe-l'oeil effects, fine antiques and magnificent beds… but in no way awesome, thanks to many personal touches. Relax in the lovely drawing room and look at family portraits, books and photos. Two signed photos are from the King of Italy, sent in 1895 to Contessa Cristina Niccolini, the last of the Naldini. She married into the current owner's family, bringing the palazzo as part of her dowry. A gem.

rooms	7: 4 doubles, 3 suites.
price	€215-€300. Singles €205-€260. Suites €300-€500.
meals	Plenty of restaurants nearby.
closed	Rarely.
directions	In Florence *centro storico*. A1 exit Firenze south; head for town centre & Il Duomo; via dei Servi off Piazza del Duomo. Park, unload & car will be taken to garage: €25-€30.

	Filippo Niccolini
tel	+39 055 282412
fax	+39 055 290979
email	info@niccolinidomepalace.com
web	www.niccolinidomepalace.com

B&B

Map 8 Entry 128

Torre di Bellosguardo
via Roti Michelozzi 2, 50124 Florence

Breathtaking in its beauty and ancient dignity. The entrance hall is cavernous, glorious, with a painted ceiling and an ocean of floor; the view reaches through a vast, plaster-crumbling sun room to the garden. Imposing, mellow buildings, georgous gardens fashioned by a friend of Dante, magical views of Florence. A water feature meanders along a stone terrace, a twisted wisteria shades the walkway to a kitchen garden, there are goats, ponies and rabbits. A pool, gym and cane tables and chairs occupy the old orangery while another pool settles into a perfect lawn. Most of the bedrooms can be reached by lift but the tower suite, with windows on all sides, demands a long climb. The bedrooms defy modern convention (no TVs, no phones) and are magnificent in their simplicity, the furniture richly authentic, the views infinite. But do ask for a room with one of the newer beds. Signor Franchetti is often here, and his manners and his English are impeccable – unlike those of the irrepressible pink parrot. All this, and Florence a 30-minute walk, or €10 cab ride, down the hill.

rooms	16: 8 doubles, 7 suites, 1 single.
price	€290. Singles €160. Suites €340–€390.
meals	Breakfast €20–€25. Supper €12. Trattoria 1km.
closed	Rarely.
directions	A1 exit Firenze Certosa for Porta Romana/Centro; left at Porta Romana on via Ugo Foscolo; keep right & take via Piana to end; right into via Roti Michelozzi.

	Signor Amerigo Franchetti
tel	+39 055 2298145
fax	+39 055 229008
email	info@torrebellosguardo.com
web	www.torrebellosguardo.com

Hotel

Map 8 Entry 129

Palazzo Magnani Feroni
Borgo San Frediano 5, 50124 Florence

Once the home of an important French dignitary, a place for the grandest and most opulent of receptions, the palace was bought by the family two centuries ago. Step off a busy street, a block away from the Arno, into a cool entrance flanked by wooden pews, marble busts and proud lions. Through the elaborate wrought-iron gates, enter a magnificent corridor that runs, cloister-like, along one side of a courtyard. The hotel is lush, elegant, a brilliant and sparkling conversion of a historic building that gives you every modern extra, from swish gym to internet. A 1900s mirrored elevator takes you up to the rooms, which are vast and high-ceilinged, luxuriously furnished with armchairs, king-size beds and Afghan rugs on polished *cotto* floors. We prefer those that look onto the street rather than the inner courtyard. Most enchanting of all: the rooftop terrace – note, the lift stops before the 60 steps up! – studded with tables and cushioned chairs, whence you gaze in a superior fashion over the rosy rooftop jumble that is Florence. The staff are young, gracious and charming: come to be utterly spoiled.

rooms	13: 12 suites for 2, 1 suite for 4.
price	€210-€590.
meals	Restaurants 200m.
closed	Never.
directions	In Florence *centro storico*. 50m from corner of via de'Serragli (1 block from Arno).

Alberto & Claudia Giannotti
tel	+39 055 2399544
fax	+39 055 2608908
email	info@florencepalace.it
web	www.florencepalace.it

Hotel

Map 8 Entry 130

Classic Hotel

viale Machiavelli 25, 50125 Florence

The hubbub of the city is so overwhelming at times that it is sheer heaven to enter the shaded, gravelled driveway of the Classic. It lies just beyond the old town gate, the Porta Romana, where Florence seems to begin and end. The area is leafy and residential, the Uffizi is a 20-minute roadside walk. The Classic is cool, friendly, secluded – elegant in a low-key way. Much of the furniture has come from the owner's parents' house in town (once a famous old hotel): interesting paintings and handsome Tuscan pieces. Its greatest charm, though, is the shaded courtyard garden with trees, shrubs and little corners where you may sit peacefully with a cappuccino and an unlavish, typically Florentine, breakfast. In winter there's a breakfast room in the basement. Bedrooms are parquet-floored and modestly attractive; some are lovely, especially those in the attic, with their heavily-beamed, sloping ceilings. Altogether an easy-going and comfortable place to stay (lift, air con, TV) for anyone visiting Florence – the feel is more villa than hotel and you're in the countryside in minutes.

rooms	20: 17 doubles, 1 suite, 2 singles.
price	€150–€200. Singles €110.
meals	Breakfast €8.
closed	Occasionally.
directions	Directions on booking. Private parking.

Dottoressa Corinne Kraft

tel	+39 055 229351
fax	+39 055 229353
email	info@classichotel.it
web	www.classichotel.it

Hotel

Map 8 Entry 131

Villa Poggio San Felice
San Matteo in Arcetri 24, 50125 Florence

The moment the gates open and you drive up past the roses, you sense this will be a special stay. Livia inherited the house from her grandparents: it's in a bewitching garden high on a hill overlooking Florence. Narrow paved paths wend their way between shrubs and tall trees, wisteria graces the walls, foxgloves border a flight of old stone steps... The villa itself, tall and immaculate, dates back to 1427. Despite its beautiful, high-ceilinged rooms, it is a friendly and approachable house. The dining room is so light and airy that it makes you smile just to be there; the drawing room has a grand piano you're welcome to play, alongide fresh flowers, big mirrors and interesting books, paintings and engravings. All the bedrooms are big, light and serene, with glossy parquet floors, family antiques, exquisite attention to detail, and views. There's also a super, well-equipped apartment right at the top, with its own terrace and lift. Livia and Lorenzo are young, hardworking and delightful. They even offer a daily 'shuttle' into Florence, to save you the hassle of driving and parking.

rooms	5: 3 doubles, 1 twin, 1 suite.
price	€200-€250.
meals	Lunch from €15. Dinner from €30. Restaurants 1km.
closed	January-February.
directions	Directions on booking.

	L. Puccinelli Sannini & L. Magnelli
tel	+39 055 220016
fax	+39 055 2335388
email	info@villapoggiosanfelice.com
web	www.villapoggiosanfelice.com

B&B

Map 8 Entry 132

Villa La Sosta

via Bolognese 83, 50139 Florence

It's a 15-minute walk to the Duomo, yet the 1892 villa on the Montughi hill stands in large landscaped gardens where songbirds lull you to sleep. The mansard-tower sitting room with sofas, books and views is a lofty place in which to relax, and there's billiards. Bedrooms, with large windows and wooden shutters, are equally stylish with striking toile de Jouy or checks and dark Tuscan pieces. Interesting, too, are artefacts gathered from the Fantonis' days in Africa – the family ran a banana plantation – including ivory carvings and wooden statues. Breakfast is served outside under an ivy-covered pergola in summer or in the dining room, just off the family's bright sitting room; over excellent coffee the young, affable Antonio and Giusy – a brother-and-sister team – help you plan your stay. If the city's treasures start to pall they will organise a day in the vineyards or local pottery villages. There's parking off the main road and the number 25 bus, which stops outside the gates, will ferry you into the city or up into the hills. *Gluten-free breakfasts available.*

rooms	5: 3 doubles, 1 triple, 1 quadruple.
price	€110-€130. Singles €85-€105. Triple €140-€160. Quad €170-€190.
meals	Dinner €30. Restaurants 800m.
closed	Rarely.
directions	Signs for Centro & Piazza della Libertà, then via Bolognese; villa on left. Bus 25 bus from r'way station; get off 800m after via Bolognese begins, just before Total Petrol. Parking.

	Antonio & Giuseppina Fantoni
tel/fax	+39 055 495073
mobile	+39 335 8349992
email	info@villalasosta.com
web	www.villalasosta.com

B&B

Map 8 Entry 133

Villa Ulivi
via Bolognese 163, 50139 Florence

At the end of a chestnut-fringed drive, the pale pink villa rests in its own park. Renovated in the 1400s, the 1800s and then, finally, in the 1930s, it's an Art Deco film set inside. Imagine wonderful mirrors and bold shapes, a circular, powder-blue velvet sofa, a bar with exquisite walnut roll top, lush Persian rugs on white marble, a piano tucked into a cosy corner. Big arched windows open to a terrace for summer breakfasts, and gardens beyond. Signora and her son are well-organised and charming, serving you fine dinner under a 1930s chandelier; Slow Food groups come for the estate wine and olive oil. Choose between B&B and self-catering – comfortable bedrooms are homely, and engaging, one with a frescoed ceiling and cherubs, another with a fine fitted wardrobe and pastel shutters. Marble bathrooms have double sinks and gold taps. The apartments, also in the villa but with their own entrances, are spacious and well-equipped with yet more Art Deco touches; Magnolia and Glicene are particularly charming. Unique B&B and Florence a ten-minute hop on the bus; the stop is just outside the gates.

rooms	6 + 3: 4 doubles, 2 triples. 4 apartments: 3 for 4, 1 for 4-6.
price	€80-€150. Apartments from €160. Entire villa on request.
meals	Dinner €30, on request. Restaurants 700m.
closed	Rarely.
directions	From Piazza Libertà take via Bolognese; entrance on left.

Sig.ra Maria Grazia Furnari
tel/fax	+39 055 400777
mobile	+39 320 0819948
email	info@villaulivi.com
web	www.villaulivi.com

B&B & Self-catering

Map 8 Entry 134

Antica Dimora Firenze
via San Gallo 72, 50129 Florence

Ring the buzzer and up you go – via the small lift or the wide stone stair. Enter the relaxed *residenza* where you come and go as you please; friendly reception is manned until 7pm. A treat to come back here, to a decanter of Vin Santo and a book of love stories by your bed. Perhaps even a four-poster or a jasmine-scented balcony... Italian love of detail is revealed in walls washed rose-pink and pistachio green, in fabrics woven by local artisans, in striped sofas, silk curtains and little vases of dried lavender. Black and white 19th-century prints and antique *cotto* floors combine beautifully with waffle towels and walk-in showers, modems and satellite TV: it's the best of old and new. Settle down in the guest sitting room, dip into almond biscuits and a cup of tea and plan where to have dinner; there's all the info. Browse a glossy book or a magazine, choose a favourite DVD, be as private or as sociable as you like. There are homemade cakes and jams at breakfast, you are on a quietish street near the university area and it's brilliant value for the centre of Florence.

rooms	6: 3 doubles, 3 twins.
price	€130–€145.
meals	Restaurants nearby.
closed	Rarely.
directions	In Florence *centro storico*. You cannot park in central Florence, ask about garage on booking.

Lea Gulmanelli
tel +39 055 4627296
fax +39 055 4634450
email info@anticadimorafirenze.it
web www.anticadimorafirenze.it

B&B

Map 8 Entry 135

La Residenza Johanna
via Bonifacio Lupi 14, 50129 Florence

Astonishingly good value in the historic centre of Florence – and what an attractive, friendly place to be. You really feel as though you have your own pad in town, away from tourist bustle. Lea's other *residenze* have been such a success that she and Johanna have opened this one in a lovely 19th-century palazzo, shared with notaries and an embassy. Up the lift or marble stairs to a big welcome from Lea and Evelyne on the second floor. Both are charming, and keen to make your stay a happy one. Graceful arches, polished floors and soft colours give a feeling of light and space to the two parallel corridors; there are comfortable sofas there, too, so you can browse through the books and guides. The bedrooms off are big, airy and cool, with excellent, stylish bathrooms. A small table holds a basic basket of biscuits, brioches, jam and tea- and coffee-making things, and you breakfast in your room (there's no dining room). Or you could slip out to a bar for a cappuccino and a panino before wandering happily off to the Duomo, the San Lorenzo leather market and the Piazza della Signoria.

rooms	11: 9 doubles; 2 singles with separate bathroom.
price	€85. Singles €50.
meals	Restaurants nearby.
closed	Rarely.
directions	In Florence *centro storico*. You cannot park in central Florence; ask about garage on booking.

	Evelyne Arrighi & Lea Gulmanelli
tel	+39 055 481896
email	lupi@johanna.it
web	www.johanna.it

Residenze Johlea I & II
via San Gallo 76 & 80, 50129 Florence

Experience living in a real Florentine *residenza*... a particularly delightful home. The restored, late 19th-century building, in an area well-endowed with musuems, has good access to train and bus stations. Nos. 76 and 80 have separate entrances – and Alexandra or Laura are there to greet you until 8.30pm. A lift transports you up to big, elegant bedrooms with long, shuttered windows, subtle colours and lovely fabrics. All are different and all are comfortable, with settees, polished floors and rugs, superb bathrooms. There are antiques and air conditioning, wooden jigsaw puzzles, books, a shared fridge. But perhaps the nicest surprise is on up the rooftop: weave your way past little reading corners, old wooden settles and chests tucked under sloping ceilings, then up a stair to a glazed-in balcony... up again to a room where you can make drinks and, finally, up a short flight of wooden steps to a wide, sun-flooded terrace. Be dazzled by a glorious, all-round panorama of Florence – superb! A very basic, do-it-yourself breakfast is included in the price.

rooms	12: 10 doubles, 2 singles.
price	€95-€120. Singles €70.
meals	Restaurants nearby.
closed	Rarely.
directions	In Florence *centro storico*. You cannot park in central Florence, ask about garage on booking.

	Lea Gulmanelli
tel	+39 055 4633292
fax	+39 055 4634552
email	johlea@johanna.it
web	www.johanna.it

Hotel

Map 8 Entry 137

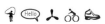

Palazzo Bombicci Pontelli
corso dei Tintori 21, Florence

Those huge, handsome doors on the streets of Florence – what lies behind them: a cool hallway, a fountained courtyard? This door heaves open to a marbled hall guarded by concièrge Maurio (on duty: 8am to 7pm) and an impressive stairway (no lift) leading to a large, luminous apartment on the first floor. Enter a small hall, then a sitting/dining room with divans for four, a new kitchen with oven, a furnished terrace (what a treat), a vast bedroom with contemporary wicker armchairs, a stunning stone fireplace – pure 16th-century palazzo – and a terrace with a view that sweeps from the Arno to the Piazzale Michelangelo. Air conditioning, central heating, a white shower; immaculate white walls, fine beams, terracotta... it's gorgeous. The second apartment on the second floor, reached via an open staircase, has much the same; no terrace, but long views and a large glazed room overlooking the courtyard below. Next door, at no 19, but on the third floor (with a lift), is a simple but comfortable and cool apartment for two with views down to Piazza Santa Croce. It all feels so central – and special.

rooms	3 apartments: 2 for 2-6, 1 for 2 + children.
price	€120-€187. €800-€1,300 per week.
meals	Self-catering.
closed	Rarely.
directions	In Florence *centro storico.* You cannot park in central Florence, ask about garage on booking.

	Signor Tuccio Guicciardini
tel	+39 0577 907185
fax	+39 0577 907185
email	info@guicciardini.com
web	www.guicciardini.com

Self-catering

Map 8 Entry 138

Relais Villa l'Olmo
via Impruneta per Tavarunzze 19, 50023 Impruneta

With a bit of luck you will be greeted by Claudia, a lovely German lady of considerable charm, married to a Florentine whose family have owned the property since 1700 (also owner of the Palazzo Magnani Feroni in Florence). The Relais is a clutch of immaculately converted apartments, all looking down over the valley, all shamelessly *di lusso*. Imagine softly-lit yellow walls beneath chunky Tuscan beamed ceilings, nicely designed kitchenettes, white china on yellow cloths, smartly checked sofas, glass-topped tables, fresh flowers – even a private pool (and plastic loungers) for the two villas if you can't face splashing with others in the main one. And there's a new communal barbecue, so you can mingle if you wish. Claudia runs a warmly efficient reception and rents out mountain bikes and mobile phones; she organises babysitting, cookery classes and wine tastings, too. There's a cheerful restaurant and a pizzeria, and farm products for sale, Florence is 20 minutes away by car or bus and it's heaven for families. *Special rates for local golf, tennis & riding clubs. Air con extra charge.*

rooms	11: 2 villas for 2-4; 8 apartments for 2-5; 1 farmhouse for 6-8.
price	Villas €160-€285. Apts €90-€240. Farmhouse €180-€380.
meals	Breakfast €10. Dinner €20-€40. Restaurants 200m.
closed	Never.
directions	A1 exit Firenze-Certosa; at r'bout, signs for Tavarnuzze; there, left to Impruneta. Track on right, signed to villa, 200m past sign for Impruneta.

	Claudia & Alberto Giannotti
tel	+39 055 2311311
fax	+39 055 2311313
email	florence.chianti@dada.it
web	www.relaisfarmholiday.it

Agriturismo

Map 8 Entry 139

Dimora Storica Villa Il Poggiale
via Empolese 69, 50026 San Casciano

This 16th-century villa is so lovely it's impossible to know where to start. Breathe in the scent of old-fashioned roses from a seat on the Renaissance loggia. Wander through the olive trees to the pool (note: some traffic hum from the next-door road) and watch the sun set. Retreat into the house and enjoy its 1800s elegance. Much loved, full of memories, it's the childhood home of two brothers, Johanan and Nathanel Vitta, who devoted two years to its restoration. The rooms are big, beautiful and full of light, and everything has been kept as it was. An oil painting of the Vittas' grandmother welcomes you as you enter; another, Machiavelli by Gilardi, hangs in the salon. Bedrooms upstairs keep their original names: the Professor's Room, the Lady's Room, the Owl's Room... all are different, all are striking. Some have frescoes and silk curtains, others fabrics specially produced in a small Tuscan workshop. The attention to detail is superb but in no way overpowering. Catarina and her staff really make you feel like wanted guests, breakfasts are ample and glorious Florence is a 20-minute drive.

rooms	20 + 3: 18 doubles, 2 suites. 3 apartments for 2-4.
price	€130–€190. Suites €190–€240. Apartments €250–€270.
meals	Restaurants nearby.
closed	February.
directions	Rome A1 exit Firenze-Certosa; superstrada Firenze-Siena, exit San Casciano; signs for Cerbaia-Empoli. After 3km, signs on left.

Catarina Piccolomini

tel	+39 055 828311
fax	+39 055 8294296
email	villailpoggiale@villailpoggiale.it
web	www.villailpoggiale.it

Hotel & Self-catering

Map 8 Entry 140

Il Poggetto
via del Poggetto 14, 50025 Montespertoli

A deliciously green and sunny Tuscan hilltop, surrounded by vineyards and olive groves. Once through the electronic gates, you'll be captivated by the views. The gardens are delightful, too: three hectares of lawns, fruit trees, azaleas, heathers and roses (always something in flower), with pines and cypresses for shade and a terrace dotted with lemon and mandarin trees. Ivana and her family moved to the 400-year-old *casa colonica* in 1974 and have renovated beautifully, using original and traditional materials. The apartments are attractive, uncluttered and full of light. All have big, comfortable beds, antique furniture and private patios. La Loggia was once a hay barn; the huge, raftered living/dining area is superb and the old triangular air bricks are still in place. La Cipressaia, characteristically Tuscan in style and very private, is a conversion of the stable block, and sleeps five. Il Gelsomino, named after the jasmine outside the door, and La Pergola join each other. Everyone has use of the pool, which is set apart in a stunning position: you can watch the sun rise and set from your lounger.

rooms	4 apartments for 2-5.
price	€340-€1,175 per week.
meals	Restaurants 1km.
closed	Rarely.
directions	Milano-Roma A1 exit Firenze Signa; right for Pisa-Livorno exit Ginestra; right for Montespertoli. In Baccaiano left uphill; left for Montagnana; signed after 1km. 1st left into via Montegufoni, left at the church into via del Poggetto.

Andrea Boretti & Ivana Pieri

mobile	+39 339 3784383
fax	+39 02 70035890
email	info@poggetto.it
web	www.poggetto.it

Locanda le Boscarecce

via Renai 19, 50051 Castelfiorentino

A sparkling star in Tuscany's firmament. Susanna is full of life and laughter, her daughter Swan is equally warm – and an accomplished sommelier. Swan's husband, Chef Bartolo from Sicily, concocts dishes that people travel miles to discover. Fruits, vegetables, herbs and olive oil come from the grounds, there are 450 wines in the cellar and, outside, the biggest pizza oven you will ever see. The 200-year-old *locanda* is on a ridge, embracing fields and farms and heavenly sunsets. Bedrooms in the farmhouse are part rustic, part refined, with bold colours and pretty lace at the windows, each space unique. Beds are modern and comfortable, furniture 18th- and 19th-century, bathrooms have bath tubs *and* showers, and some rooms have kitchenettes. Tennis, cycling, swimming – all are possible – or you may relax under the dreamy gazebo and dip into a book on art history from the library. Even the location is enticing, in a charmed triangle formed by Florence, Siena and Pisa. Heart-warming, creative, special. *Ask about cookery courses and wine-tastings.*

rooms	14: 10 doubles, 3 triples, 1 quadruple.
price	€100-€145.
meals	Dinner €35.
closed	20 November-26 December.
directions	From Castelfiorento, via A. Vivaldi for Renai; right after dirt road, signed. Over bridge road curves left, stay on paved road for 'di Pizzacalada'; T-junc left; signed.

	Susanna Ballerini
tel	+39 0571 61280
fax	+39 0571 634008
email	info@leboscarecce.com
web	www.leboscarecce.com

B&B

Map 8 Entry 142

Fattoria Barbialla Nuova

via Castastrada 49, 50050 Montaione

At the end of a long, cool, forest drive, an exciting arrival: a 500-hectare farm specialising in Chianina cattle, olive oil and white truffles. Guido, Gianluca and Marco have worked hard to provide somewhere beautiful to stay in this glorious nature reserve. 'Doderi' has three apartments, simple and minimalist with clean lines, fine linen, books, music and the occasional black and white photo. Bedcovers designed by Gianluca, stable doors, Roman blinds and 60s-style furniture in Tuscan colours add style, originality and colour. The three apartments in 'Brentina', deeper in the woods, are a touch more primitive; perhaps too much so for some, though others will love the simplicity of the whitewashed walls and the handmade staircase, and all have delicious bathrooms. Outside: pergola, patio and pool, cheerful with deckchairs and decking, and orchard and hens. Marco or Guido is always around to help if you need anything, and October and November are the times to go if you fancy a spot of truffle-hunting: you will be accompanied by an expert and his dog. We love this place. *Minimum stay three nights.*

rooms	7 apartments: 2 for 2, 3 for 4, 2 for 6. 1 villa for 8.
price	Apt for 2: €440. Apt for 4: €1150. Apt for 6: €880. Villa: €2200. Prices per week.
meals	Self-catering.
closed	10 January-10 March.
directions	From A1, exit Firenze Signa, follow signs to 'S.G.C. FI-PI-LI' direction Pisa, exit San Miniato up hill to Montaione; 4km after Corazzano, on right opp. white 6km sign.

	Àrghilo Società Agricola
tel/fax	+39 0571 677004
mobile	+39 335 1406577
email	info@barbiallanuova.it
web	www.barbiallanuova.it

Self-catering

Map 8 Entry 143

Fattoria del Bassetto
via Avanella 42, 50052 Certaldo

Authentic, atmospheric and fun. The Benedictine monks who lived here opened their doors to pilgrims and that tradition of hospitality has been kept alive by la Duchessa and her three sons. And how! Most guests find themselves, like Pozzo in *Waiting for Godot*, unable to leave. It is still a working farm making olive oil and honey and samples are on display in reception – along with guide books, backpackers and sleeping dogs. In the villa are six genuinely old-fashioned bedrooms; in the old *convento*, five small dorms. The feel is house-party rather than hotel, with wine tastings on Friday night, a bar on Saturday with a band, a twice-weekly barbecue and a kitchen for communal use (breakfast ingredients supplied). Two terraces and a sofa'd library are available for guests in the villa; the pool and hammocks are shared. This is Tuscan countryside at its least rose-tinted and the proximity of road and rail cannot be disguised – but there are innumerable hidden and visible rewards, and the glories of Florence and Siena are a train ride away. Great value. *Minimum stay two nights.*

rooms	6: 2 doubles, 2 twins, 2 family; bathrooms shared. Hostel: 5 dormitories for 3-6.
price	Villa €70-€80. Singles €60. Hostel €22.
meals	Trattorias 10-minute walk. Kitchen available.
closed	November-March.
directions	Florence-Siena exit Poggibonsi Nord for Poggibonsi; SS429 for Certaldo; 5.2km, Fattoria signed on right.

Duchessa Guicciardini di Zoagli

tel	+39 0571 668342
fax	+39 0571 663939
email	info@fattoriabassetto.com
web	www.fattoriabassetto.com

B&B & Self-catering

Map 8 Entry 144

Le Filigare
50020 Barberino Val d'Elsa

Overlooking vineyards, surrounded by green-cloaked hills, pretty gardens, shady patios and a statue-strewn terrace, this is an immaculate Tuscan estate. Now the Burchis have converted part of the main villa and farm buildings into stylish apartments with an authentic feel and architect Deborah has worked hard to combine traditional materials with a contemporary penchant for space. Beams, raftered ceilings, archways, terracotta floors, cool white walls set the tone, rustic furniture does the rest – simple wrought-iron or wooden beds (some four-poster), painted wardrobes, scrubbed tables, copper pans. Modern sofas and art works add elegance; living areas are open-plan with smart kitchens tucked into corners. Some apartments have patios, others a mezzanine level, others jacuzzi baths. Choose 'Girasole', up the hill, for romance and a private garden. You get a summer swimming pool, tennis court, peacocks, wines on tap – it's perfect! Shops and restaurants are a ten-minute drive, Florence and Siena under an hour and your energetic hosts are most welcoming.

rooms	12 apartments for 2, 4 and 6.
price	€500-€750 per week.
meals	Restaurant 1km.
closed	Rarely.
directions	A1 exit Certosa; superstrada for Siena; exit San Donato in Poggio; well signed from Panzano road.

Alessandro Cassetti Burchi

tel	+39 055 8072796
fax	+39 055 8072135
email	info@lefiligare.it
web	www.lefiligare.it

Self-catering

Map 8 Entry 145

Fattoria Casa Sola

via Cortine 5, 50021 Barberino Val d'Elsa

Count Giuseppe Gambaro and his wife Claudia tend the wine and olive oil production as the family has done for generations. The estate grows a variety of grapes; gates are shut at night to prevent wild boar from snaffling them! The two-storey apartments, 700 metres from the main house and pool, are cool, fresh and comfortable with whitewashed walls, tiled floors, traditional country bedspreads and vineyard views. Named Red, White, Yellow, each has a garden with roses to match. Your hosts are charming and courteous and passionate about their wine, and give you a bottle on arrival. Once a week they take guests round the vineyards and wine-making facilities, rounding off the visit with a glass of Vin Santo and *cantucci* biscuits. Claudia is very fond of children and organises weekly races and games. There are cookery and watercolour classes for grown-ups, and you can also play tennis and ride. Order a takeaway meal for your supper, or eat out in Barberino and San Donato. Or drive the 30 minutes to Florence or Siena.

rooms	6 apartments: 1 for 2-3, 2 for 4, 2 for 4-6, 1 for 8.
price	€600–€2,300 per week.
meals	Self-catering.
closed	Rarely.
directions	Firenze-Siena exit San Donato in Poggio; SS101 past S. Donato church; 1.5km, right to Cortine & Casa Sola.

Conte Giuseppe Gambaro

tel	+39 055 8075028
fax	+39 055 8059194
email	vacanze@fattoriacasasola.com
web	www.fattoriacasasola.com

Sovigliano

Strada Magliano 9, 50028 Tavarnelle Val di Pesa

Walking distance from Tavarnelle, down a country lane, this ancient farmhouse stands among vineyards, olives, cypresses and pines. Though the setting is secluded you are in the middle of some of the most popular touring country in Italy; on a clear day, you can see the towers of San Gimignano. Every view is breathtaking. Sovigliano has been renovated by the family with deep respect for the architecture and traditional materials. The self-catering apartments – one palatial, with a glorious stone fireplace – are very attractive, all white walls, ancient rafters, good beds and country antiques. If you choose to go B&B, the double rooms are equally charming, and dinner can be arranged. A big, delightfully rustic kitchen, with a private fridge for each guest, makes an excellent place for you to meet others. Relax under the pines in the garden, take a dip in the pool, work out in the exercise area (where children must be supervised), enjoy a pre-dinner drink. Vin Santo, olive oil and grappa are for sale, Signora is most helpful and you'll find it hard to tear yourself away. *Min. three nights.*

rooms	4 + 4: 2 doubles, 2 twins. 4 apartments for 2-4.
price	€100-€120. Apartments €120-€250.
meals	Dinner €31.
closed	Rarely.
directions	SS2 Firenze-Siena exit Tavarnelle; on entering town, right & follow Marcialla. Sovigliano just out of town: left at 4th r'bout down lane signed Magliano; follow signs.

Signora Patrizia Bicego

tel	+39 055 8076217
fax	+39 055 8050770
email	info@sovigliano.com
web	www.sovigliano.com

B&B & Self-catering

Map 8 Entry 147

Azienda Agricola Il Borghetto Country Inn
via Collina S. Angelo 23, 50020 Montefiridolfi

A tall hedge, private gates, lofty cypress trees – you could drive past and miss this. Slip inside and you feel you've stumbled on a lost world. The 15th-century building, all sloping pantiled roofs around a central tower, was rescued by the Cavallini family and restored, along with the olive groves and vineyards. Step into rooms of timeless elegance, rich but welcoming. The airy dining room opens onto a covered veranda, perfect for breakfasts of brioche, local cheeses and homemade jams. Dinner – from a fine Tuscan chef – is by request. Bedrooms, with their tiled floors and beamed ceilings, are understatedly luxurious with soft colours, antiques, fresh flowers and individual touches; perhaps a pretty wallpaper or a sleigh bed, a writing desk or a hand-painted wardrobe. Florence and Siena are close: borrow a bike and explore. Or wander the gardens with their terraces, pond, orchard and Etruscan tomb. The Cavallinis are quiet and easy-going while Tim, the UK wine-maker, is happy to explain his work. Raise a glass of Chianti from the pool to far-reaching Tuscan views. *Cookery courses available.*

rooms	8: 3 doubles, 5 suites.
price	€130–€260.
meals	Dinner, 3 courses, €50. Light lunch €15–€35.
closed	November–April.
directions	A1 exit Firenze-Certosa; after toll, Firenze-Siena exit Bargino; right; 200m, then left for Montefiridolfi; 500m after church, leave gate with columns on right; 20m signed.

	Roberto Cavallini
tel	+39 02 804725
fax	+39 055 8244247
email	info@borghetto.org
web	www.borghetto.org

Agriturismo

Map 8 Entry 148

Palazzo Malaspina B&B

via del Giglio 35, 50020 San Donato in Poggio

A special find. The medieval walls of San Donato are tucked away behind an arch, while the Renaissance façade belies a modern and spacious interior. Enter the big hall with its fine wooden doors and stylish staircase: sense the history. The palazzo is listed and Maria Pellizzari is enthusiastic about all she has to offer. She was born here, in Room 3, and now lives in the apartment downstairs with her pet dog. Breakfast, in your bedroom – or set by Maria at a huge table on white runners and china – includes fruits, cheeses, croissants, jams. (Do try her delectable chocolate cakes.) Each of the bedrooms has a classic Tuscan charm with family antiques and fabrics from the House of Busatti in Anghiari. Luxurious bathrooms have mosaic tiles and huge white towels bearing the palazzo's emblem; three have a jacuzzi. From some of the rooms you can just glimpse the towers of San Gimignano, from others, little gardens that guide the eye to the countryside beyond and its treasures. There's a very small garden to the rear. Drop your baggage off outside; car parks are a five-minute walk.

rooms	5: 3 doubles, 2 twins/doubles.
price	€85–€120.
meals	Restaurant next door.
closed	Occasionally.
directions	A1 exit Firenze-Certosa; SS Firenze-Siena for Siena; exit San Donato; signs for San Donato; thro' arch into *centro storico*; via del Giglio, on left.

	Maria Pellizzari
tel	+39 055 8072946
fax	+39 055 8092047
email	info@palazzomalaspina.it
web	www.palazzomalaspina.it

B&B

Map 8 Entry 149

Corte di Valle

via Chiantigiana, loc. Le Bolle, 50022 Greve in Chianti

The British ambassador in the 1920s, Sir Ronald Graham (a reputed pro-fascist) lived here, and what was good enough for him… But it did go downhill, and Marco, who left banking after 35 years to pursue this dream, has had to pour money into it as well as affection. He has succeeded brilliantly: the old Tuscan farmhouse is a handsome, even stylish, place to stay and has not lost any of its dignity and character. Bedrooms are large, the décor is uncluttered but lovely, the shower rooms are immaculate and the beds very comfortable. The room at the top has its own terrace – an idyllic spot from which to watch the sun set and rise. Downstairs is a huge sitting room where you can gather with your friends and a cavernous hall; outside is a pool with a view. Occasional dinner is served in their hunting lodge restaurant across the yard. Marco enjoys food and wine and may offer tastings of his own vintage; Irene, gentle and shy, is proud of the herbs and saffrons she sells. All around you lies the lush and lovely Chianti countryside, and the idyllic little town of Greve is five kilometres away.

rooms	8: 7 doubles, 1 twin.
price	€95-€115.
meals	Dinner €25, on request.
closed	Rarely.
directions	5km north of Grève in Chianti, on west side of S222, north of turning to Passo dei Paccorai. House visible from road.

Irene Mazzoni

tel	+39 055 853939
fax	+39 055 8544163
email	cortedivalle@cortedivalle.it
web	www.cortedivalle.it

Agriturismo

Map 8 Entry 150

Fattoria Viticcio

via San Cresci 12/a, 50022 Greve in Chianti

You're on a hill above Greve in Chianti Classico country. Alessandro's father, Lucio, bought the farm in the 1960s and set about producing fine wines for export. It was a brave move at a time when people were moving away from the countryside. Now managed by Alessandro, the vineyard has an international reputation. Visit the vaults and taste for yourself. Nicoletta runs the agriturismo, helped by their young daughters. The apartments, each named after one of them – Beatrice, Arianna, Camilla – lie at the heart of the estate and much thought has gone into them. Plain-coloured walls, brick arches, beams and terracotta floor tiles give an attractively simple air; the rooms have well-made furniture and some carefully selected antiques; kitchens are delightful. The pool rests in a walled garden, with a small play area for children, and a second pool and tennis court in the olive groves are planned. You may hear the occasional tractor – this is a working estate – but the farmyard is tidy and well-kept, with tubs of flowers everywhere. There's a lovely family atmosphere, too, and wonderful views.

rooms	3 + 5: 3 doubles.
	5 apartments for 2-6.
price	€80.
	Apartments €90-€155;
	€515-€850 per week.
meals	Restaurants 15-minute walk.
closed	Rarely.
directions	A1 exit Firenze Sud; via Chiantigiana SS222. In Grève, signs for pool (piscina): over small bridge past pool on right; take track for Viticcio, signed.

	A. Landini & N. Florio Deleuze
tel	+39 055 854210
fax	+39 055 8544866
email	info@fattoriaviticcio.com
web	www.fattoriaviticcio.com

Agriturismo & Self-catering

Map 8 Entry 151

Poggio all'Olmo
via Petriolo 30, 50022 Greve in Chianti

A small, ten-hectare Tuscan farm, six kilometres from Greve, where wine and olive oil are produced in the traditional way. Three generations of Vannis still toil, grandfather tending fat tomatoes in the kitchen garden and pruning the vines. Francesca enjoys having people to stay and looks after you well. The farmhouse, which goes back to the 17th century, has two guest bedrooms, each with a kitchenette – basic, no frills – while the old hay barn has been converted into a couple of simple but comfortable apartments with beams and terracotta. The lower of the two has an extra bed and its own patio; the views, across vineyards and olive groves to the hills beyond, are superb. The undulating landscape is typical Chianti, the air as pure as can be, and the swimming pool, fragrant with the scent of herbs and roses, a delight. Witness the day-to-day activities of a working farm without stirring from your chair – though there is a guide in nearby Lamole who will take you for walks. Peace and tranquillity, genuine family life, home-produced wine and olive oil. *Minimum stay three nights in apartment.*

rooms	2 + 2: 2 doubles. 2 apartments: 1 for 2-3, 1 for 2-4.
price	€75. Apartments €90.
meals	Breakfast on request. Restaurant 4km.
closed	Rarely.
directions	From Greve in Chianti SS222 for Panzano. After 2km, left for Lamole & on for 5km. House between Vignamaggio & Lamole, signed.

	Francesca Vanni
tel	+39 055 8549056
fax	+39 055 853755
email	olmo@greve-in-chianti.com
web	www.greve-in-chianti.com/olmo.htm

Agriturismo & Self-catering

Map 8 Entry 152

Podere Torre

via di San Cresci 29, 50022 Greve in Chianti

At the end of a long bumpy track, a little farmstead that exudes contentment; no wonder the roses do so well. They are coaxed and charmed by Cecilia, who has the same effect upon her guests. Hers is no run-of-the-mill B&B: here everything is intuitively presented. Next to the main house is 'La Stalla', a cool, ground-floor bedroom in the watchtower. 'Concimaia' (the name referring to its unpoetical origins as a manure store) is reached across a flowery terrace with table and chairs for two, and interconnects with 'Fienile', an apartment in the small barn – a useful set-up for a party of four. Cecilia gives you fluffy towels, cotton bed linen, blocks of Marsiglia soap, lavender bags and candles for evening relaxation. Swallows nest in the laundry room, where you can wash and iron, and you get the basics needed to rustle up a picnic supper and eat outside. Cecilia and Paolo run a small vineyard producing good-quality wine and olive oil. There is a taverna a mile away that you can walk to; at breakfast time we advise you stay put and be spoiled.

rooms	2 + 1: 2 doubles. 1 apartment for 2.
price	€70 (€450 per week). Apartment €85 (€550 per week).
meals	Breakfast €7.50. Restaurants 2km.
closed	Rarely.
directions	From Grève in Chianti for Pieve di San Cresci; 3km on minor road, signed.

Signora Cecilia Torrigiani

tel/fax	+39 055 8544714
mobile	+39 347 3130901
email	poderetorre@greve-in-chianti.com
web	www.greve-in-chianti.com/poderetorre.htm

Castello di Lamole
via di Lamole 82, Lamole, 50022 Greve in Chianti

Heavy rafters, tiny windows, floors of granite, stunning old stone walls – history seeps from every cranny. The 13th-century fortress is an intriguing, stepped maze of nooks and alleys, arches and passageways, trailing vines and dripping wisteria. You are surrounded by 13 hectares of ancient chestnut woods, a small vineyard and olive groves; lovely views sweep down terraces past rosemary and lavender to a pool and across the valley. The apartments vary in size and character and have patios and much rustic charm. Expect good solid furniture and pretty fabrics, tapestry cushions, rush mats, perhaps a sink decorated with straw hats or a noble old fireplace. Jacopo's grandfather bought the castello years ago; now it has been restored and your young host is relaxed among guests. A grocer's shop is a walk away, the castle sells wine, grappa and olive oil, and a bus transports you to Grève. In the hayloft restaurant there's good farmhouse cooking, the estate's fine wines and the background music of Riccardo Marasco – famous folk singer and Jacopo's dad. *Minimum stay two nights. Tricky parking some distance away.*

rooms	9 apartments: 2 for 4, 7 for 2.
price	B&B: €120-€200.
	Self-catering: €680-€1,050 per week.
meals	Breakfast €8. Dinner €22.
	Restaurant 1km.
closed	January-February.
directions	From Florence SS222 for Grève in Chianti; 1km after Grève left for Lamole; follow signs for Castello di Lamole.

	Jacopo Marasco
tel	+39 055 630498
fax	+39 055 630611
email	info@castellodilamole.it
web	www.castellodilamole.it

B&B & Self-catering

Map 8 Entry 154

Podere La Casellina
via Poggio alla Croce 60, 50063 Figline Valdarno

Come here for life's slow rhythm – and for the gentle family. The Bensi grandparents moved here in 1936 (see picture below), when the local church put the *podere* into their careful hands; the family and young Michelangelo have worked the land ever since. Anyone wishing to experience the 'real' side of peasant life – and learn something of its history – should come here; so little has changed at La Casellina, inside or out, and there are few concessions to modernity. Guest bedrooms are in the old hayloft and stables, simple but comfortable, with views of the little San Pietro al Terreno church. The landscape, between Chianti and Valdarno, is exquisite; you have the chestnut woods of the Chianti mountains to one side, and oaks, cypresses and olives to the other. Learn to prune vines and pick olives on the farm; gather chestnuts and wild mushrooms in the woods. Go riding or biking, then return to Grandma's recipes – the grape flan is delicious. There's passion fruit for breakfast, and Michelangelo is a dear who speaks brilliant English. *Minimum stay two nights.*

rooms	3 doubles.
price	From €76.
meals	Lunch €18. Dinner €24.
closed	10 January-28 February.
directions	Leave A1 at Incisa; Figline road. Just before Figline, right to Brollo & Poggio alla Croce; 4km, on right.

	Michelangelo & Silvia Bensi
tel	+39 055 9500070
mobile	+39 333 7192139
email	poderelacasellina@tin.it
web	www.poderelacasellina.it

Agriturismo

Map 9 Entry 155

Villa Le Barone

via San Leolino 19, 50020 Panzano in Chianti

The Marchesa, who has now passed away, wrote a delightful book about her passion for the countryside and the lovely old manor house that has been in the family for 400 years. It's a gorgeous place, with old-fashioned comforts and no TVs: truly unspoiled. Staff bustle with an easy-going friendliness under the supervision of the owners, a charming couple who spend part of the year here. Bedrooms vary, some in the villa, others in outbuildings around the estate; some are small, others on a grand scale; most have a warm Tuscan style and some charming pieces of furniture. The sitting room has an irresistible comfort, with a log fire for chilly nights and vast coffee-table books to whet your appetite for Italy. The airy dining room – once the wine cellar – is a fitting setting for leisurely Tuscan dinners and local wines. The gardens are no less appealing, full of roses, olive trees and lavender; you have tennis for the active, a parasoled terrace for the idle and a pool that is far too seductive for anyone intent upon a cultural holiday. That said, do visit the exquisite church of San Leolino, a step away.

rooms	28: 27 twins/doubles, 1 single.
price	€170–€270.
	Half-board €95–€145 p.p.
meals	Light lunch €16.
	Dinner €34.
closed	November–March.
directions	Panzano (not marked on all maps) 7km from Grève in Chianti; hotel signed from Greve.

Conte & Contessa Aloisi de Larderel

tel	+39 055 852621
fax	+39 055 852277
email	info@villalebarone.it
web	www.villalebarone.it

Hotel

Map 8 Entry 156

Podere Le Mezzelune
via Mezzelune 126, 57020 Bibbona

A treat to find this house in the north Maremma. After a long, winding track, big wooden gates; ring the bell and they swing open to reveal a tree-lined drive… Miele the labrador is the first to greet you. The Chiesas have turned their home into a delightful B&B where you feel as though you are visiting friends. Downstairs, a huge dining table for breakfasts of fresh, home-baked pastries and seasonal fruits, and an open fire for winter. Upstairs: bedrooms, each at a corner of the house with a wisteria-clad terrace (two look out to sea). Painted white and cream, they have linen curtains, wooden floors, furniture made to Luisa's design… charming with candles, fresh fruit and vintage wooden pegs hung with an antique shawl. Bathrooms, too, are perfect. For longer stays you have two little cottages in the garden, comfortable with open fires, dishwashers and beams. You are surrounded by cypresses, vines, flowers, herbs and 2,000 olive trees. A magical place, five minutes from the historic centre, not far from the sea and blissfully free of newspapers and TV. *Minimum stay two nights; three nights in cottages.*

rooms	4 + 2: 4 twins/doubles. 2 cottages for 2-3.
price	€146-€176. Cottages €166-€176 (€1,162-€1,232 p.w.).
meals	Breakfast in cottages €13-€15, on request. Good restaurants 5km.
closed	Rarely.
directions	Exit SS1 at La California towards Bibbona. Just before village, signs for Il Mezzelune on left. Follow for approx 2km to farm gate.

	Luisa & Sergio Chiesa
tel	+39 0586 670266
fax	+39 0586 671814
email	relais@lemezzelune.it
web	www.lemezzelune.it

B&B & Self-catering

Map 8 Entry 157

Villa la Bandita

Tenuta la Bandita, via Campagna Nord 30, 57020 Sassetta

There's still a magical, undiscovered feel about the high Maremma – sunny hills, spectacular views and ancient forest with deer, porcupine and wild boar. The sense of space is wonderful. Villa la Bandita was once Daniella's family's summer retreat. As a teenager she had a vision of turning the house into a small hotel or guest house; now she and her husband live on the 85-hectare estate. Staying in the elegant, 17th-century, two-storeyed villa is like being a guest in a private country house, with an approachable, humorous and charming hostess. It's all very quiet, relaxing and civilised. The restaurant walls are hung with huge tapestries, there are fresh flowers, a collection of vintage jugs and some interesting antiques. Dino and Daniella join guests for meals at the great glass table supported by two lions whenever they can. Gracious bedrooms look out over open countryside and the estate's cedar and pine woods, olive groves, vineyards, vegetable gardens, orchards and two small lakes. From some places you can catch a distant, tantalising glimpse of the Tyrrhenian Sea.

rooms	11: 10 doubles, 1 suite.
price	€90-€140. Suite €135-€165.
meals	Dinner €30. Restaurant 3-6km.
closed	November-March.
directions	SS1 Aurelia South - exit Donoratico. Follow signs for Castagneto Carducci then Monteverdi. Before Sassetta, left for Monteverdi. After 2km, La Tenuta on right.

Dino & Daniella Filippi

tel	+39 0565 794224
fax	+39 0565 794350
email	bandita@tin.it
web	www.labandita.com

B&B

Map 11 Entry 158

Pieve di Caminino

via prov. di Peruzzo, 58028 Roccatederighi

A fallen column lying deep in the grass, woods, a quiet lake... so peaceful that it's hard to believe what a history this settlement has had since it was first recorded in 1075. Set in a huge natural amphitheatre, ringed by hills and medieval fortresses, it has seen battles rage and monks and hermits come and go. There's even a magic spring. Once you've driven through the big, rusty gates and down the tree-lined drive, you'll be greeted by your hosts in an 11th-century church - part of the owners' private quarters. It's the most lovely, airy space, with battered columns, soaring arches and elegant furniture - a subtle study in cream, gold and brown. The apartments, too, are beautiful. Each has its own terrace or balcony and is simply furnished with family antiques and fine old paintings. Enchanting windows look over the grounds; the massive walls are rough stone or plaster, the ceilings beamed or vaulted. The 500-hectare estate produces its own olive oil and wine and has distant views to the sea and the isle of Elba. *Minimum stay three nights in peak season.*

rooms	7 apts: 2 for 3, 3 for 4, 2 for 5.
price	€90-€120 for 2-3(€455-€805 per week). €160-€210 for 4-5 (€700-€1099 per week).
meals	Restaurant 7km.
closed	Rarely.
directions	From Milan m'way Bologna - Firenze exit Firenze Certosa, for Siena-Grosseto, exit Civitella Marittima for Follonica. 5km before Montemassi right for Sassofortino. On right 1km.

Piero Marrucchi & Daniela Locatelli

tel	+39 0564 569737
fax	+39 0564 568756
email	caminino@caminino.com
web	www.caminino.com

Self-catering

Map 11 Entry 159

Azienda Agricola Montebelli
loc. Molinetto, 58023 Caldana Bivio

Step outside and breathe in the scents of myrtle and juniper. Wander up to the ancient oak at the top of the hill and watch the sun set. And explore this whole lovely area on horseback: Montebelli has nine horses and three ponies (and mountain bikes, too). Little tracks lead you past gnarled oaks to vineyards, olive groves and a small lake. The farm is run by a lovely family: Carla, her husband and their son Alessandro, back from a life in South Africa. Loungers line the elegant pool; jars of the farm's produce – honey, jam, olive oil, grappa and wine – are displayed in reception, alongside a blackboard announcing the day's menu. The cooking is Tuscan/Neapolitan, the produce home-grown and organic, the quality outstanding. If you're lucky, cookery courses may be in the offing – do ask. Breakfast is served on the big, covered terrace; on a summer evening there could be a concert or a barbecue. Bedrooms are cool, clean and welcoming, their white walls, wooden floors, understated furnishings and interesting pictures striking the perfect note of simplicity in an unspoiled place. Superb value.

rooms	21: 11 doubles, 2 suites, 8 triples.
price	Half-board €85-€108 p.p.
meals	Half-board only.
closed	January-March.
directions	From SS1 exit Gavorrano Scalo for Ravi-Caldana; 5km, turn for Caldana. After 2.5km, sign for Montebelli.

Carla Filotico Tosi

tel	+39 0566 887100
fax	+39 0566 81439
email	info@montebelli.it
web	www.montebelli.com

B&B

Map 11 Entry 160

Antico Casale di Scansano
loc. Castagneta, 58054 Scansano

The food is delicious and breakfasts are quite a spread – and the restaurant gets full marks for not overwhelming you with a long menu. Be idle, by all means – but when you see your fellow guests scooting off to various parts of this mini-resort to ride, hike or cook the day away, you may wish to join them. There are morning courses in Tuscan cookery with Mariella Pellegrini, while down at the stables lessons and pony treks take place under the watchful eye of Athos. The bedrooms in the old building vary in size while those in the new are large, light, fresh and clean, with balconies and breathtaking views; the cheapest lie closest to the road. There's satellite TV for the evenings and air con for sultry nights. In the restaurant, picture windows pull in the light and the views, the sitting room is welcoming with big sofas, open fire and games, there's a super outdoor pool and a wellness centre dedicated to relaxing treatments and enhanced by delightful perfumes. The Pellegrini family and their staff are warm and gracious; this is a happy place, wonderful for families.

rooms	32: 21 doubles, 5 suites, 6 singles.
price	Half-board €120-€170; suites €195-€240; singles €80-€95.
meals	Half-board only.
closed	Rarely.
directions	From Scansano towards Manciano (SS322). House 2.5km east of Scansano.

Signor Massimo Pellegrini

tel	+39 0564 507219
fax	+39 0564 507805
email	info@anticocasalediscansano.com
web	www.anticocasalediscansano.com

Hotel

Map 11 Entry 161

Villa Bengodi
via Bengodi 2, loc. Bengodi, 58010 Fonteblanda

A house that matches its owners: gentle and with old-fashioned charm. Great-aunt Zia Ernesta lived in the room with the angel frescoes for most of her life; now Caterina, who lives in Florence, shares the running of the B&B with her brother and his wife. The villa and its gardens are their pride and joy. Bedrooms are generous, light and spotless and house a hotchpotch of furniture from past decades; one has a ceiling painted in 1940, another a terrace; all have original floor tiles in varying patterns. Modern bathrooms are excellent, views are to the garden or sea. While away the days in the enchanting palm-fringed garden, or on the terrace where views reach to Corsica on a clear day. Beaches and mile upon mile of surf are a hop away – or you could walk the full mile to Talamone, where a family friend takes you out on his boat to fish and to swim; tuck into what you catch. The apartment is newly done up and has its own garden. Dine in summer on the terrace, in winter under a chandelier made of antlers and pine cones. A personal home in a magical setting. *Minimum stay three nights.*

rooms	6 + 1: 6 doubles. 1 apartment for 5.
price	€100–€150. Apartment €500–€1,500 per week.
meals	Dinner €30.
closed	Rarely.
directions	From Grossetó-Roma superstrada, towards Talamone. First left & where road ends near station right into via Bengodi. First right again.

	Famiglia Orlandi
mobile	+39 335 420334
fax	+39 0564 885515
email	villabengodi@toskana.net

B&B & Self-catering

Map 11 Entry 162

Il Pardini's Hermitage

loc. Cala degli Alberi, 58013 Isola del Giglio

You arrive by sea; the trip around the coast from Giglio Porto, sometimes choppy, takes 20 minutes. Once on the island, your mode of transport is on foot or by donkey! It's quite a hike up to the villa, but there are plenty of little areas to sit and catch your breath along the way. The island is a wonder of flora and fauna – peregrine falcons, kestrels and buzzards if you're lucky, gorgeous wild flowers.... This once-hermitage, now a private villa, is far from any village or coastal resort: perfect seclusion. Bedrooms are simple, pale-walled and delicious, the doubles with stunning sea views. Find a quiet spot in the well-kept gardens, colourful with cacti and flowers, or indulge in a bout of sea-water therapy – there's a beautiful platform to dive from and the water is crystal-clear. Paint or pot, play an instrument or a game, ride a donkey, visit a beach on the other side. And dress up for dinner, a formal affair of stiff white napery and hushed conversation. *Minimum stay three nights. Watercolour, ceramics and raku (pottery) courses available; also health and beauty weeks.*

rooms	13: 10 doubles, 2 singles, 1 suite.
price	Half-board €95-€155 p.p. Full-board €110-€170 p.p.
meals	Half-board or full-board only.
closed	October-March, but open as a retreat.
directions	Accessible by boat from Giglio Porto: 20-min ride. If seas rough, on foot or by mule. Full details at time of booking.

	Federigo & Barbara Pardini
tel	+39 0564 809034
fax	+39 0564 809177
email	info@hermit.it
web	www.hermit.it

Hotel

Map 11 Entry 163

Villa Marsili

viale Cesare Battisti 13, 52044 Cortona

Always refreshing to come to Cortona, set so magnificently on the top of a hill. And the site of this beautifully run palazzo-hotel is steeped in history: in the 14th century the church of the Madonna degli Alemanni stood here, built to house the miraculous image of the Madonna della Manna. Beneath, an Oratory was linked by a flight of stairs (still to be seen in the breakfast room); in 1786 the church was demolished and an elegant mansion built on the site. The owners have carefully preserved many of the original architectural features hidden over the centuries, and the hall and the light-filled bedrooms are immaculately and individually decorated with trompe l'œils and hand-painted borders. Colours are gentle yellows, bathrooms are gorgeous, most rooms are large, some are tiny, all windows have views. The front of the house looks onto a garden with a pergola where an excellent breakfast buffet is enjoyed – along with a stunning panorama of the Valdichiana and Lake Trasimeno. On the northern side is a winter garden, with the Borgo San Domenico a mesmerising backdrop. *Complimentary evening aperitif.*

rooms	26: 18 doubles, 3 suites, 5 singles.
price	€132-€217. Suites €260-€310. Singles €90-€110.
meals	Good restaurant 10-minute walk uphill.
closed	9 January-February.
directions	Leave A1 at Val di Chiana, take Siena/Perugia m'way; 2nd exit for Cortona. Follow signs for Cortona Centro. Parking nearby.

	Stefano Meacci
tel	+39 0575 605252
fax	+39 0575 605618
email	info@villamarsili.net
web	www.villamarsili.net

Hotel

Map 9 Entry 164

Casa Bellavista

loc. Creti C.S. 40, 52044 Cortona

A glass of wine at a table in the orchard. Birdsong for background music – or occasionally foreground, if the family rooster is feeling conversational. And a panorama of Tuscan landscape. Bellavista is well-named: its all-round views take in Monte Arniata, Foiano della Chiana and the old Abbey of Farneta. Next door is a field of sunflowers. There was a farm here for 200 years but the house was extensively restored about 30 years ago. It still has the original brick exterior, now softened by creepers, and a welcoming, family atmosphere (Simonetta and her husband have two young children). There's an assured, uncluttered country elegance to the rooms, and pretty, airy bedrooms are furnished with family antiques and interesting engravings. Simonetta's kitchen has a huge marble table top for kneading bread and she cooks farmhouse food for her guests. She also gives cookery lessons for a maximum of four, so if you want to learn how to make gnocchi, fresh pasta, focaccia… Her husband, who's in the restaurant business, sees to the wines. Vespas and mountain bikes are free! Real Italian family B&B.

rooms	3: 1 double, 2 twins/doubles.
price	€115-€140.
meals	Dinner €35.
closed	Rarely.
directions	Autostrada Valdichiana exit Perugia; exit Foiano. After 400m, right for Fratta-S.Caterina. On for 2.8km, right next to ruined building. After 1km, right at junc.; keep to left-hand road. After 600m, right onto a dirt road.

	Simonetta Demarchi
tel	+39 0575 610311
fax	+39 0575 610749
email	info@casabellavista.it
web	www.casabellavista.it

B&B

Map 9 Entry 165

La Palazzina
Sant'Andrea di Sorbello, 52040 Mercatale di Cortona

There is an English inflection to La Palazzina, with its quirky 14th-century watch tower planted inexplicably beside the main house. It makes a most unusual self-contained retreat with luscious views across the wooded valley. You have a well-equipped kitchen, a woodburner for cosy nights, a winding stair to a half-moon double and, at the top, a twin with a stunning, brick-beehive ceiling. The honeysuckle-strewn terrace is just as you would wish, with cypress trees marching sedately up the hill and birdsong to disturb the peace. There's also an apartment for two at one end of the farmhouse, with its own private entrance under a loggia. The grounds, including a swimming pool with views, are for you to explore and lead to some of the loveliest walks in the valley. David and Salina are great company and will cook dinner for you on your first evening. Hannibal defeated the Roman army at nearby Lake Trasimeno and there is little that David doesn't know about the historical importance of this area – his enthusiasm is contagious. *Minimum stay one week in tower, three nights in farmhouse.*

rooms	2 apartments: 1 for 2, 1 for 4.
price	Tower €893–€1,193 (£595–£795). Farmhouse €599–€893 (£399–£595). Prices per week.
meals	Self-catering. Dinner first evening, €25 with wine. On request.
closed	Rarely.
directions	Directions on booking.

	David & Salina Lloyd-Edwards
tel/fax	+39 0575 638111
mobile	+39 335 572 7812
email	italianencounters@technet.it
web	www.italianencounters.com/lapal.htm

Self-catering

Map 9 Entry 166

Relais San Pietro in Polvano

loc. Polvano 3, 52043 Castiglion Fiorentino

Paradise high in the hills. The adorable Signor Protti and his wife run this enchanting hotel with their son and daughter-in-law and the care they lavish on the place is apparent at every turn. Bedrooms have shutters and gorgeous old rafters, wide wrought-iron beds, elegant painted wardrobes, rugs on tiled floors, straw hats on white walls. For cool autumn nights there are cream sofas and a log fire. The pool, on a terrace just below, must have one of the best views in Tuscany: keep your head above water and you are rewarded with the blue-tinted panorama for which Italy is famous. There is a restaurant for guests serving delicious local food and their own olive oil; bread comes fresh from the bread oven. In summer you dine at beautifully dressed tables on a terrace overlooking the gardens, full of cool recesases and comfy chairs, and the olive-grove'd valley beyond. An atmosphere of luxurious calm and seclusion prevails, and your hosts are a delight. For those who choose to venture forth, note that gates close at midnight.
Children over 12 welcome. Minimum stay two nights.

rooms	10: 4 doubles, 1 single, 5 suites.
price	€170–€230.
	Single €130–€140.
	Suites €230–€300.
meals	Lunch or dinner €30–€45.
closed	November–March.
directions	A1 Rome-Milan exit Monte San Savino for Castiglion Fiorentino. At 3rd lights, left for Polvano. After 7km, left for Relais San Pietro.

	Signor Luigi Protti
tel	+39 0575 650100
fax	+39 0575 650255
email	info@polvano.com
web	www.polvano.com

Hotel

Map 9 Entry 167

Villa i Bossi
Gragnone 44-46, 52100 Arezzo

Fifty people once lived on the ground floor of the old house and everything is still as it was – the great box which held the bread, the carpenter's room crammed with tools, the rich robes hanging in the Sacristy, the old oven for making charcoal… Francesca loves showing people round. Her husband's family have lived here since 1240 and the house is full of their treasures. There's even a fireplace sculpted by Benedetto da Maiano in the 1300s – his 'thank you for having me' to the family. Sleep in ornate splendour in the main villa or opt for the modern comforts of the Orangery: simple yet beautiful. This really is a magical place, full of character and memories, with lively, friendly hosts. The park-like gardens, set among gentle green hills, are a delight, and have been altered and enriched over the centuries. To one side of the pool, a hill covered in rare fruit trees; to the west, Italian box hedges four metres high, and camellias, peonies and old-fashioned roses, avenues, grassy banks and shady trees, a pond and enticing seats under arching shrubs, olives and vines: they make their own Chianti and oil.

rooms	10 + 1. Villa: 2 doubles, 2 twins. Orangery: 2 doubles, 2 triples, 2 quadruples. 1 apartment for 3.
price	From €125.
meals	Restaurant 2km.
closed	Rarely.
directions	In Arezzo follow signs to stadium. Pass Esso garage & on to Bagnoro. Then to Gragnone. 2km to villa.

Francesca Viguali Albergotti

tel	+39 0575 365642
fax	+39 0575 964900
email	franvig@ats.it
web	www.villaibossi.com

B&B & Self-catering

Map 9 Entry 168

Castello di Gargonza

loc. Gargonza, 52048 Monte San Savino

A fortified Romanesque village in the beauty of the Tuscan hills, whose 800-year-old steps, stones, rafters and tiles remain virtually intact. Today it is a private, uniquely Italian marriage of exquisitely ancient and exemplary modern. Seen from the air it is perfect, as if shaped by the gods to inspire Man to greater works: a magical maze of paths, nooks and crannies, castellated tower, great octagonal well, a heavy gate that lets the road slip out and tumble down, breathtaking views. No cars, no shops, but a chapel, gardens, pool and old olive press for meetings, concerts or breakfasts, cosy with big fireplace and comfy chairs. An excellent restaurant sits just outside the walls. The count and countess and their staff are passionate about the place and look after you well. Choose between self-catering and B&B — bedrooms and apartments are 'rustic deluxe' with smart modern furnishings, white-rendered walls, superb rafters, open fireplaces, tiny old doors. Intriguing, delightful and sociable too: a perfect place for families. *Minimum stay two nights; apartments one week.*

rooms	24 + 8: 21 doubles, 3 suites. 8 apartments for 2-10.
price	€110-€171. Suites €163-€181. Apartments €672-€1,715 per week.
meals	Lunch €25. Dinner €35.
closed	10 January-1 March; November.
directions	Exit A1 at Monte S. Savino; SS73 for Siena. Approx 7km after Monte S. Savino right for Gargonza; signed.

	Conte Roberto Guicciardini
tel	+39 0575 847021
fax	+39 0575 847054
email	gargonza@gargonza.it
web	www.gargonza.it

B&B & Self-catering

Map 9 Entry 169

Borgo Iesolana

loc. Iesolana, 52021 Bucine

At the centre of an immaculate patchwork of fields, vineyards and woods, this irresistible group of old buildings. Mellow stone and warm brick blend, flowers tumble from terracotta pots, arches invite you in out of the sun, a pool beckons. Giovanni and Francesco inherited the estate from their grandfather and live here with their young families. They have created nine apartments, all different, from the farm buildings, and it is a solid, sensitive conversion. The décor is an upmarket, uncluttered mix of traditional and new: good beds and fabrics, super kitchens, thoughtful lighting. And if you prefer not to self-cater, you can breakfast in the 'wine bar' across the way. This, too, is an impeccable restoration, with modern Italian furniture and big windows. Lunch and dinner are available on request: local produce and traditional Tuscan fare. The farm is beautifully run (the very vines are edged with roses) and produces wine, olive oil, grappa and honey. It lies alongside an old Roman road that once linked Siena with Florence, with views on all sides of Chiantishire. *Minimum stay 2-7 nights depending on season.*

rooms	9 apartments: 3 for 2, 3 for 4, 2 for 6, 1 for 8.
price	€490-€2,100 per week.
meals	Breakfast €8. Lunch or dinner €25-€30, on request.
closed	Never.
directions	A1 Firenze-Roma exit Valdarno; at toll, right for Montevarchi; dir. Levane/Bucine; thro' Bucine; left to Pogio; left for Iesolana; 150m left; over narrow bridge; cont. to Borgo.

Giovanni & Francesco Toscano

tel	+39 055 992988
fax	+39 055 992879
email	info@iesolana.it
web	www.iesolana.it

Rendola Riding
Rendola 66, Montevarchi, 52025 Arezzo

One of the forerunners of agriturismo in Tuscany, Jenny started Rendola back in the 70s and gives you the best possible way of seeing Chianti – on horseback. You need to be able to ride, and the minimum age for riders is ten. Equestrians will appreciate the beautiful conditions and the English, not western, style. There are lessons with set timetables, relaxed rides and treks and three-day forays. After a long, hot day in the saddle it is wonderful to return to showers and homely rooms. At the rustic ring of a cow bell, guests, family and stable workers gather in the dining room for dinner, where sprightly Pietro serves wholesome organic Tuscan dishes washed down with Chianti – and regales the assembled company with many a tale. It's all delightfully laid back: chickens, ducks, turkeys, horses, dogs in the courtyard; music, books an open fire in the sitting room; jackets on the backs of chairs… Non-riders will appreciate generous Jenny's advice on what to see and do in the area. *Minimum stay two nights. Guests can be collected from Montevarchi train station.*

rooms	6 + 2: 3 doubles/twins, 2 family, 1 single. 2 apartments for 2.
price	€80. Single €40. Half-board €60 p.p. Full-board €80 p.p. Apartment €90 with breakfast.
meals	Lunch or dinner €15–€20, with wine.
closed	Rarely.
directions	From autostrada del Sole exit 25 for Montevarchi & Mercatale Valdarno. After 5km right for Rendola; house 200m from village.

	Jenny Bawtree
tel	+39 055 9707045
fax	+39 055 9707045
email	info@rendolariding.it
web	www.rendolariding.it

Agriturismo & Self-catering

Map 9 Entry 171

Odina Agriturismo
loc. Odina, 52024 Loro Ciuffenna

You are 650 metres above sea level and feel on top of the world – the Arno valley reaches out before you and the air is pure. Antonella takes great pride in this solid, pale-blue-shuttered house and its surrounding gardens. Each bush, tree and herb has been chosen with care, and the interiors of house and apartments are delightfully rustic and contemporary. Each is different: some kitchen surfaces are of granite, others of local *pietra serena*; bathroom walls are softly ragged in varying shades; all have French windows to a patio with wooden outdoor furniture. Oil, vinegar, sugar, coffee, salt and washing-up liquid are provided, and if you ask in advance they will lay on more for which you would pay. The reception is in a beautifully restored, de-consecrated chapel, with an old bread-making chest and a 'shop' selling Odina olive oil and beans. Take a dip in the pool, go for long, lazy walks in the olive groves and chestnut woods, prepare a barbecue. Garden courses and visits – highly recommended – are held here in May. *Minimum stay seven nights.*

rooms	4 apartments for 2, 5, 6, 7. Also farmhouse for 8-10.
price	€400-€750 for 2. €700-€1,500 for 4-5. Farmhouse €1,800-€3,200. Prices per week.
meals	Self-catering. Restaurants 8-10km.
closed	15 January-mid-February.
directions	Florence-Roma A1, exit Valdarno. In Terranuova, follow Loro Ciuffenna.

	Signor Paolo Trenti
tel	+39 055 969304
fax	+39 055 969305
email	info@odina.it
web	www.odina.it

Casa Simonicchi

via Simonicchi 184, Caprese Michelangelo, 52033 Arezzo

After a blissful drive through the Casentino National Park you arrive at a hamlet of stone houses. This one is a farmhouse with a barn attached, carefully and lovingly restored by sculptress Jenny. Warm, generous, knowledgable, she can tell you about the the historic towns to visit; the countryside of Michelangelo and St Francis of Assisi; the friendly taverna down the road. Reached via her hall, on the quaint top floor, is a 'gallery' apartment simply and charmingly furnished, with natural colours, cotton rugs, some oak pieces from England, paintings, sculptures and ceramics. Best of all: a roof terrace with an awning for shade and panoramas of that heavenly countryside celebrated in the paintings of Piero della Francesca. This will suit – and captivate – those with children: a room with four single beds, a sitting room with dining area and new kitchen, two showers. For a party of six, there's an option to rent the double that leads to the terrace. Outside, long garden terraces, lavender and olives, and a telescope for the stars. Dinners, on request, are cooked by friend Vittorio at the outdoor pizza oven.

rooms	1 apartment for 2-6. Extra room available.
price	€300-€870 per week.
meals	Dinner on request. Restaurant nearby.
closed	Christmas-3rd week March.
directions	Exit A1 Arezzo; north for Sansepolcro; signs for Caprese Michelangelo; left for Lama; right for Chiusi della Verna; after cypress-filled cemetery, house on 3rd right-hand bend; sharp descent.

Mrs Jennifer Frears-Barnard

tel	+39 0575 793762
fax	+39 0575 793762
email	jenniferbarnard@libero.it
web	www.simonicchi.com

Self-catering

Map 9 Entry 173

Fortezza de' Cortesi

loc. Monti 26, 53037 San Gimignano

Restoring the ruins of this lovely place was a labour of love for Cledy. The project took nine years, the results are stunning. An actress, Cledy has given the 10th-century *fortezza*-turned-villa a charm and distinction all of its own. Captivating features – vaulted ceilings, arched windows, rich stone, chestnut beams – mix with fabrics and colours in the most harmonious manner. The five double rooms, all different, have sumptuous bathrooms and unforgettable views; up in the tower is the most tempting of suites, with a big fireplace and a bath from which you gaze on the hills as you soak. There's a tiny kitchen area, too, for hot drinks. Come for two nights of perfect B&B – or rent the entire lovely place. And if you're into self-improvement, Cledy can rustle up a course or two, on cookery, ceramics or wine tasting. The house stands high in 12 hectares of land, with a terraced garden, gazebo, pool and views of the celebrated towers of San Gimignano. Worth the drive to get here, but leave the children behind: this place is exquisite! *B&B minimum stay two nights.*

rooms	6: 5 doubles, 1 suite.
price	€140-160.
	Suite €210-240.
	Whole villa €6,000-€7,000 per week.
meals	Good restaurant 5km.
closed	Rarely.
directions	Exit Florence-Siena m'way at Poggibonsi Nord; signs for San Gimignano; after 8km, road forks, right for San Gimignano; 50m left into gravel road; signed.

Cledy Tancredi

tel/fax	+39 0577 940123
mobile	+39 338 7732761
email	info@fortezzacortesi.com
web	www.fortezzacortesi.com

Hotel L'Antico Pozzo

via San Matteo 87, 53037 San Gimignano

Step inside – and the hustle and bustle of San Gimignano vanishes. It's like entering another era: one of grace, elegance and calm. The interiors of the hotel, a medieval house bang in the heart of the city, are a study in soft Tuscan colours. The cool bedrooms are restrained, luxurious, inviting, all with fine fabrics and special ceilings, some frescoed, others vaulted or white-painted wood. The wrought-iron bedsteads are exquisite, the bathrooms are excellent. Breakfast is in the Sala Rosa, a ballroom in its heyday, renowned for 18th-century society gatherings. The old well that gives the place its name is still here, too, secure, water-filled and artfully lit by concealed lighting. Approach it via a sequence of little passageways and stairs and note the holes in the walls – the 15th-century equivalent of air con! Outside, the pretty terracotta terrace, bright with scarlet geraniums, has shady arches for escaping the sun. Emanuele and his sisters are in charge and run the hotel with youthful charm and efficiency. It is deliciously soothing to return to after busy forays into town.

rooms	18: 17 doubles, 1 single.
price	€125–€160.
meals	Restaurants nearby.
closed	Rarely.
directions	A1 exit Firenze-Vertosa for Siena; exit Poggibonsi-Nord; follow signs for S. Gimignano; use car park no. 3 in *centro storico*.

	Emanuele Marro
tel	+39 0577 942014
fax	+39 0577 942117
email	info@anticopozzo.com
web	www.anticopozzo.com

Hotel

Map 8 Entry 175

Il Casale del Cotone
loc. Cellole 59, 53037 San Gimignano

A relief to escape the heaving crowds of San Gimignano and to look back from Il Casale del Cotone over the glorious vineyards and olive groves to that Manhattan of Tuscany. The house is 17th century, and it was in this parish that Puccini composed *Suore Angelica*. Inspiration may strike here in other ways and certainly the landscape is such to tempt many an artist. The old family house has been carefully restored and furnished with family pieces and the occasional reclamation find. Big double rooms are done up in simple Tuscan style, with tiled floors, very good bathrooms and comfortable wrought-iron beds; those on the ground floor have patios where pots of jasmine scent the air, those above, views of the hills. The apartments, too, are attractive. Breakfast is served by the housekeeper in the courtyard opposite the little chapel or in the hunting room; dinners are generous. Outside, a pretty garden patio by the pool; across the road, the coach house annexe, also restored to its former glory and once again hosting weary travellers on the well-trodden route between San Gimignano and Certaldo.

rooms	11 + 2: 9 doubles; 2 triples. 2 apartments: 1 for 2, 1 for 3.
price	€92–€105. Triples €120–€135. Apartments €98–€130.
meals	Dinner with wine from €35.
closed	Rarely.
directions	From S. Gimignano for Certaldo. Casale del Cotone 3km on left.

Signor Alessandro Martelli

tel/fax	+39 0577 943236
mobile	+39 348 3029091
email	info@casaledelcotone.com
web	www.casaledelcotone.com

B&B & Self-catering

Map 8 Entry 176

Fattoria Guicciardini

viale Garibaldi 2/A, Piazza S. Agostino 2, 53037 San Gimignano

A visit to San Gimignano is a must and this makes a charming base: eight self-catering apartments right in the centre, immaculately converted from a 15th-century complex of farm buildings. Two were granaries in a former life (their bedrooms on a mezzanine floor), another was the farm cook's house. Lovely cool rooms have huge raftered ceilings, others arched windows or original fireplaces and tiles; all have been furnished in a contemporary style with new sofas, kilim-style rugs, white curtains and the occasional antique. There are entrances from both outside the city walls and from the Piazza S. Agostino (and do sneak a look at the church's altar frescoes by Benozzo Gozzoli). Get up early and watch the mists fall away to reveal the vineyards all around, then drink in the astonishing art of San Gimignano before the army of tourists descends. Evening in the city is magical, too, when the city's fairytale towers are floodlit. This is the time of day at which San Gimignano – honey pot of Tuscan tourism, deservedly so – is at its most lovely.

rooms	8 apartments: 5 for 2-4, 3 for 4-6.
price	€120-€187 for 2-6 per night. (€800-€1303 per week).
meals	Restaurants nearby.
closed	Rarely.
directions	Leave Florence-Siena m'way at S. Gimignano & Poggibonsi Nord exit. Fattoria in centre of S.Gimignano.

	Signor Tuccio Guicciardini
tel/fax	+39 0577 907185
mobile	+39 329 2273120
email	info@guicciardini.com
web	www.guicciardini.com

Self-catering

Map 8 Entry 177

Podere Il Sasso - Rosae Villa

loc. Fabbricciano 50, 53034 Colle di Val d'Elsa

A Tuscan kitchen: dried herbs hanging from the beams, dressers painted with fruit and flowers. Anna makes much of her guests, spoiling them with silver cutlery, crystal and fine linen. She's energetic, full of fun and a great cook; she has no English but has a daughter living close by who does. This is a real family home, full of photos and ornaments, surrounded by olive trees, orchards and garden. There are lemon trees in big terracotta pots, patios to sit out on and plenty of trees for shade. A black cockerel and his harem peck contentedly around. The house is 16th century in origin, with attractive, flexible accommodation, full of the scent of fresh flowers and lavender. The smaller apartment, in a separate little building, has a tiny kitchen with an exposed rock wall and a woodburning stove; the larger one – in the house but with its own entrance – has a living area with wide brick arches, terracotta floor and an open fireplace. (The bedrooms in either can also be let on their own.) From the bedroom in the house you can glimpse the extraordinary towers of San Gimignano. *Minimum stay two nights.*

rooms	4 doubles (can also be let as 2 apartments).
price	€88 (€450 per week).
meals	Restaurants nearby.
closed	November.
directions	A1 exit Firenze & Certosa; superstrada Firenze/Siena, exit Colle di Val d'Elsa. Follow signs for centre; go to Piazza Arnolfo & call, Anna will come & meet you in 5 minutes.

Anna Piccolo Giunco

tel	+39 0577 920377
fax	+39 0577 920674
email	info@rosaevilla.it
web	www.rosaevilla.it

B&B & Self-catering

Map 8 Entry 178

Fattoria Tregole
loc. Tregole 86, 53011 Castellina in Chianti

A vineyard and a private family chapel. What could be more Italian? The delightful Kirchlechners – he an architect, she a restorer – make Chianti Classico, grappa and olive oil from their Tuscan manor farm. They spent seven years restoring the buildings, keeping original features – raftered ceilings, terracotta floors, large fireplaces – and furnishing with a light, country-house touch. The airy apartments and the bedrooms, including a ground-floor suite with a terrace, feel like the family's rooms; all are lovely. Walls are eye-catching with Edith's hand-painted stencils, painted brass bedsteads are cleverly restored; there are traditional lampshades, dried flowers, patchwork quilts and crochet cushions. It is light, warm and inviting. Breakfast in the sunny dining room or on the patio; twice a week Edith cooks a Tuscan dinner, accompanied by the wine from the Tregole cellars. A beautiful pool, quiet views over olive groves and vine-clad hills, a garden with shady nooks, a tiny Renaissance chapel – it is intimate and homely. *B&B: over 12s welcome. Apartments minimum stay three nights.*

rooms	5 + 2: 4 doubles, 1 suite for 2. 2 apartments: 1 for 4, 1 for 5.
price	€110. Suite €120. Apartments €180-€200.
meals	Dinner €30, book ahead.
closed	5 November-March.
directions	From Florence SS222 for Grève-Panzano-Castellina; 5km after Castellina in Chianti; sign for Tregole; 1km.

	Edith Kirchlechner
tel	+39 0577 740991
fax	+39 0577 741928
email	fattoria-tregole@castellina.com
web	www.fattoria-tregole.com

B&B & Self-catering

Map 8 Entry 179

Palazzo Leopoldo
via Roma 33, Radda, 53017 Radda in Chianti

In a corner of the hall is a stone carving of a swaddled baby – 14th-century evidence of the hospital this was. For the last few centuries Palazzo Leopoldo has been a manor house. It's surprisingly peaceful here, in the middle of beautiful, hilltop Radda – and you can walk to several *enotecas* nearby to taste the finest Chiantis. The whole house has a delightful feel. The hall is light, with white-painted arches, an old tiled floor, the occasional bright rug, fresh flowers. Stroll onto the terrace, where Vittorio offers welcoming drinks, and gaze over the lovely hills. Bedrooms range from suites to doubles in the eaves; all are big, generously equipped and have a rustic Tuscan feel. Some have the old bell-pulls for service, others the original stoves and frescoes: the owner has preserved as much as possible. Remarkable breakfast is served in a remarkable kitchen, replete with 18th-century range. Add to that an indoor pool and spa, a restaurant serving delicious food and truly delightful staff. Well worth the steep and winding road to get here. *Ask about cookery classes.*

rooms	17: 12 doubles, 5 suites.
price	€160–€220.
	Suites €220–€380.
meals	Lunch €25.
	Dinner €35.
closed	January & February.
directions	Signed in centre of
	Radda in Chianti.

	Vittorio Trevisan
tel	+39 0577 735605
fax	+39 0577 738031
email	info@palazzoleopoldo.it
web	www.palazzoleopoldo.it

Hotel

Map 8 Entry 180

La Locanda
loc. Montanino, 53017 Radda in Chianti

Admire the view from the pool – both are stunning. This is a magical place – a soft green lawn edged with Mediterranean shrubs slopes down to the pool, a covered terrace overlooks medieval Volpaia. (Some of the best Chianti is produced here; the village is a 20-minute walk.) The house vibrates with bold colour and lively fabric. The beautiful raftered living room, with open fireplace, big, stylish sofas and pale terracotta floor, reveals photos of Guido and Martina, he from the South, she from the North. They scoured Tuscany before they found their perfect inn, renovated these two houses and filled them with fine antiques, delightful prints, candles and fun touches, like the straw hats in the entrance hall. There's a library/bar where you can choose books from many languages and where Guido is generous with the grappa. The bedrooms are in a separate building and have big beds, great bathrooms and whitewashed rafters, as was the custom here. Martina cooks and gardens while Guido acts as host – they are a charming pair. Once settled in you'll find it hard to stir. *Minimum stay two nights.*

rooms	7: 3 doubles, 3 twins, 1 suite.
price	€200-€260. Singles €170-€225. Suite €280.
meals	Dinner €30. Restaurants 4km.
closed	Mid-November–mid-April.
directions	From Volpaia village square take narrow road to right which becomes track. On for 2km past small sign for La Locanda to left; 1km further to group of houses.

	Guido & Martina Bevilacqua
tel	+39 0577 738833
fax	+39 0577 739263
email	info@lalocanda.it
web	www.lalocanda.it

Hotel

Map 8 Entry 181

Hotel Villa la Grotta
Brolio, 53013 Gaiole in Chianti

There are many treats in store. The first, glimpsed on your way in, is the marvellous Castello di Brolio. The second is the hotel itself, on the castle's 4,000-acre estate. Originally a ninth-century manor house and later a nunnery, it has been restored and converted into a delightful small hotel by its Swiss owner. A bottle of wine will be waiting to welcome you in a cool, inviting bedroom – all pastel walls, soft lighting, lovely old beds, colourful kilims on terracotta-tiled floors. All have four-posters and many have vineyard views, making this a popular honeymooners' retreat. General manager Doogie runs it all with panache and her own inimitable style – it's informal and fun. You're pampered, too, with a Turkish bath, jacuzzi baths and two swimming pools, the outdoor one with pillars sculpted by a famous artist. But perhaps the biggest treat of all is the restaurant, where fish and meat dishes are cooked to perfection, accompanied by well-priced wines and served in a stylish dining room (or alfresco, under an ancient walnut tree). No surprise that people travel from as far as Florence.

rooms	12: 10 doubles, 2 suites.
price	€230-€270. Suites €325-€345.
meals	Dinner €35-€40.
closed	December-March.
directions	From Gaiole to Castello di Brolio; left of castle for Castelnuovo Berardenga, signs 1km, hotel on right.

Doogie Morley-Bodle

tel	+39 0577 747125
fax	+39 0577 747145
email	info@hotelvillalagrotta.it
web	www.hotelvillalagrotta.it

Hotel

Map 9 Entry 182

Borgo Argenina

loc. Argenina, S.M. Monti, 53013 Gaiole in Chianti

Weeds smothered the stone walls and there was no running water or electricity: the tiny hamlet of Borgo Argenina had been abandoned for 20 years when Elena bought it. Much hard labour has gone into restoration and the results show all the creativity you'd expect from a former fashion designer. Elena's artistry appears in patchwork tablecloths and delicately stencilled arches and ceilings – exquisite. Rooms are scented with lavender, sage and roses, bedrooms have quilts and cushions made from fabrics found in antique markets, furniture is hand-painted by Elena in Tuscan colours. In the pretty breakfast room, old grilled doors open on to a bright garden. The house and villa, set slightly apart, are equally refreshing, full of imaginative detail, and have plenty of privacy; you may prepare your own meals if you wish. Elena is an engaging hostess and she and her daughter Fiorenza look after you well; if you're a castle enthusiast, she'll draw you a map of all the castles in the area (and there are many!). An unusual place, hidden well away from the rest of Chianti. *Minimum stay three nights.*

rooms	6 + 3: 4 doubles, 2 suites. 2 houses for 2-3, 1 villa for 4.
price	€150. Suites €180-€200. House €200. Villa €400-€450.
meals	Osteria 5km.
closed	October-March.
directions	From Gaiole towards Siena follow signs for San Marcellino Monti. Left to Argenina.

	Elena Nappa
tel	+39 0577 747117
fax	+39 0577 747228
email	borgoargenina@libero.it
web	www.borgoargenina.it

B&B & Self-catering

Map 9 Entry 183

Borgo Casa Al Vento
loc. Casa al Vento, 53013 Gaiole in Chianti

Comfortable agriturismo in green Chianti; the approach to the hamlet down the long, sandy track is stunning. Proceed to your airy rooms and prepare to unwind in this secluded retreat, surrounded by wooded hills, tree-fringed lake, olives and vineyards. The property is made up of a hotch-potch of old buildings, medieval in origin, that were given a makeover some years ago and are now packed with jolly families. Exposed beams, stone walls and red-tiled floors create a rustic mood, while the décor, though not stylish – dralon and velour are in much evidence – is as neat as a new pin and as comfortable as can be. Each apartment is different, some have patios and all are a short walk from a lake. The B&B rooms are in two separate houses and share a beamy lounge; the cellar restaurant is jolly with red tablecloths and Italian radio. Come for the gardens and terraces, ducks, geese, goats, mini-playground, tennis (extra charge) and pretty pool. For good, well-priced restaurants there's Gaiole, a ten-minute drive up a steep, twisting road.

rooms	8 + 9: 8 suites. 8 apartments: 3 for 6, 3 for 4, 2 for 2. Villa for 2.
price	Suite €140-€250. Apartments €542-€1,600 per week. Villa €4,000 per week.
meals	Breakfast €10. Dinner, 3 courses, €30.
closed	Rarely.
directions	Exit A1 at Valdarno. Follow signs for Siena & Gaiole in Chianti, about 20km. At Gaiole, signs to Casa al Vento, about 3km.

	Signor Giuseppe Gioffreda
tel	+39 0577 749068
fax	+39 0577 744649
email	info@borgocasaalvento.com
web	www.borgocasaalvento.com

B&B & Self-catering

Map 9 Entry 184

Castello di Tornano

loc. Tornano, 53013 Gaiole in Chianti

The first thing you see is the ancient stone tower, peeking above the wooded hills and vineyards. Inside, a beautiful restoration that has enriched the glorious stonework, the spaciousness and the sense of history. Rooms are positively regal with deep rugs on tiled floors, sparkling chandeliers and richly coloured drapes and linen (plum, raspberry, royal blue, vermilion). The opulent Tower Room has its own jacuzzi and a terrace with stunning views. Self-catering apartments are uncluttered with exposed beams and stone walls, some with lovely vaulted ceilings. Bathrooms are a treat: neutral-toned mosaics blend in with the original stone, there are big mirrors and fluffy white towels and robes. Relax downstairs in the living room with its old font, soft-lighting and plush red drapes; request dinner and you are served fine Tuscan food. You're on an agriturismo so chianti, olive oil, grappa and sweet Vin Santo are all produced here. Come for the friendly atmosphere and the lovely pool and garden, the wine tastings, the riding on the estate, the luxuriousness of it all, and the peace.

rooms	11 + 7: 7 doubles, 2 triples, 2 suites. 7 apartments.
price	€215–€450.
meals	Breakfast €12. Dinner €35, on request.
closed	10 January–10 February.
directions	A1 exit Valdarno for Cavriglia-Gaiole on road 408. Pass Gaiole, cont. for Siena for 5km; signed on left.

Patrizia & Francesco Gioffreda

tel	+39 0577 746067
fax	+39 0577 746094
email	info@castelloditornano.it
web	www.castelloditornano.it

B&B & Self-catering

Map 9 Entry 185

Castello di Spaltenna
53013 Gaiole in Chianti

Live like a lord, dine among popes. This medieval castle, with its neighbouring bell-towered church, was the centre of a feudal hamlet and still has a regal feel. Walls are solid, doors are carved, ceilings beamed and vaulted, passageways dotted with armour, wall sconces and cushioned seats in arched alcoves. The tapestry-hung dining room trumpeting over 400 wines – originally a refectory when the castle was a monastery – is hung with papal portraits still. There is nothing medieval about the comfort, however; luxurious bedrooms have been slipped into the grand spaces, the feel being more Italian country castle than swish hotel. Fabrics are rich – silks, bold stripes, soft muslins – and each room is different; some with four-posters, others with beds on a dais, perhaps a fireplace, wooden ceiling, stone wall or archway. Indulge yourself in the two pools (one indoor), sauna, gym and Turkish bath, gaze over the Chianti valley, play tennis, stroll to the village bars, dine – superbly – in the candlelit courtyard. Guido, the director, played here as a child and is charming, hard-working and full of energy.

rooms	36: 26 doubles, 10 suites.
price	€195-€540.
meals	Lunch or dinner €45.
closed	8 January-March.
directions	Exit A1 at Valdarno. Well signed from Gaiole at top of hill.

	Guido Conti
tel	+39 0577 749483
fax	+39 0577 749269
email	info@spaltenna.it
web	www.spaltenna.it

Hotel

Map 9 Entry 186

L'Ultimo Mulino

loc. La Ripresa di Vistarenni, 53013 Gaiole in Chianti

The sense of space is stunning – the vast, medieval hall, lofty ceilings, stone walls, flights of stairs... Original arches give glimpses of passageways beyond and many of the rooms are connected by little 'bridges' from which you can see the millstream far below. Outside the restored watermill is a large terrace for delicious breakfast, a lovely long pool, and a small amphitheatre where occasional concerts are held. You're surrounded by trees and it's immensely quiet – just the sound of water and birds. All feels fresh and clean, welcoming and lived-in, and nothing is too much trouble for the staff. Sparsely, elegantly and comfortably furnished, the great hall makes a cool, beautiful centrepiece to the building – and there's a snug with a fireplace where you can roast chestnuts in season. Excellently equipped bedrooms have terracotta tiled floors and good, generously sized beds. You dine in the conservatory, overlooking the stream, on mainly Tuscan dishes, tempted by truffles and local delicacies. Historic Radda is a ten-minute drive.

rooms	13: 12 doubles, 1 suite.
price	€175–€232. Suite €230–€284.
meals	Dinner €35.
closed	November–March.
directions	From Gaiole in Chianti 1st right on road to Radda. Mill on right after bend.

	Massimiliano Draghi
tel	+39 0577 738520
fax	+39 0577 738659
email	info@ultimomulino.it
web	www.ultimomulino.it

Hotel

Map 9 Entry 187

Antico Borgo Poggiarello
strada di San Monti 12, Monteriggioni

The 17th-century farm buildings in the woods – the *borgo* – have been transformed into holiday homes and linked by a circuit of well-considered paths. Poggiarello is a family set-up. Signora Giove does the cooking, and is happy, son Roberto does front of house and is even happier – he once worked in a tax office and has no regrets! Nino, Paolo and Duke – the perfectly behaved English setter – are there when you need them. You can self-cater or do B&B here: arrangements are flexible. Most apartments are for two; some interconnect and are ideal for eight. Rooms are big and comfortable with brand-new wrought-iron beds, cream curtains and covers, new tiles; all have private patios and great views. Two are excellent for wheelchair-users. Days are spent lolling by the pool, evenings sunset-gazing on the terrace. Though the treasures of Siena, Monteriggioni and Volterra lie a short drive away, it's hard to leave… there's a beautifully-lit bath housed in a cave that's heated all year to 38 degrees, and a dear little restaurant where you can sample the best of Tuscan home cooking.

rooms	2 + 12: 2 suites. 12 apartments: 8 for 2-4, 3 for 4-6, 1 for 6-8.
price	Suites €123-€174. Apartments €102-€150 for two.
meals	Dinner, 5 courses, €25.
closed	Never.
directions	From Florence-Siena m'way exit Monteriggioni. Right after stop sign, 1.4km, left for Abbadia a Isola & Stove. After 6km, left for Scorgiano. On for 4km, left at 'Fattoria di Scorgiano'. Left on track after 2km.

	Roberto Giove
tel/fax	+39 0577 301003
mobile	+39 335 1281584
email	info@poggiarello.com
web	www.poggiarello.com

B&B & Self-catering

Map 8 Entry 188

Frances' Lodge
strada di Valdipugna 2, 53100 Siena

You stay in a converted hilltop lemon-house – a ten-minute bus ride into the city. Catch your breath at views that soar across olive, lemon and quince groves to the Torre del Mangia of Siena. The old farmhouse was bought by Franca's family as a summer retreat. Now she and Franco – warm, charming, intelligent – have filled the lofty, light-filled *limonaia* with beautiful things: an oriental carpet, a butter-yellow leather sofa, vibrant art by Franca. Guests may use this lovely room until 8.30pm. A glass partition etched with a lemon tree leads to the kitchen, Franca's domain. Breakfasts at the long table – or on the loggia in summer – are for lingering over: Tuscan salami and pecorino, fresh figs, delicious coffee. Bedrooms burst with personality and colour – one, funky, cosy and Moroccan, another huge, white and cream, with a terrace. Chic coloured bed linen, huge walk-in showers, a fridge stocked with juice and water, towels for the pool. And what a pool – curved, it lies on the edge of the house, filled with views. A special place with a big heart. *Minimum stay two nights. Children over 10 welcome.*

rooms	4 + 2: 3 doubles, 1 family room for 4. 1 suite for 2, 1 family suite for 4, both with kitchenette.
price	€180–€220. Suite €240.
meals	Restaurants 2km.
closed	10 January–10 February.
directions	Pass by Siena on Tangenziale (ring road) for Arezzo-Roma; exit Siena Est to big r'bout 'Due Ponti'; road to S. Regina; 1st right Strada di Valdipugna; signed on right.

	Franca Mugni
tel	+39 0577 281061
fax	+39 0577 281061
email	info@franceslodge.it
web	www.franceslodge.it

B&B & Self-catering

Map 8 Entry 189

La Grotta di Montecchino

via Grossetana 87, S. Andrea a Montecchino, 53010 Costalpino

A fantastic position, high on a hill five kilometres above Siena, with views over olive groves, cornfields and sunflowers. You can glimpse Siena in the distance, but why base yourself in the city when you can escape here? La Grotta is a 25-acre organic farm producing wine, olive oil and corn. The owners stay here as often as they can, in their own quarters 400 metres away. Guests have a lovely old farm building converted into holiday lets. Each one, although simple, is roomy with some special touches: stencil decorations, woodburning stoves, the odd antique. Some of the furniture is makeshift and the lighting barely enough to read by, but this is a good place for families in summer: there's a pool surrounded by jolly parasols and plastic loungers, a football pitch and masses of open space. There's also a new and characterful little restaurant in the old cellar; Simonetta loves baking and makes spectacularly good tarts. You won't be short of things to do: cookery classes here, wine-tastings nearby, and history and culture in Siena, a bus ride away.

rooms	6 apartments for 2-4.
price	€300-€450 for 2. €400-€620 for 4. Prices per week.
meals	Dinner €18. Self-catering.
closed	15-30 November.
directions	From Siena, SS73 to Roccastrada. At Costalpino towards S. Rocco a Pilli & Grosseto. At S. Andrea, 'Montecchino' signed, right. Follow farm track, 1km.

Dottor Agostino Pecciarini

tel	+39 0577 394250
fax	+39 0577 394256
email	info@montecchino.it
web	www.montecchino.it

Self-catering

Map 8 Entry 190

Borgo Casabianca

SP 10, loc. Casabianca, 53041 Asciano

A medieval hamlet on top of a hill, meticulously restored. In theory a farm, this has more the feel of a country estate. Signora Alba Ines Calusi has seen to all the detail, discreet staff see to the rest. In the padronal villa – with a tiny chapel standing alongside – are terracotta-tiled bedrooms grandly endowed with elaborate ceilings, rich drapes and chandeliers; some have the original 18th-century wall decorations. The surrounding stables and barns have been made into 20 self-contained, individually furnished apartments, nicely rustic with white walls, old beams and chunky terracotta. Each has its own little garden; many have balconies or terraces with stupendous views that reach over the forested estate to the Atlantic. You are far from shops but this is an otherwise ideal set-up for self-caterers, especially families. There are wonderful walks in the surrounding countryside and bikes for further afield; you can meander down to the lake to fish, relax at the pool-side bar or hide away in the secluded cloister garden. The formal restaurant in the old wine cellars still has the original vats and press.

rooms	9 + 20: 3 doubles, 6 suites. 20 apartments: 15 for 2, 5 for 4-6.
price	€163. Suites €293-€353. Apartments €922 for 2 per week; €1,356 for 4-6 per week.
meals	Dinner €25-€55. Breakfast €12 for self-caterers. Restaurant 9km.
closed	January-March.
directions	A1 exit 28 for Valdichiana, Sinalunga, Asciano. After Asciano, 6km on left.

	Signora Alba Ines Calusi
tel	+39 0577 704362
fax	+39 0577 704622
email	casabianca@casabianca.it
web	www.casabianca.it

Bosco della Spina
Lupompesi, 53016 Murlo

The road sign for 'pizzeria' is misleading: nothing so ordinary here! Tables overlook a magical garden of pergolas, waterfalls, tumbling vines and creeping wisteria; Murlo Castle hangs in the distance. Imaginatively restored and landscaped, these former farmhouse cellars in medieval Lupompesi have strikingly modern interiors and old Tuscan beams and terracotta. It is an arctitecturally interesting and imaginative restoration. The restaurant, a cool space of open arches, raftered ceiling and sleek furniture, serves classic regional dishes (pizza in the summer only) accompanied by 180 wines. The minimalist mini-apartments (each with fridge, sink and dual hob) have terraces and big divans and furniture made by local craftsmen; blankets are neatly rolled, colours are white and conker brown, beds are hi-tech four-poster, shower rooms are designer-special. All this and a wine bar, library, small gym, exquisite slimline pool (good for lengths) and garden spots filled with tinkling water and views. A chic but friendly family affair, where Mum cooks and daughter is the confident manager.

rooms	14 apartments: for 2-4, 4-6, 4-8. All with kitchenette.
price	€120–€200.
meals	Dinner €30.
closed	Rarely.
directions	A1 for Siena; exit Siena south; SS2 for Rome; 15km; Monteroni d'Arbia; right to Vescovado di Murlo just before Lucignano d'Arbia; 8km; right for Casciano di Murlo; 1km; in Lupompesi, on left, signed 'Residence'.

	Brigida Meoni
tel	+39 0577 814605
fax	+39 0577 814606
email	bsturist@boscodellaspina.com
web	www.boscodellaspina.com

B&B

Map 11 Entry 192

Azienda Agricola Podere Salicotto

Podere Salicotto 73, 53022 Buonconvento

Watch sunsets fire the Tuscan hills; catch the sunrise as it brings the valleys alive. Views from this hilltop farmhouse roll off in every direction. It is peaceful here, and beautiful. Breakfast is a feast that merges into lunch, with produce from the organic farm, and Silvia and Paolo, a well-travelled, warm and adventurous couple, are happy for you to be as active or as idle as you like. Eat in the big farmhouse kitchen or under the pergola, as deer wander across the field below. Paolo is full of ideas and will take you sailing in his six-berth boat that has crossed the Atlantic – or organise wine-tasting and cycling trips. The beamed and terracotta tiled bedrooms are airy and welcoming, full of soft, Tuscan colours and furnished with simplicity but care: antiques, monogrammed sheets, great showers. B&B guests are in the main house (private entrance) while the apartment is in the converted barn. Visit Siena, medieval Buonconvento, Tuscan hill towns. Come back, rest in a hammock, laze around the pool with a glass of wine and a fabulous view.

rooms	6 + 1: 6 doubles. 1 studio for 2-4.
price	€130-€150. Studio €1,330 per week.
meals	Lunch or dinner, €15-€20, on request. Restaurants 3km.
closed	Mid-December-mid-March.
directions	From Siena via Cassia to Buonconvento; with the Consorzio Agraria on your left, turn immed. left; follow road to Podere on right.

Silvia Forni

tel	+39 0577 809087
fax	+39 0577 809535
email	info@poderesalicotto.com
web	www.poderesalicotto.com

Agriturismo & Self-catering

Map 11 Entry 193

La Locanda del Castello

Piazza V. Emanuele II 4, 53020 San Giovanni d'Asso

Antique clocks and white truffles are just two of the treats here; the former are collected by your excellent host Silvana, the latter are a rare delicacy for which the region is famous. The hilltop village of San Giovanni d'Asso acts as a bridge between the Val d'Orcia (home of the celebrated truffle) and the breathtaking countryside of the Crete Senesi. At the heart of the town is an imposing 16th-century castle, and tucked into its walls lies La Locanda Del Castello. There are only nine bedrooms in this lovely hotel; all are beautifully decorated and furnished with Silvana's family hierlooms. Bathrooms are luxurious and, as with everything in the hotel, built into the original shape of the castle. But the jewel in this particular crown is the restaurant – open to the public – where the chefs cook to old Tuscan recipes and guests feast on pecorino cheese, fine meats and an intoxicating selection of regional wines. And, of course, truffles. On balmy evenings, the canopy over the patio can be rolled back to allow diners to marvel at the moon. Breakfasts are every bit as delicious.

rooms	9 doubles.
price	€110-€150.
meals	Lunch or dinner €30.
closed	10 January-10 March.
directions	Florence-Roma A1, exit Valdichiana; 5km to Sinalunga; 10km Trequanda-Montisi; 5km to hotel. Park below castle.

	Signora Silvana Ratti Ravanelli
tel	+39 0577 802939
fax	+39 0577 802942
email	info@lalocandadelcastello.com
web	www.lalocandadelcastello.com

Hotel

Map 11 Entry 194

Residenza d'Arte

Poggio Madonna dell'Olivo, 53049 Torrita di Siena

Sleep in an art gallery: a big, bold, historic space filled with big, bold, contemporary art. Around one thousand sculptures, paintings and installations litter the 14th-century Residenza's unique bedrooms, salons and terraces. They are the works of Anna Izzo, whose family spent five years restoring the mellow stone buildings. Cool spaces of vaulted and raftered ceilings, chunky stone and brick walls and elegant arches, they form the perfect backdrop for her striking work. Bedrooms range from large to vast; small shower rooms reveal ancient brickwork. Furnishings are minimal and characterful: a sleek modern sofa by an antique chest, a red glass vase filled with twigs, a fuchsia bedspread on a big bed. Breakfast on the terrace where bronze sculptures vie for attention with views of medieval Torrita di Siena on the hill. Enrico, Anna's son, can arrange riding, wine tours, cycling trips, spa treatments at Montepulciano, swimming in a nearby private pool, hot-air ballooning. Enthusiastic and friendly, the family are a delight. Not for the sedate and conventional – a place to fire the senses.

rooms	8 doubles.
price	€135-€200.
meals	Restaurant 500m.
closed	November-mid-March.
directions	From A1 exit Valdichiana until Torrita di Siena; signed. Outside *centro storico*.

Enrico Ferretti

tel	+39 0577 684252
fax	+39 0697255730
email	residenzadarte@fastwebnet.it
web	www.residenzadarte.com

B&B

Map 12 Entry 195

Villa Poggiano
via di Poggiano 7, 53045 Montepulciano

It's the gardens that capture the imagination – six enchanting hectares of them. Centuries-old cypresses line the paths, a stone table in a secluded alcove overlooks a breathtaking view, flowers tumble out of stately pots on the terrace. The house and gardens once belonged to a German general and it was he who imported the magnificent stone statues, dating back to the 1900s, and built the memorable pool. Austerely beautiful, it is made of travertine stone, with more statues presiding over the patio and walls. There's a fountain, too, in what was once the children's pool. Stefania's family bought the place in 2000. Five years on, it is immaculate, and elegantly and traditionally furnished with antiques and old paintings. The suites are luxurious and the bathrooms sumptuous – they have space and marble in plenty, and pretty tiles from Capri. Three of the rooms, in lodges in the grounds, are independent. One has a terrace, another a garden and all have wonderful views to Monte Amiata and the Torre di Montichiello. *Minimum stay two nights. Beauty treatments available.*

rooms	6: 1 double, 5 suites. Lodges: 2 doubles, 1 suite.
price	€190–€210. Suites €230–€300.
meals	Restaurants 2km.
closed	December–March.
directions	From A1 exit Valdichiana for Montepulciano. After 5km left at lights in Torrita di Siena for Montepulciano. On for 8km SS146 for Pienza. 2km further left at Relais Villa Poggiano. Left to Villa after 800m.

	Stefania Savini
tel	+39 0578 758292
fax	+39 0578 715635
email	info@villapoggiano.com
web	www.villapoggiano.com

B&B

Map 12 Entry 196

Il Piccolo Bordello

Montepulciano

The architect, dispatched abroad after a brothel he designed in Camberwell collapsed revealing half the Cabinet, spent a formative year on a Grand Tour and fell in love with Palladio's work. However, he never found another client and retired to live squalidly in Italy. But Palladio remained with him, rooted in his soul; this little villa is the result. Money ran out before the stucco could be applied, and the stonemasons – local lads – were not quite up to the delicate carving required for the capitals, yet the place carries – does it not? – a touch of Palladio's magic: a hint of the massive entrance portico, the classical proportions, the grandiosity. You can imagine the carriages sweeping up to the entrance for a ball. When our hero died the place became a sanctuary for goats nimble enough to jump through that door. Now it has been lavishly converted to reflect the mood of the times: it is a pint-sized 'agriturismo', dignified in its distress. The vehicle in the picture below is available for trips into town and can do practically any job you ask of it.

rooms	By the hour.
price	Escort dependent.
meals	Pork scratchings only.
closed	Rarely.
directions	Ask your MP.

	Madame Desideri Carnali
tel	+39 0000 112233
fax	+39 0000 112233
email	clinets@ilbordello.com
web	www.piccolo_bordello.it

Agriturismo

Map 12 Entry 197

Montorio
strada per Pienza 2, 53045 Montepulciano

As you come up the drive, you will be inspired by the Temple of San Biagio. A Renaissance masterpiece designed by Antonio Sangallo the Elder, it is an unforgettable backdrop to Montorio. The house stands on top of its own little hill, 600m above sea level, overlooking a vast green swathe of Tuscany. All warm stone walls and roofs on different levels, it was once a *casa colonica*. It is now divided into five attractive apartments, each named after a celebrated Italian artist or poet, each with a well-equipped kitchen and an open fire. White walls, beams and terracotta floors set a tone of rural simplicity; antiques, paintings and wrought-iron lights crafted by Florentines add a touch of style; leather chesterfields and big beds guarantee comfort. The terraced gardens – full of ancient cypress trees, pots of flowers and alluring places to sit – drop gently down to olive groves and vineyards. Stefania's other villa, Poggiano, is ten minutes away and historic Montepulciano, full of shops and eating places, is close enough to walk. *Minimum stay three nights.*

rooms	5 apartments: 3 for 2, 2 for 4.
price	€120–€180 for 2 (€500–€1200 per week). €180–€250 for 4 (€1,100–€1,700 per week).
meals	Restaurants 500m.
closed	December-January.
directions	A1 exit Valdichiana for Montepulciano. In Torrita di Siena, left at lights to Montepulciano. There, follow signs to Chianciano. Right at x-roads bilvio di S. Biagio.

Stefania Savini

tel	+39 0578 717442
fax	+39 0578 715635
email	info@montorio.com
web	www.montorio.com

Self-catering

Map 12 Entry 198

Agriturismo Poggio all'Olmo
str. della Chiana 39, 53042 Chianciano Terme

A little bit of Pompeii in untouched Tuscany. Friendly owners Franceso and Luisa come from modern Pompei – and brought with them two big volcanic balls which now sit by the child-friendly pool. Created from a restored farmhouse, these agritourisimo apartments are the real thing – simple, spotless and well-priced. Brilliant for families, each apartment has typical terracotta floors, white walls and generous windows. Furniture, some from the family, is oldish and furnishings homely; gingham tablecloths here, lace trims there, nothing fancy, all just fine. Each has a kitchen/dining area and separate bedrooms, plus some divan beds for extra guests. Bathrooms are white and spick and span. Step outside and cook supper on the barbecue, or bake a pizza in the wood oven (organic oil, wine and honey from the 12-hectare estate are for sale); then retreat to your small, private terrace. If cooking is too much of a strain, Luisa offers her own pasta and tempting local dishes, as well as breakfast – wonderful. Lose the children in the wooden play area, enjoy the well-tended garden, succumb to the silence.

rooms	5 apartments: 1 for 2, 3 for 2-4, 1 for 2-5.
price	€56-€130 for 2.
meals	Breakfast €5. Light meals €6. Restaurants 1km.
closed	15-31 January.
directions	From Chianciano Terme for *centro storico*; 500m; left for Montalese; 800m, signed; follow track, 300m.

	Francesco & Luisa Nastri
tel/fax	+39 0578 30125
mobile	+39 335 5613581
email	info@poggioallolmo.it
web	www.poggioallolmo.it

Agriturismo

Map 12 Entry 199

Il Rigo

Podere Casabianca & Poggio Bacoca, 53027 San Quirico d'Orcia

The fame of Lorenza's cooking has spread so far that she's been invited to demonstrate her skills in the US. (She runs courses here, too.) So meals in the big, beamed dining room at pretty check-clothed tables are a treat. Irresistible home-grown organic produce, 60 local wines to choose from and a gorgeous Tuscan setting. There are two houses on the family farm, named after the stream running through it. 'Casabianca', reached via a cypress-flanked drive, is ancient and stone built. A vine-covered pergola shades the entrance; beyond the reception area is a courtyard full of climbing roses. The second house, 'Poggio Bacoca', is about 600 metres away. Once home to the farmworkers, it's red-brick built and has two sitting rooms and panoramic views. You walk (600m) to 'Casabianca' for those wonderful meals. Bedrooms are homely, pretty and inviting; all have embroidered sheets, appealing colour schemes and matching bathrooms. No televisions: it's not that sort of place. Lorenza and Vittorio hope and believe that their guests will prefer a relaxed chat over a glass of wine.

rooms	15 doubles.
price	€100-€108. Half-board €144-€156.
meals	Lunch or dinner €22-€25, on request.
closed	Never.
directions	Exit A1 Certosa; follow superstrada, exit Siena South. SS.2 (via Cassia) 2km south of S Quirico d'Orcia; on left on 2km track, signed.

Signor Vittorio Cipolla & Lorenza Santo

tel	+39 0577 897 291
fax	+39 0577 898236
email	info@agriturismoilrigo.com
web	www.agriturismoilrigo.com

Agriturismo

Map 11 Entry 200

Castello di Ripa d'Orcia
via della Contea 1/16, 53027 Ripa d'Orcia

As you drive up the long, white road, the castle comes into view: a thrilling sight. Ripa d'Orcia dates from the 13th century, one of Siena's most important strongholds. The battlemented fortress (closed to the public) dominates the *borgo* encircled by small medieval dwellings. The family are descendants of the Piccolominis who acquired the estate in 1484 and are hugely proud of their heritage; Signor Rossi runs it all with efficiency and charm. Grand banquets and knights in shining armour may come to mind… children would love it here. Rooms and apartments have huge raftered ceilings and are furnished simply and well; many have breathtaking views. There's also a day room, filled with lovely furniture and heaps of books to browse. You breakfast in a small annexe off the main restaurant, and there's a cellar for wine-tastings. The area is a paradise for walkers and there is enough on the spot to keep lovers of history and architecture happy for hours – before the 'official' sightseeing begins. *Minimum stay two nights; one week in apartments.*

rooms	6 + 8: 6 twins/doubles. 8 apartments: 5 for 2, 3 for 4.
price	€110-€135. Singles €89-€110. Apts for 2, €490-€575; for 4, €649-€750. Apt prices per week.
meals	Dinner à la carte, €25. Closed Mondays.
closed	November-February.
directions	From SS2 for San Quirico d'Orcia; right over bridge. Follow road around town walls for 700m. Right again, signed; 5.3km to Castello.

	Famiglia Aluffi Pentini Rossi
tel	+39 0577 897376
fax	+39 0577 898038
email	info@castelloripadorcia.com
web	www.castelloripadorcia.com

B&B & Self-catering

Map 11 Entry 201

La Locanda del Loggiato
Piazza del Moretto 30, 53027 Bagno Vignoni

You wouldn't know this was here. An inconspicuous door off the Piazza del Moretto leads to a delightful, unexpected room of muted colours and fine furniture. Grandma's baby grand piano stands in one corner; she was much loved and there are reminders of her everywhere. On one wall is the 1473 coat of arms of the Chigi family – one of many discoveries made when this delectable house was renovated. A spiral staircase takes you up to a little, beamed mezzanine but the bedrooms all open off the main room. They are graceful and pretty, with big, antique beds, soft neutral fabrics and stencilled borders. Some look out to the square, others onto the old thermal bath – the house was once an inn for people who visited Bagno Vignoni for the terme. Breakfast is across the square and down a few steps to the little wine bar, Il Loggiato. A stable in the 14th century, later a refectory for the monks next door, it now guards huge jars of mushrooms in oil and herbs and olives bottled by Barbara and Sabrina. There are other good eating places in this tiny, beautiful village, too.

rooms	6: 1 double, 5 twins/doubles.
price	€130.
meals	Restaurants nearby.
closed	Rarely.
directions	From North A1 exit Certosa. Superstrada for Firenze, exit Siena sud, take La Cassa for Roma. Through San Quirico D'Orcia, at crossroads to Bagno Vignoni; house in centre.

Barbara & Sabrina Marini

tel	+39 0577 888925
fax	+39 0577 888370
email	locanda@loggiato.it
web	www.loggiato.it

B&B

Map 11 Entry 202

Hotel Terme San Filippo
via San Filippo 23, 53020 Bagni San Filippo

Arthritic Pope Pio II came here in 1462. The Italians still adore hot thermal springs, and this is one of the best, sited in the gorgeous, rolling Orcia valley. People come from all over to test for themselves the healing properties of what many believe to be miraculous minerals – don't be alarmed by the occasional wafts of sulphur. There's a pool heated to 40 degrees (that's hot), a superb waterfall, cold showers and a well-being centre offering massages, mud baths, saunas and a whirlpool. Work out in the woods, stroll to the extraordinary and calcareous Fosso Bianco nearby. Bedrooms are comfortable, nothing fancy. Well-presented regional dishes are served in the yellow dining room, whose hand-written menus can be scanned each morning. Walls are faux-marble – "for fun", says Gabriella, who is as delightful as her team. The atmosphere is bustling yet relaxed, with white towelling robes de rigueur. A great place for a healthy, pampering weekend, and a fine starting point for an excursion to Mount Amiata, central Tuscany's most majestic peak. *Minimum stay two nights.*

rooms	27: 23 doubles, 4 singles.
price	€94-€114.
	Singles €55-€65.
	Half-board €62-€72 p.p.
	Full-board €70-€80 p.p.
meals	Lunch or dinner €20.
closed	November-Easter.
directions	From Siena SS2 for Rome, then to Bagni S. Filippo. via S. Filippo is main road through village.

	Gabriella Contorni
tel	+39 0577 872982
fax	+39 0577 872684
email	info@termesanfilippo.it
web	www.termesanfilippo.it

Hotel

Map 11 Entry 203

Le Radici Natura & Benessere

loc. Palazzone, 53040 San Casciano dei Bagni

The densely-wooded, unmade road that leads to Le Radici gives little away. It twists and curves and, just when you think you'll never make it, opens into a small oasis. The owners' conversion of this solitary 15th-century stone farmhouse into a small hotel has been a labour of love; Alfredo scoured the antique markets and raided his stock of family heirlooms to furnish the rooms; now the decoration is 'elegant country'. No sitting room, few staff, but bedrooms are a good size, with delicately toned, hand-finished walls and colour from armchairs and kilims. Breakfasts are basic; instead, Alfredo indulges his passion for cooking with the small restaurant he has created in the vaulted former pigsty, making good use of the rich array of ingredients that Tuscany offers. The geraniums thrive in this microclimate and bloom even in November, tumbling down from large urns, window sills and balconies. A pool blends into the landscape, and a little winding footpath takes you up to the wooded crown of the hill where you can sit and enjoy the views. *Minimum stay two nights.*

rooms	10 + 1: 7 doubles, 3 suites. 1 apartment for 2.
price	€130-€200. Suites €184-€220.
meals	Lunch or dinner €33.
closed	9 November-March.
directions	Exit A1 at Chuisi for S. Casciano & Palazzone. Left for Palazzone. Through village; track uphill past small church on right. Le Radici signed down narrow track to right.

Alfredo Ferrari

tel	+39 0578 56038
fax	+39 0578 56033
email	leradici@leradici.it
web	www.leradici.it

B&B & Self-catering

Map 12 Entry 204

La Crocetta

loc. La Crocetta, 53040 San Casciano dei Bagni

Inauspiciously sited in the middle of a housing estate, the 900 farmed acres nevertheless spill over with good things: cereals, wine, olive oil… dinners are fabulous. The large stone building dates from 1835, and was completely restored in 1993. Though next to a main road, it is shielded by oak trees and a large garden that feels wonderfully secluded. The interior is furnished with attractively colourwashed or stencilled walls and rush-seated chairs. Open fires add warmth in winter. Bedrooms are simple but cosy, with good modern shower rooms; some are country-Italian in style, others traditional-English, with floral fabrics and chintz. Cooking is a strong point – mouthwatering aromas drift in from the kitchen towards mealtimes and there's always a choice, including vegetarian. Cristina and Andrea are engaging hosts and conversation is easy; he's the cook, she's the designer. There's a brand new pool, and it's a five-minute walk to the spa in town. Note: if you're allergic to cats there were ten around at the last count! *Minimum stay three nights.*

rooms	8: 4 doubles, 3 twins, 1 single.
price	€110. Singles €58. Half-board €77 p.p.
meals	Dinner €28.
closed	Mid-November-March.
directions	Exit A1 motorway at Chiusi towards S. Casciano dei Bagni. There, La Crocetta signed.

	Andrea & Cristina Leotti
tel	+39 0578 58360
fax	+39 0578 58353
email	agriturismolacrocetta@virgilio.it
web	www.agriturismolacrocetta.it

Agriturismo

Map 12 Entry 205

Photo Lois Ferguson

umbria

Locanda Palazzone
loc. Rocca Ripesena, 05010 Orvieto

An imposing palazzo in the Umbrian countryside, Locanda Palazzone is full of contrasts. Built by a cardinal as a resting place for pilgrims to Rome, it was designed with an urban sophistication: buttressed walls, mullioned windows, vaulted hall. It later fell from grace and became a country farmhouse – until Ludovico's family rescued it, planting vineyards and restoring the buildings. Despite the rusticity of the setting, the interiors are cool, elegant, chic. The sitting room (once the Grand Hall) is light and airy, its huge windows overlooking the garden. Bedrooms – split-level suites, mostly – are understatedly luxurious, their modern and antique furnishings set against pale oak floors, cream walls, exposed stone. Red, claret and purple cushions add warmth; white linen sheets, Bulgari bath foams and specialist herb soaps soothe. Meals – regional, seasonal – are served on rainbow porcelain on the terrace, accompanied by the estate's wines. Your generous hosts are eager to please, the pool is surrounded by delphiniums and roses, and views sweep to vineyards and forests. A remarkable place.

rooms	7: 5 suites for 2, 2 suites for 4.
price	€156–€340.
meals	Dinner, 4 courses, €34. On request.
closed	15 January-15 March.
directions	A1 Florence-Roma, Orvieto exit; 1.8km toward Orvieto; at bridge for funicular, right for Allerona; cont. to Sferracavallo junc.; again follow Allerona; 200m, left toward Castel Giorgio, keeping petrol station on right; 2.5km, signed.

	Lodovico Dubini
tel	+39 0763 393614
fax	+39 0763 394833
email	info@locandapalazzone.com
web	www.locandapalazzone.com

Agriturismo

Map 12 Entry 206

Locanda Rosati
loc. Buonviaggio 22, 05018 Orvieto

From the moment you turn off the road – whose proximity is quickly forgotten – the atmosphere is easy. The house has been gently modernised but remains firmly a farmhouse; the summer-cool rooms on the ground floor – with open fires in winter – have been furnished with an eye for comfort rather than a desire to impress, and wild flowers, books and magazines are scattered. Dinner is the thing here; it's rustic, delectable and Giampiero and Paolo are natural hosts, full of stories and enthusiastic advice on what to do and where to go. Tables are laid with simple cloths, glass tumblers and butter-coloured pottery, the recipes have been handed down the Rosati generations and the wines come from a wonderful cellar carved out of the tufa seven metres below ground. Bedrooms are simple, with new wooden beds, pristine bed linen, spotless showers. Much of the furniture comes from the famous Bottega di Michelangeli in Orvieto, whose jigsaw-like carved animal shapes characterise this region. From the gardens you can see the spiky skyline of Orvieto: delightful. *Ask about cookery courses for guests.*

rooms	10: 4 doubles, 5 family, 1 single.
price	€110-€130. Singles €90-€110. Half-board option.
meals	Dinner €30.
closed	7 January-February.
directions	Exit A1 at Orvieto; for Viterbo, Bolsena & Montefiascone; 10km; on right.

	Signor Giampiero Rosati
tel	+39 0763 217314
fax	+39 0763 217314
email	info@locandarosati.orvieto.tr.it
web	www.locandarosati.orvieto.tr.it

Agriturismo

Map 12 Entry 207

La Palombara Maison d'Hôtes

strada di Collicello 34, Castel Dell'Aquila, 05020 Terni

Picture a valley in gently rolling farmland in a hidden corner of Umbria. Nothing grand or pretentious, just an 18th-century farm, an ancient mulberry tree, the nightingale's ballad… Marie France and Massimo retired here recently after running a hotel in Amelia. They live in the main house with Mouette, their bouncy young golden retriever, and are gentle, unobtrusive and charming. The old stone-built piggery has been converted into two attractive, white-shuttered apartments. The airy rooms are simply and pleasingly furnished with a mix of old and new: antique china cabinets and modern pine cupboards, marble-topped tables and the odd pretty item of painted furniture. There is a washing machine but don't expect mod cons and luxuries — it's not that sort of place, and the beds are decidedly firm! Each apartment has its outside sitting area and the pool is fringed with lavender and rosemary. The garden is still in its infancy — tiny olive trees, roses, wisteria — and there's a little orchard with apricots and peaches, cherries and figs: pick your own. *Minimum stay three nights low season.*

rooms	2 apartments for 5.
price	€900-€1,100 per week.
meals	Restaurant & pizzeria 3km.
closed	Rarely.
directions	Exit Amelia from Terni-Perugia; follow signs to Avigliano; left to Collicello for 500m; signed left.

	M. Ralli & M. France de Boiscuille
tel/fax	+39 074 4988491
mobile	+39 335 484311/+39 335 6137768
email	info@lapalombara-umbria.it
web	www.lapalombara-umbria.it

Self-catering

Map 12 Entry 208

Locanda di Colle dell'Oro
strada di Palmetta 31, 05100 Terni

Candles flicker alongside the path, illuminating your way as you return from the garden restaurant. It's an imaginative touch, in keeping with the Locanda's ethos. Gioia delights in her family's country home and you will too, from the moment you step into the striking entrance hall and breathe in the heady scent of jasmine. In spite of occasional music and four lively dogs, the restored 19th-century house feels harmonious and calm. Large, lovely bedrooms, named after plants, have neutral colour schemes and bleached wooden furniture, hand-painted with flowers by Gioia; ask for one with a good view. Sheets and towels are of the purest linen and the bathrooms are beautifully planned. The luxury is real and understated. French windows lead from the breakfast room to the terrace looking down over sprawlling Terni, and a garden full of birdsong and geraniums, jasmine, roses, hydrangeas; the swimming pool is hidden on a lower terrace. Yoga classes three times a week, cookery classes out of season. *Minimum stay two nights.*

rooms	12: 7 doubles, 4 triples, 1 suite.
price	€70–€100.
	Triples €110.
	Suites €130.
meals	Lunch or dinner €30.
closed	Rarely.
directions	From A1 exit Terni Ovest. Follow signs for Norcia Cascia until signs for Locanda.

Gioia Iaculli

tel	+39 0744 432379
fax	+39 0744 437826
email	locanda@colledelloro.it
web	www.colledelloro.it

Hotel

Map 12 Entry 209

La Fontana

strada di Palazzone 8, 05022 Amelia

Your heart lifts as you approach these three small vine-clad cottages in their olive-grove setting. The outskirts of historic Amelia are not promising, but here you are enveloped by beautiful old trees. Each cottage fits two comfortably, and each has its own furnished eating out area. Indoors, furnishings are an intriguing, jostling mix of styles, as are the pictures, *objets* and many books. One cottage, Limonaia, has both open fire and central heating: a winter break here would be wonderfully cosy. Rosetto too has an open fire, and beautiful Russian icons on its walls; Pergola has a pretty sitting out area and a small double bed. Set in seven acres of hillside, the lovely mature gardens flow through a small orchard and down to a rose-strewn pergola, barbecue area and swimming pool. The drinking water, from a private source and pure enough to be bottled and sold, is yours for free – no need to lug plastic bottles from the supermarket. The English owners live in Amelia but are full of advice should you need it: the town is lively and unspoilt and one of the oldest in Italy. *Minimum stay one week.*

rooms	3 cottages: 2 for 2, 1 for 2-3.
price	€450-€550 per week.
meals	Self-catering. Restaurants 2km.
closed	Rarely.
directions	Exit A1 for Orte; follow Terni; exit Amelia. In front of main walls follow Giove to 1st intersection. Left & immed. right. 1st left to Strada di Palazzone.

Philip Corsano

tel	+39 0744 983465
email	pcorsano@yahoo.com
web	www.umbriandream.com

Self-catering

Map 12 Entry 210

La Porta del Tempo

via del Sacramento 2, 05039 Stroncone

Enter the substantial front door on the untouched, medieval street. Step inside: the marble staircase reveals that this was a grand 15th-century palazzo. In a later reincarnation it became a police station (note the original cell doors), now it is managed by a young, charming and welcoming couple. The building was renovated in 1996, without the help of architects, and the whole place glows with warmth and good humour. The vaulted stairwell has colourwashed walls; the terracotta floors have been unevenly laid to recreate a sense of history. Old paintings, sepia prints – all of it is lovely. In the breakfast room, homemade pastries and jams are served on pretty checked cloths. Bedrooms have curved brick ceilings, warm rugs and heavy cream curtains; in the loft is a room with low beams and views straight from the bed to the street below. The bathrooms are done in simple Italian style, the towels are voluminous. And your hosts, who live next door, can organise almost anything, from mountain biking to horse riding.

rooms	8 + 1: 6 doubles, 1 single, 1 triple. 1 apartment for 4.
price	€85–€120. Apartment €500–€750 per week.
meals	Two restaurants in village. Picnics possible.
closed	Rarely.
directions	E45 or A1 exit Orte, then Terni Ovest; signs for Stroncone; park outside walls & walk through town gate under loggia following black & white signs.

	Rosanna Russo
tel	+39 0744 608190
fax	+39 0744 609034
email	info@portadeltempo.com
web	www.portadeltempo.com

Antica Dimora alla Rocca

Piazza Rocca, 26039 Trevi

Perched at the top of the lovely hill town of Trevi, this is one of very few *palazzi* in Umbria to have been turned into a hotel. Built in 1650, it was the family home of the Valenti. (Livio Bordoni, the manager, cares passionately about the place, and is hugely knowledgeable.) Four years were spent restoring the building before it opened in 2002, and the work has been beautifully done. Original frescoes on the first floor represent the seasons, though Winter is unaccountably missing (perhaps theft, perhaps wishful thinking). The bedrooms, the largest quite magnificent, have exquisitely painted wooden ceilings, rich fabrics and deliciously sybaritic, if dimly lit, bathrooms. Throughout, the interior is elegant and sophisticated, but not oppressively so: there's a charming, lively atmosphere and the staff are attentive and friendly. The vaulted dining room, once Trevi's olive press, has a glass viewing panel in the floor – gaze down on the press itself; the hooks in the ceiling were used for drying prosciutto. It's a memorable room to dine in and the food and wines are excellent.

rooms	34: 22 doubles, 2 suites. Annexe: 7 doubles, 3 suites for 2-4.
price	€104-€164. Annexe €55-€80.
meals	Dinner, 5 courses, €30.
closed	Monday.
directions	From Rome A1 for Orte, then Terni Spoleto-Trevi. At Foligno S3 to Trevi, signed.

	Livio Bordoni
tel	+39 074 238541
fax	+39 074 278925
email	hotelallarocca@libero.it
web	www.hotelallarocca.it

Hotel

Map 12 Entry 212

Abbazia San Pietro in Valle

via Case Sparse di Macenano 4, 05034 Ferentillo

Ancient, venerable, spectacular. Originally founded in the eighth century, the abbey sits tranquilly on the side of a wooded valley, way way beyond the industrial outskirts of Terni. The church is full of good things; look out for the lion rampant which you'll find carved on much of the abbey's furniture, the *stemma* of its first secular owners. These days the daughters of the present owners gently run the place. Most of the serenely furnished rooms have views over the valley and stunning ancient-tiled floors; most open off a courtyard, so if it's raining you'll need an umbrella for that mad dash from room to restaurant. Dinner at convent tables is rustic-refined: true Umbrian. The cloisters are lovely, the setting beautiful: find a perch and watch the light changing round the towers and cypresses. Below is the river Nera – you can go rafting from Scheggino – and across the valley is the deserted village of Umbriano a Rocca di Protenzione, said to be the first human settlement in Umbria. You can truffle-hunt in autumn here (by request), then cook your spoils! Return to sauna, billiards, sofas. Special.

rooms	12: 10 twins/doubles, 2 suites.
price	€98–€125.
	Suites €130–€165.
meals	Dinner à la carte, €35.
closed	3 November–March.
directions	Florence-Roma A1, exit Orte; E55 to Terni, exit Terni Est; take SS209 (Visso, Norcia, Cascia); 20km; follow sign to abbey.

Letizia & Chiara Costanzi

tel	+39 0744 780129
fax	+39 0744 435522
email	abbazia@sanpietroinvalle.com
web	www.sanpietroinvalle.com

Hotel

Map 12 Entry 213

Monte Valentino
06026 Pietralunga

On top of the world in Umbria. Woods fall away, hills climb to snow-scatttered heights. It's the perfect escape, the only route in a steep, winding, two-kilometre dirt track. All around you lie 60 hectares of organically farmed land – mushrooms are gathered from the woods, cereal and vegetables from the fields, fruit from the trees. These new apartments are contemporary yet cosy with simple wooden furniture, tiled floors and throws on the striped sofas. All have small balconies and kitchens and clean, fresh shower rooms; two have access to beautifully designed, red-brick terraces, where the views sweep and soar away. The swimming pool is delightful, surrounded by deck chairs and olive trees. Fabrizia, who lives next door, is enthusiastic and charming with an engaging smile, and proud of her new venture – meet her over simple breakfast in her homely kitchen. This is perfect cycling terrain – for the experienced! You can also swim in the river, horse riding is six miles away, cookery lessons can be arranged, and Fabrizia's husband Nicola will give you archery lessons if you fancy something different.

rooms	4 apartments for 2-3.
price	€65-€75 per night.
meals	Restaurants 12km.
closed	Never.
directions	SS E45 Orte-Cesena exit Montone-Pietralunga; SP201 to Pietralunga. At km12, Carpini (before Pietralunga); right at x-roads, signed.

	Fabrizia Gargano & Nicola Polchi
tel	+39 075 9462092
mobile	+39 320 2394995/6
email	info@montevalentino.it
web	www.montevalentino.it

Agriturismo & Self-catering

Map 9 Entry 214

Casale

S. Faustino, Montone, Pietralunga

Both house and setting are spectacular – and the garden is on its way. Tim and Austin, who have another Special Place in the Yorkshire Dales, have renovated beautifully. Behind the old Umbrian stones lie three cosy bedrooms, pristine bathrooms and a kitchen and living area worthy of a glossy interiors' magazine. The country dining table seats eight, there are sofas and an open fire, a stainless steel oven, masses of workspace and a sink with a view. Preparing your *tartufi neri arrosto* – Umbrian black truffles wrapped in pancetta – would be no hardship here. Nothing is busy or overdone, the views are amazing – there's a new 'look out' gazebo – and the saltwater pool, with terraces and wooden loungers, is impossible to resist. Visit Umbertide for provisions, hilltop Montone for narrow streets tumbling with geraniums, restaurants, bars and ancient-rampart views. At the end of a rough two-mile road this is remote – but Perugia, San Sepolcro, Cortona and Assisi are only an hour's drive. If you're more than eight, put your friends up at the agriturismo up the hill. *Minimum stay three nights.*

rooms	House for 6 + sofabed.
price	£140 (£850–£1,800 per week).
meals	Self-catering.
closed	Rarely.
directions	From Carpini signs for Monte Valentino, right at 3rd sign up to house.

Austin Lynch & Tim Culkin

tel	+44 (0)1748 823571
fax	+44 (0)1748 850701
email	oztim@millgatehouse.demon.co.uk
web	oztiminitaly.com

Self-catering

Map 9 Entry 215

Pereto

fraz. Carpini Sopra, 06014 Montone

All but hidden in the Carpina valley, lost in 900 hectares of private estate, these lovely buildings are far from any madding crowd yet only a couple of rough-track miles – and two possible fordings of the river – from Montone. Televisions and telephones are delightfully absent – it's that sort of place. Sharing the same swathe of lawn as the *casa padronale* where your host lives, the holiday homes are the quintessence of carefree country living. Generous, comfortable and stylish, each has a large fireplace and a free supply of wood for chilly days. In early May, when we visited, diaphanous curtains billowed at wide open windows and the sun beat down on the old terracotta roofs. Antique country furniture, painted wrought-iron beds, attractive rugs and prints combine harmoniously with bold coloured kitchen tiling and ancient rafters. And if you don't feel like cooking, there a stunning new glass dining room overseeing the valley; painted white furniture, a roaring fire in winter, organic olives and wine, barbecued lamb – reason alone for visiting this remote and beautiful hideaway.

rooms	2 apartments: 1 for 4, 1 for 6.
price	€450–€1,100 per week. Weekend rates on request.
meals	Dinner €25.
closed	Rarely.
directions	Exit E45 at Montone for Pietralunga. After 5km left to Pereto.

	Signor Giulio della Porta
tel	+39 075 9307009
fax	+39 075 9307009
email	pereto@pereto.com
web	www.pereto.com

Self-catering

Map 9 Entry 216

La Preghiera
via del Refari, 06018 Calzolaro

Shady terraces, a sunken garden, a flower-filled loggia and a private chapel. So many tranquil spots in which to recharge batteries. This glorious 12th-century monastery, hidden in a wooded valley near Gubbio and Cortona, was a pilgrim's resting place. Now it is owned by the Tunstills (architect and interior designer) who have restored with English country-house flair and Italian attention to detail. The large sitting and dining rooms are elegantly scattered with sofas, paintings and antiques; there are a billiard room and a library of books and DVDs. Bedrooms combine original features – beamed and raftered ceilings, terracotta floors, wooden shutters, exposed stone – with sophisticated details. Bed linen is cotton and silk, furniture is hand-crafted, wardrobes have interior lights, bathrooms are marbled. Breakfast on the terrace, take afternoon tea by the pool, dine by candlelight on local boar and truffles. There are vintage bikes to borrow, horse riding and golf, medieval hilltop towns to visit, lovely staff to look after you. You can even book a massage by the pool. *Ask about half-price deals.*

rooms	11 twins/doubles.
price	€275-€630.
meals	Dinner with wine, 4 courses, €50. On request.
closed	Rarely.
directions	Exit E45 at Promano; for Città di Castello; left at r'bout; next r'bout right thro' Trestina; right to Calzolaro; before bridge left to Vecchio Granaio; road bears right, hotel on left.

	Liliana & John Tunstill
tel	+39 075 9302428
fax	+39 075 9302363
email	promotions@lapreghiera.com
web	www.lapreghiera.com

Hotel

Map 9 Entry 217

Casa San Martino

San Martino 19, 06060 Lisciano Niccone

Perhaps this is the answer if you are finding it impossible to choose between Tuscany and Umbria – a 250-year-old farmhouse on the border. Sit with a glass of wine in your Umbrian garden, watch the sun set over the Tuscan hills. The lovely, rambling house is alive with Lois's personality and interests: she's a remarkable lady who has lived in Italy for years and a fluent linguist. Her charming big kitchen is well-equipped; an arch at one end leads to a comfortable family room, a door at the other to a pretty veranda with a stone barbecue. Up the narrow staircase is a large light sitting room with flowery sofas, books and an open fireplace – perfect for roasting chestnuts. The whitewashed bedrooms and bathrooms are cosy and attractive. Lois lives next door, is there when you need her and offers guests a rich number of courses to choose from (cookery, fresco-painting, hiking, the history of Italian gardens); she can even book you a chef. The big garden with its dreamy pool looks across the Niccone valley and there are two villages with shops close by. *Minimum stay three nights.*

rooms	4: 1 double, 1 twin/double; 2 twins/doubles sharing bath.
price	€140. Whole house €2,500-€3,000 per week.
meals	Dinner with wine €30. Restaurants 3km.
closed	B&B Nov-April only. Self-catering May-Oct only.
directions	A1 exit Valdichiana. Then '75 bis' for Perugia, then for Tuoro & for Lisciano Niccone.

Lois Martin
tel +39 075 844 288
fax +39 075 844 422
email csm@tuscanyvacation.com
web www.tuscanyvacation.com

B&B & Self-catering

Map 9 Entry 218

Castello di Montegualandro

Montegualandro 1, 06069 Tuoro sul Trasimeno

The castle, perched on one of the highest hills overlooking Lake Trasimeno, feels ancient and remote. Yet the 21st century lies minutes down the hill. What we see now was begun in the ninth century, and its first known owner was Charlemagne: the castle was a mini-estate with its own penal system and dungeons (still to be seen). It is a privilege to stay in such a unique place, and a pleasure too: the apartments are comfortable and your hosts attentive and delightful. (Accept their offer to collect you from Tuoro when you first arrive: this is not an easy place to find.) Rooms in the apartments, once simple dwellings, are not large but are peaceful and stylish, with whitewashed walls, stone or brick floors, beams, open fires and country antiques. Two have extra beds on a mezzanine reached by a stepladder – not for the young or infirm. All have small kitchens with a well-stocked fridge and a complimentary bottle of the estate's own exceptional olive oil. You are well placed for Perugia, Assisi and Florence, and tempting food markets and restaurants are a ten-minute drive. *Minimum stay three nights.*

rooms	4 apartments: 3 for 3, 1 for 4.
price	€600–€700 per week.
meals	Self-catering. Many restaurants 5km.
closed	Rarely.
directions	Exit Bettolle-Perugia m'way at Tuoro. Right for town, then left for Arezzo. 2.2km on, right at 'Vino Olio' sign, to Castello. Right before 'strada della caccia' sign, on to iron gate.

	Claudio & Franca Marti
tel	+39 075 8230267
fax	+39 075 8230267
email	info@montegualandro.com
web	www.montegualandro.com/index.html

Self-catering

Map 9 Entry 219

Chiesa Pagano Country House

strada vicinale Rocca di Rasina, Spedalicchio, 06019 Umbertide

Slip into the elegant pool, sample the best of local wines in the cellar bar, set off to explore Gubbio, Assisi, Spello, Cortona and Perugia. This is a sophisticated and intriguing Anglo-Italian set-up, and Anne and Carlo are a kind, talented and generous couple. Their house – once a church, later a warehouse for drying tobacco, now meticulously restored – has been stylishly sprinkled with *objets d'art* from far-flung places. Electronically gated, encircled by a perimeter fence, it is reached via a glorious, cypress-lined drive. The garden is yet young but the views stretch for miles, over olive groves, vineyards and woods. The sitting room, a museum piece in its own right, is one of the loftiest in this book, its huge golden sofas and illuminated sculptures dwarfed by ecclesiastical ceilings. Bedrooms, not large, have an international flavour and are very comfortable; a chestnut desk here, a brocade-covered chair there, down duvets, heavy curtains, subdued lighting, satellite TV. Most seductive of all are the breakfast room and terrace from which sensational views sweep down the valley.

rooms	7: 5 doubles, 2 suites.
price	€130–€180.
meals	Snack lunch available. Restaurant 6km.
closed	24-26 December.
directions	From Umbertide, take 'Tiberina 3 bis' road for 3km until Niccone; SS416 left, 5.5km. At Spedalicchio, right at Chiesa Pagano sign; up hill 1km.

Anne Rogers

tel	+39 075 9410730
fax	+39 075 9410730
email	chiesapagano@tiscali.it
web	www.chiesapagano.com

B&B

Map 9 Entry 220

Prato di Sotto

Santa Giuliana, 06015 Pietrantonio

The visitors' book glows: some have called Prato di Sotto "heaven on earth".
Penny has nurtured the hilltop farmhouse and its 14th-century outbuildings
resplendently back to life – French beams were imported for the ceilings, the
doors leading to the library come from a monastery, some fireplaces are Umbria.
Sri Lankan armchairs live harmoniously alongside antique mirrors, deep sofas,
cushions, kilims and deliciously comfortable beds, and no expense has been spared
in the kitchens, designed with serious cooking in mind – one of Penny's passions.
'Casa Antica' is deeply luxurious with many bedrooms and bathrooms, dining
terrace and upstairs balcony/terrace with stupendous views. 'La Terrazza' has a
large terrace draped in wisteria and white roses; the ancient olive mill is a
romantic studio with a huge veranda; the cottage, too, has a vibrant terrace and a
glorious view. Borrow a labrador for your rambles across the hills, swim, sail on
Lake Trasimeno, return to gorgeous gardens. Penny cares for you as family friends
and brings you fresh-laid eggs for breakfast.

rooms	4 cottages: 2 for 2, 1 for 4, 1 for 8.
price	€800–€2,750 per week. Shorter breaks possible.
meals	Self-catering. Breakfast & dinner on request.
closed	Rarely.
directions	Exit N3 (S) at Badia Monte Corona. Under bridge, left aT-junction.; 3km after Badia left onto track. On for 4km veering left near S. Giuliana; 1st house on right. Phone to be met.

	Penny Radford
tel	+39 075 9417383
fax	+39 075 9412473
email	pennyradford@libero.it
web	www.umbriaholidays.com

Self-catering

Map 9 Entry 221

Casa San Gabriel

CP No 29, V. Petrarca No 2, 06015 Pierantonio

Enjoy David's wine on arrival, absorb the view of cultivated and wooded hills and unwind. Chrissie and David, warm, generous, thoughtful, bought the farmstead in a ruinous state and did it up all up in under a year. The little 'houses', private but close, each with its own terrace, are suitable for singles, couples or families so take your pick. For further space there's a living room in the main house with books and open fire. The restoration is sympathetic, unpretentious, delightful, the off-white décor and soft furnishings enhancing undulating beams and stone walls; the bathrooms are so lovely you could spend the day in them. Supplies are left for breakfast on your first morning and should last until you're ready to venture out. You may also pluck produce from the vegetable gardens. David cooks on Tuesdays, Thursday is pizza night – your chance to use an original wood-fired oven. Bliss to have Perugia so near by – a 20-minute drive – and to return to a pool with views down the valley all the way to Assisi, a bottle of chilled Orvieto by your side. *B&B option Oct-April.*

rooms	3 apartments: 1 for 2, 1 for 2-4, 1 for 4.
price	B&B: €80. Self-catering: €400-€875 per week.
meals	Dinner €20 (Tues); pizza €15 (Thurs). Restaurant 5-minute drive.
closed	Rarely.
directions	E45, exit Pierantonio for Antognolla Castle; after 4.5km, left for Santa Caterina; 1.5km on white road.

	Christina Todd & David Lang
tel	+39 075 9414219
fax	+44 (0)870 432 1331
email	chrissie@casasangabriel.com
web	www.casasangabriel.com

B&B & Self-catering

Map 9 Entry 222

Locanda del Gallo
loc. Santa Cristina, 06020 Gubbio

A restful, almost spiritual calm emanates from this wonderful home. In a medieval hamlet, the *locanda* has all the beams and antique tiles you could wish for. Light, airy rooms with pale limewashed walls are a perfect foil for the exquisite reclaimed doors and carved hardwood furniture from Bali and Indonesia; your charming hosts have picked up some fabulous pieces from far-flung places, and have given the house a colonial feel. Each bedroom is different, one almond with Italian country furniture, another white, with wicker armchairs and Provencale prints; some have carved four-poster beds. Bathrooms are gorgeous, with deep baths and walk-in, glass-doored showers. A stunning veranda wraps itself around the house: doze off in a wicker armchair, sip a drink at dusk as the sun melts into the valley. The pool is spectacular, like a mirage clinging to the side of the hill. Jimmy the cook conjures up food rich in genuine flavours, with aromatic herbs and vegetables from the garden; he and his wife are part of the extended family. As guests you will be made to feel every bit as much at home.

rooms	9: 6 doubles, 3 suites for 4.
price	€112-€122.
	Suites €204-€224.
	Half-board €75-€80 p.p.
meals	Dinner €25.
closed	December-March.
directions	Exit E45 at Ponte Pattoli for Casa del Diavolo; for S Cristina 8km. 1st left 100m after La Dolce Vita restaurant, continue to Locanda.

	Signora Paola Moro
tel	+39 075 9229912
fax	+39 075 9229912
email	info@locandadelgallo.it
web	www.locandadelgallo.it

Hotel

Map 9 Entry 223

Le Cinciallegre
fraz. Pisciano, 06020 Gubbio

This was once a tiny 13th-century hamlet on an ancient crossroads where local farmers met to buy and sell their produce. It's an incredibly peaceful spot, overlooking the valley, meadows and woods, and reached via a long, unmade road. Fabrizio used to be an architect and his conversion of these old houses is inspired – it feels authentic and delightful. In the cool, beamed living room, comfortable seats pull up around a 200-year-old woodburning stove; there's lots of pleasantly rustic furniture and a fine old dresser. The simple, comfortable bedrooms, named after birds, have their own terrace areas and immaculate bathrooms. Cristina is a wonderful cook, serving real country foods and Umbrian wines. Afterwards, guests settle down to enjoy *rosolios* and *ratafias* (homemade liqueurs). Fabrizio and Cristina are warm, hospitable, interesting people, passionate about the environment, their lovely, natural garden and the ten hectares of land full of wildlife. Fabrizio will be happy to tell you about the walking – indeed, he'll be disappointed if you don't have time to explore.

rooms	7: 3 doubles, 2 triples, 1 family, 1 single.
price	€96.
meals	Half-board €70 p.p.
closed	15 December–15 March.
directions	A1 exit Val di Chiana for Perugia & follow E45 to Cesena. Exit Umbertide Gubbio. Follow 219 for Gubbio. Signposted from Mocaiana.

	Fabrizio & Cristina De Robertis
tel	+39 075 9255957
fax	+39 075 9272331
email	cince@lecinciallegre.it
web	www.lecinciallegre.it

Agriturismo

Map 9 Entry 224

I Mandorli / Agriturismo
loc. Fondaccio 6, 06039 Bovara di Trevi

I Mandorli is aptly named: there's at least one almond tree outside each apartment. The blossom in February is stunning and, in summer, masses of greenery shades the old *casa padronale*. Once the centre of a 200-hectare estate, the shepherd's house and the olive mill in particular are fascinating reminders of days gone by. Mama Wanda is passionate about whole, lovely, rambling place and will show you around, embellishing everything you see with stories about its history. Widowed, she manages the remaining 47 hectares, apartments and rooms, *and* cooks, aided by her three charming daughters: home-grown produce and excellent gnocchi every Thursday. Bedrooms are sweet, simple affairs with new wrought-iron beds and pale patchwork quilts; small bathrooms are spotless. Children will love the wooden slide and seesaw, the old pathways and steps on this shallow hillside, the new pool – wonderful to return to after cultural outings to Assisi and Spoleto. This is olive oil country so make sure you go home with a few bottles of the best. *Laundry facilities: small charge.*

rooms	3 + 3: 3 twins/doubles.
	3 apartments: 1 for 2, 2 for 4.
price	€40-€85 (€265-€600 per week).
	Apartments €65-€150
	(€360-€600 per week).
meals	Dinner €20 (not Sun or winter).
	Self-catering in apartments.
closed	Rarely.
directions	SS3 exit Trevi for Bovara;
	signed from main road.

	Famiglia di Zappelli Cardarelli
tel	+39 0742 78669
fax	+39 0742 78669
email	info@agriturismoimandorli.com
web	www.agriturismoimandorli.com

Agriturismo & Self-catering

Map 12 Entry 225

Hotel Palazzo Bocci

via Cavour 17, 06038 Spello

A beautiful townhouse in Spello's cobbled centre, whose pale yellow façade, dove-grey shutters and modest dront door barely hint at the grandeur inside. Enter a tranquil courtyard with a tiny, trickling fountain; then through to a series of glorious reception rooms, most with painted friezes. The most impressive is the richly-decorated drawing room, the *sala degli affreschi*; and there's a reading room filled with old tomes and travel magazines. The whole building is multi-levelled and fascinating with its alcoves, nooks and crannies. Guest bedrooms are immaculate, with serene cream walls, polished chestnut beams, big comfortable beds, simple drapes. The suites have frescoed ceilings, the bathrooms are a delight. Delicious breakfasts are served on the herringbone-tiled terrace in warm weather; it overlooks Spello's ancient rooftops and makes a lovely spot for a sundowner. Step across the cobbled entrance to the restaurant, Il Molino – once the village olive mill – and dine under an ancient, brick-vaulted ceiling. A charming hotel in a charming town, run by delightful people.

rooms	23: 15 doubles, 2 singles, 6 suites.
price	€130–€160.
	Singles €80–€100.
	Suites €180–€270.
meals	Lunch or dinner approx. €30.
closed	Rarely.
directions	From Assisi for Foligno. After 10km, leave main road at Spello. Hotel opp. Church of Sant'Andrea in town centre. Private parking.

	Signor Fabrizio Buono
tel	+39 0742 301021
fax	+39 0742 301464
email	info@palazzobocci.com
web	www.palazzobocci.com

Hotel

Map 12 Entry 226

Brigolante Guest Apartments

via Costa di Trex 31, 06081 Assisi

In the foothills of St Francis's beloved Mount Subasio, the 16th-century stone farmhouse has been thoughtfully restored by Stefano and Rebecca. She is American and came to Italy to study, he is an architectural land surveyor – here was the perfect project. The apartments feel very private but you can always chat over an *aperitivo* with the other guests in the garden. Rooms are light, airy and delightful, full of Grandmother's furniture and Rebecca's kind touches: a welcome basket of goodies from the farm (wine, eggs, cheese, honey, olive oil, homemade jam), handmade soap and sprigs of lavender by the bath. Pretty lace curtains flutter at the window, kitchens are well-equipped, and laundry facilities are available on request. This is a farm with animals, so ham, salami and sausages are produced as well as wine. Feel free to pluck whatever you like from the vegetable garden – red peppers, fat tomatoes, huge lettuces. A lovely, peaceful place for families and walkers; you are deep in the Mount Subasio National Park and there are dozens of trails to explore. *Minimum stay two nights; one week in summer.*

rooms	3 apartments: 1 for 2, 2 for 2-4.
price	€255-€440 per week.
	Short stays possible in low season.
meals	Self-catering.
	Restaurant 1km.
closed	Rarely.
directions	Assisi ring road to Porta Perlici, then towards Gualdo Tadino, 6km. Right, signed Brigolante. Over 1st bridge, right, over 2nd wooden bridge, up hill 500m, right at 1st gravel road.

	Signora Rebecca Winke Bagnoli
tel	+39 075 802250
fax	+39 075 802250
email	info@brigolante.com
web	www.brigolante.com

Self-catering

Map 12 Entry 227

Hotel e Agriturismo Le Silve

loc. Armenzano, 06081 Assisi

The setting, deep in the heart of the Umbrian hills, takes your breath away. It's as beauitful and as peaceful as Shangri-La – so remote you'd do well to fill up with petrol before leaving Spello or Assisi. The medieval buildings have been beautifully restored and the whole place breathes an air of tranquillity. Superb, generous-sized bedrooms have stone walls, exquisite terracotta floors, beautiful furniture, old mirrors and (a rarity, this!) proper reading lights. Bathrooms with walk-in showers are similarly rustic with terracotta floors and delicious pampering extras. The apartments are spread across three converted farm buildings. We loved the restaurant, too – intimate and inviting both indoors and out. The produce is mostly organic, the bread is homemade, the cheeses, hams and salami are delectable. There are tennis and table-tennis, a pool with a bar, a hydromassage and a sauna and hectares of hills and woods in which to walk or ride or walk. A happy, friendly place, and popular – be sure to book well in advance.
Minimum stay two nights.

rooms	20 + 13: 20 doubles. 13 apartments for 2-4.
price	€83-€91. Half-board €112-€120 p.p. Apartments €60-€90.
meals	Dinner €30-€40.
closed	November-March (open 20 December-2 January).
directions	Milan A1 exit Valdichiana for Perugia, then Assisi. Signs for Gualdo Tadino then Armenzano, km12; signs for hotel, 2km.

Signor Marco Sirignani

tel	+39 075 8019000
fax	+39 075 8019005
email	info@lesilve.it
web	www.lesilve.it

Agriturismo & Self-catering

Map 12 Entry 228

Agriturismo Alla Madonna del Piatto
via Pieve San Nicolo' 18, 06081 Assisi

The road winds up through woods and off the isolated track to a simple, centuries-old farmhouse in a hidden corner of Umbria. The position is stupendous, the views stretching over olive groves and forested hills to Assisi and its basilica. The old farmhouse was abandoned for decades until these Italian-Dutch owners fell in love with the view, then restored the building with sympathy and style, then replanted the olive groves. Bedrooms are large, airy, uncluttered, their country antiques mixed with Moroccan bedspreads, pottery or decorative wall lights picked up on Letizia's travels. One room has a loo with a view. Breakfasts served on generous white china are enjoyed at mosaic-topped tables in the sitting/dining room, a fresh, modern space of white and rose-coloured walls and a warm sofa by an open fire. Your hosts – approachable, hugely helpful – share their home gladly. If you can tear yourself away from the terrace and its panorama, there are walks, medieval hill towns and all of Umbria to explore. *Ask about cookery classes. Minimum stay two nights; three in high season.*

rooms	6: 5 twins/doubles, 1 family room for 3.
price	€80-€110.
meals	Trattoria 2km.
closed	Last 2 weeks January-February.
directions	From Assisi SS147 for Perugia; after Ponte San Vittorino turn right, Via San Fortunato; uphill 6.5km; right; Via Petrata.

	Letizia Mattiacci
tel	+39 075 8199050
mobile	+39 328 7025297
email	letizia.mattiacci@libero.it
web	www.incampagna.com

Agriturismo

Map 12 Entry 229

Corbine di Sotto

strada vicinale delle Spinale 6, 06077 Ponte Pattoli

Mellow stone buildings cluster round a courtyard, overlooked by tall cypresses, enveloped by wooded hills. It's an entrancing place. Twelfth century in origin, it has been restored by Frederik and Wendy using local craftsmen and materials: old Umbria meets new and the result is heaven. Soft curves and arches, beams and old-style plastering give the apartments their restful, traditional character. Flagged or terracotta floors, harmonious hues, understated furniture and secluded terraces suggest a sense of style and space. Each apartment is extremely well equipped and has a stunning kitchen – and if you fancy a night off, catering can be arranged. Frederik has a wine cellar, too, of which he is immensely proud, and will organise wine-tasting evenings for enthusiasts. The swimming pools are magnificent: splash indoors under beautiful high brick arches or outside, surrounded by lavender. The imaginatively terraced gardens are as inspired as the interiors, with stone walls and huge terracotta urns, olive trees and pines. Come in early summer and the hillside above is red with poppies.

rooms	2 apartments: 1 for 2, 1 for 4.
price	€1,195–€1,995 per week.
meals	Restaurants 5km.
closed	1 October–1 June.
directions	From Bologna A14 for Ancona, exit Cesena Nord; E45 exit Ponte Pattoli, through village left for Ponte Felcino. Right on Strada Vicinale delle Spinale, right through gates.

Frederik & Wendy Meijer

mobile	+39 338 3778867
fax	+39 075 5914182
email	info@corbinedisotto.com
web	www.corbinedisotto.com

Self-catering

Map 12 Entry 230

Castello dell'Oscano

strada della Forcella 37, 06010 Cenerente

At the turn of the century, Count Telfner visited England and was so taken by the opulent intimacy of its grand country houses that he went straight back to Italy and did up his own place. Hence Oscano: a glorious, lovable parody of England. There's a grand, balustraded central staircase, suitably creaky, huge oils on most of the walls, a grand piano in the drawing room and a proper library – for afternoon tea. The sitting room would not look out of place in Kent. Owner Maurizio has nurtured the house almost since its rebirth. He returned from Belgium with a trompe l'œil, commissioned ceramics from Deruta and stocked the cellars with the best Umbrian wines. Bedrooms have a faded baronial elegance in the National Trust spirit: floral wallpapers, period furnishings and large windows which look over the garden and park. Bathrooms are big and modern. The rooms in the Villa Ada next door, though less stylish, are best described as 'well-appointed' and are hugely comfortable. The whole experience is one of comfort, unpretentious refinement, and tranquillity. And the food is excellent.

rooms	30 + 13: 20 doubles, 10 suites. 13 apartments for 2-5.
price	€150-€230. Suites €290-€310. Apartments €325-€775 per week.
meals	Dinner €35.
closed	Rarely.
directions	Exit E45 Perugia Madonna; from Perugia for San Marco. Take small road for Cenerente. Signed.

	M. Ravano & M. Bussolati
tel	+39 075 584371
fax	+39 075 690666
email	info@oscano.com
web	www.oscano.com

Agriturismo & Self-catering

Map 12 Entry 231

Castello di Petroia

Scritto di Gubbio, 06020 Perugia

Brave the loops of the Gubbio-Assisi road and arrive at the castle at dusk. The front gate is locked, you ring to be let in; an eerie silence, and the gates creak open. Inside, dim lighting, stone walls, a splendid austerity. Come morning, you will appreciate the vast-fireplaced magnificence of the place, and the lovely terrace that catches the all-day sun. With a full house, dinner is a sociable affair, graciously presided over – in English and Italian – by the tweed-clad count. It takes place in one of two grand dining rooms and is rounded off by the house speciality, a fiery liqueur. Then up the stairs – some steep – to bedrooms with polished floors and shadowy corners, dark furniture and flowery beds. A feeling of feudalism remains – four staff serve 12 guests – and the landscape is similarly ancient. The castle is set on a hillock surrounded by pines in beautiful, unpopulated countryside and a marked footpath running through it. Walk to Assissi – it takes a day – then taxi back. Or take the bus into Gubbio and the funicular into the hills – the views are stupendous. And return to your 900-acre estate.

rooms	6: 2 doubles, 4 suites (1 in tower).
price	€110-€140.
	Suites €150-€200.
meals	Dinner with wine €28-€34.
closed	January-March.
directions	S298 from Gubbio south for Assisi & Perugia. After Scritto, just before Biscina & Fratticiola, take stony road signed to Castello.

	Conte Carlo Sagrini
tel	+39 075 920287
fax	+39 075 920108
email	castellodipetroia@castellodipetroia.com
web	www.castellodipetroia.com

Hotel

Map 12 Entry 232

Le Torri di Bagnara

str. della Bruna 8, Solfagnano, 06080 Perugia

Aided by a staff of 30, Signora Giunta runs her family empire with professionalism and pride. Hers is a huge and magnificent estate, 1,500 acres of pastoral perfection with vast views, a pristine pool (floodlit at night), a 12th-century tower, an 11th-century abbey, three castles and many terraces. It is a medieval framework for a modern, holiday enterprise and you feel you're on top of the world. Four rustic but elegant apartments fill the tower, each on a different floor. They have barrow-vault ceilings and Romanesque windows, strokeable fabrics and fine old furniture, swish galley kitchens and wonderful views. On the ground floor is a communal dining and sitting area for the sociable; outside, figs, peaches, olives, herbs and a shared laundry. Bedrooms in the abbey feed off a delightful paved courtyard with small church and tower and are as luxurious as the rest. You're three miles from restaurants but one is planned here and the motorway is conveniently close. Cookery classes, chefs, wine-tastings, free mountain bikes… Giunta has thought of everything. *Bus stop 500m.*

rooms	8 + 4: 4 doubles, 3 suites.
	4 apartments: 1 for 2, 2 for 4, 1 for 5.
price	€100–€160.
	Apartments €380–€1,142 per week.
meals	Restaurant 2km.
closed	Never.
directions	E45 exit Resina; north for
	Pieve San Quirico Bagnara;
	2km, signed on left.

	Zenaide Giunta
tel	+39 075 5792001
fax	+39 075 5793001
email	info@letorridibagnara.it
web	www.letorridibagnara.it

Agriturismo & Self-catering

Map 9 Entry 233

Villa Rosa

voc. Docciolano 9, Montemelino, 06060 Magione

The beautifully restored farmhouse looks out over fields and farms to the villages of Solomeo and Corciano, with Perugia in the distance. Distant church bells, the hum of a tractor, the bray of a donkey… yet you are five kilometres from the superstrada. You couldn't find a better spot from which to discover Tuscany and Umbria. Megan, who is Australian, and Lino are a helpful and hospitable couple, and will help you enjoy every aspect of your stay: hunt for truffles (or cashmere, in Solomeo!), book in for a twice-weekly cookery class with a chef from Perugia, take advantage of a personalised tour. There are three apartments here. For a family, the two-storey *casetta* at the end of the garden is perfect – a delightful mix of recycled beams and terracotta tiles, with open fire, air con, jacuzzi and perfect views. The flat on the ground floor of the farmhouse is similarly good – new bunk beds in the living area, cool in summer, a great terrace. There's a saltwater pool to cool you down, and the views from two of the apartments are wonderful.
Apartments: minimum stay three nights.

rooms	1 cottage for 6. 2 apartments, 1 for 3, 1 for 4.
price	Cottage €160-€175 (€600-€1,100 p. w.). Apartments €95-€115 (€425-€725 p.w.) each.
meals	Restaurant 1km.
closed	Rarely.
directions	Exit Perugia-Bettolle at Corciano, for Castelvieto through village (via underpass & bridge) to shrine. Left & on to 2nd shrine; right uphill; house after couple of bends.

	Megan & Lino Rialti
tel	+39 075 841814
fax	+39 075 841814
email	meglino@libero.it

Self-catering

Map 12 Entry 234

Villa Aureli

via Luigi Cirenei 70, 06071 Castel del Piano

Little has changed since the Villa was built in the 18th century and became the country house of the Serègo Alighieri family 100 years later. The ornamental plasterwork, floor tiles and decorative shutters reflect its noble past, it is known to all the locals and is full of precious and historic treasures (walled up by a perspicacious housekeeper during the Occupation) which inspire the interest, attention and care of Pietro, son and heir of Sperello. The house in fact has its origins in the 16th century, and the grounds are suitably formal – overgrown here, tamed there, with lemon trees in amazing 18th-century pots in the *limonaia* and a swimming pool created from an irrigation tank. The apartments are big and beautiful, the one on the second floor the largest and grandest, with balconies and views. Floors have mellow old tiles, ceilings are high and raftered, bedrooms are delightfully faded, one with aqua-blue bedsteads, raspberry covers and an antique painted wardrobe. You are a step away from the village, so can walk to the few shops and bar. A quietly impressive retreat, wonderfully peaceful – and special.

rooms	2 apartments: 1 for 4-6, 1 for 4-8.
price	€950-€1,200 per week.
meals	Self-catering. Occasional dinner €36.
closed	Never.
directions	From A1, exit Valdichiana for Perugia, exit Madonna Alta towards Città della Pieve. At square, sign for Bagnaia; on left after 200m. Alternatively, go to centre of Castel del Piano and ask.

	Sperello di Serègo Alighieri
mobile	+39 340 6459061
fax	+39 075 5149408
email	villa.aureli@libero.it
web	www.villaaureli.it

Self-catering

Map 12 Entry 235

The Country House Montali

via Montali 23, 06068 Tavernelle di Panicale

It's an irresistible combination – a gorgeous place, mouthwatering vegetarian food. Alberto's expertise in restoring historic buildings and his desire to give vegetarians something more inspired than brown rice have resulted in the creation of Montali. It stands on a plateau surrounded by woodland, reached by a long, bumpy track. From the gardens you can walk straight over the hills or down to Lake Trasimeno – spectacular. The guest rooms, in three single-storey buildings, have verandas, wide views and a pleasantly colonial air. White walls show off hand-carved teak furniture and oil paintings by Alberto's talented brother; terracotta floors are strewn with Indian rugs. And not a TV in sight. As for the food – it's exquisite. Served with good local wines in the serene little restaurant, it's mainly mediterranean, with touches of nouvelle and haute cuisine. Malu, Alberto's wife, is the head chef and Montali is fast making an international name for itself. (Cookery courses available on request.) Alberto and Malu are both delightful; they are also keen musicians and sometimes organise evening concerts.

rooms	10 doubles.
price	Half-board €160–€200 for two.
meals	Half-board only.
closed	Rarely.
directions	A1 from Rome, exit Fabro, for Tavernelle. 2km after Tavernelle, left for 'Colle San Paolo'. Up hill 7km, following signs. Left at top of hill, hotel 800m on left.

Alberto Musacchio

tel	+39 075 8350680
fax	+39 075 8350144
email	montali@montalionline.com
web	www.montalionline.com

Villa di Monte Solare

via Montali 7, Colle San Paolo, 06070 Fontignano

A hushed, stylish, country retreat in a perfect Umbrian setting. This noble villa, encircled by a formal walled garden, has been transformed into a small hotel with uniformed staff, elegant rooms and fine restaurant. The grounds, which include the little chapel of Santa Lucia and a small maze, envelop the hotel in an atmosphere of calm. Bedrooms are spacious and lovingly tended, full of local fabric and craftmanship. The public rooms have kept their charm, their painted cornices and friezes, huge fireplaces, ancient terracotta floors. The restaurant, a gorgeous beamed room with a roaring fire in winter, seats bedroom capacity, so non-residents may only book if guests are dining out. Cappuccino from a bar machine at breakfast; at dinner, superb designer food and a choice 380 wines. The owners live for this place and eat with guests every night, the mood is refined and jackets are usually worn, though not insisted upon. In the old glass *limonaia* is a new beauty spa, for guests only. There are bikes to rent, pools to swim, even concerts and talks on Umbrian history. The view stretches out in every direction.

rooms	28: 21 doubles, 5 suites, 2 family.
price	€150–€210.
	Suites & family rooms €200–€240.
	Singles €90–€105.
meals	Lunch €15–€26. Dinner €35–€45.
closed	Never.
directions	Exit A1 at Chiusi-Chianciano; right to Chiusi; right for Città della Pieve; signs for Perugia, wall on left; left for Perugia-Tavernelle (SS220); 1km after Tavernelle, left for Colle S. Paolo. 4km to villa.

	Rosemarie & Filippo Iannarone
tel	+39 075 832376
fax	+39 075 8355462
email	info@villamontesolare.it
web	www.villamontesolare.it

Villa Lemura

Villa Le Mura 92, 06064 Panicale

Live like an aristocrat but without the pomp or circumstance. This 18th-century building, once the country villa of Umbrian nobility, has an opulent but faded grandeur. Delightful Emma, Luca and family have made it their home: don't be surprised to find a bicycle propped against the gracious pillars of the entrance hall. Rooms will make you gasp – frescoed ceilings, richly tiled floors, Murano chandeliers – yet it all feels charmingly lived-in. Furniture is a comfortable mismatch of antiques and brocante finds. The high-ceilinged, elegant bedrooms might include an antique French bed, a chaise-longue or a painted ceramic stove. Most have frescoes, one has a private terrace. Sink into sofas in the ballroom-sized salon, browse a book in the library, breakfast on the terrace above the Italian garden. Dinner can be arranged – or you may rustle up your own in the delightful orangery. Lake Trasimeno, Perugia and Assisi wait to be discovered; or find a quiet spot in the villa's shady gardens, full of terraced pool, mossy statues, fountains, olive grove and views.

rooms	7: 3 doubles, 1 twin, 1 triple; 1 double, 1 twin sharing bathroom.
price	€90–€150. Whole house on request.
meals	Dinner €25 (min 8), on request.
closed	Occasionally.
directions	From A1 exit Chiusi for Perugia; exit Perugia/Magione (not Panicale); signs to Panicale; thro' Macchie & Colgiordano (not up to Panicale); left to Lemura, villa 1st on left.

	Emma & Luca Mezensio
tel	+39 075 837134
fax	+39 075 837134
email	villalemura@libero.it
web	www.villalemura.com

B&B & Self-catering

Map 12 Entry 238

Agriturismo Madonna delle Grazie
Madonna delle Grazie 6, 06062 Città della Pieve

Children who love animals will be in heaven. There are rabbits, dogs, horses, ducks and hens, and Renato will pluck a cicada from an olive tree and show them how it 'sings'. This is a real farm – not a hotel with a few animals wandering about – so don't expect luxury; it's agriturismo at its best and you eat what they produce. The simple guest bedrooms in the 18th-century farmhouse are engagingly old-fashioned; all have their own terraces or balcony and the bathrooms are spotless. The farm is now fully organic, and the food in the restaurant delicious, so make the most of Renato's own salami, chicken, fruit and vegetables, olive oil, grappa and wine. There's also a big playground for children, and table-football in the house. The youngest offspring, free from the tyranny of taste, will appreciate the Disney gnomes incongruously dotted around the picnic area. For the grown-ups there's riding, archery, a discount at the San Casciano Terme spa… and views that stretch to Tuscany in one direction, Umbria in the other. A great little place.

rooms	6 doubles.
price	€90–€120.
meals	Dinner €20.
closed	Rarely.
directions	From A1 North: exit Chiusi-Chianciano, rigth to Chiusi & Città della Pieve. From A1 South: exit Fabro, turn left; left after 1km to Città della Pieve.

Signor Renato Nannotti
tel	+39 0578 299822
fax	+39 0578 297749
email	info@madonnadellegrazie.it
web	www.madonnadellegrazie.it

Agriturismo

Map 12 Entry 239

Fattoria di Vibio

loc. Doglio, 06057 Montecastello Vibio

Get away from it all at this farmhouse in a magical setting – you are miles from anywhere. The collection of sensitively restored outbuildings is more 'residential complex' than agriturismo, with outside lighting, a brand-new spa, a swish pool and occasional late-night muzak keeping nature at bay. The spa, tucked into the hillside, is fabulous. Bedrooms are comfortable, simple, stylish, some with room for additional beds, all with heavenly views. Mezzanine apartments are perfect for families. The charming sitting room is cosy with chunky beams, big lamps and open fire – bliss to return to after some exceptional walks. Ask to borrow one of the large-scale maps of the area, book a picnic and discover the virtually uninhabited valleys and hills. The brothers produce organic olive oil, honey and fruit which you can buy; their mother runs cookery courses – take her cookbook *Entriamo in Cucina* away with you for inspiration at home. Limited English is reluctantly spoken, so translators are brought in for the courses and other themed happenings. *Minimum stay two nights, or one week in August.*

rooms	13 + 4: 13 twins/doubles. 3 apartments for 4-5, 1 for 6.
price	Half board €80-€105 p.p (€455-€735 per week). Apartments €800-€1,900 per week.
meals	Lunch €25. Dinner €30.
closed	10 January-28 February.
directions	Florence-Roma A1, exit Orvieto. SS448 for Todi. Left for Prodo-Quadro (SS79); signed.

	Filippo & Giuseppe Saladini
tel	+39 075 8749607
fax	+39 075 8780014
email	info@fattoriadivibio.com
web	www.fattoriadivibio.com

Agriturismo & Self-catering

Map 12 Entry 240

Relais Il Canalicchio

via della Piazza 4, 06050 Canalicchio di Collazzone

Not only a pleasant detour between Perugia and Orvieto but a charming retreat. Once known as the Castello di Poggio, this pretty 13th-century hamlet high on an Umbrian hilltop is almost a principality in itself: 51 rooms, two pools, gym, tower, gardens with white roses, ancient fortress walls. The decoration is a surprisingly international mix, a quirk reflected in the names of the bedrooms (Isabelle Rubens, the Countess of Oxford); note some of the décor is tired and awaits revival. Many rooms are tucked under white-painted rafters, others open onto little balconies or terraces and the bathrooms are a treat; those in the tower have views that sweep over an endless valley of olive groves, vineyards and woods. We liked the rooms in the new wing, with their sponged walls and hand-stencilled details. Downstairs, play a frame of billiards over a glass of grappa – having dined first at Il Pavone, where the views at sunset are breathtaking. Others may prefer to retreat to the quiet of the library. There's character here, masses of space, and Dorine masterminds her flurry of staff beautifully.

rooms	49: 35 doubles, 14 suites.
price	€160-€195. Singles €125-€155. Suites €230-€260.
meals	Lunch or dinner €45. Restaurants 15km.
closed	Rarely.
directions	Rome A1 for Firenze, exit Orte. E45 Perugia-Cesena, exit Ripabianca for Canalicchio.

	Federico Pittaluga
tel	+39 075 8707325
fax	+39 075 8707296
email	relais@relaisilcanalicchio.it
web	www.relaisilcanalicchio.it

Hotel

Map 12 Entry 241

Casale Campodoro

fraz. Viepri 106, 06056 Massa Martana

A feast for the eyes. The interior of this restored 18th-century building has been embellished with style and a quirky humour. Imagine an Indonesian hippo's head over a fireplace and a plastic goose as a lamp. Piero, a gentle, humorous and intelligent Italian, lives here with Carolina, four cats and three daft, friendly and boisterous dogs. In one bathroom, a muscular plaster-cast juts out of the wall and serves as a towel rail; elsewhere, Piero's Scottish grandmother's clothes – lace interwoven with scarab beetles – have been framed and hung. By the pool are plastic yellow Philippe Starck sofa and chairs; on the walls, religious icons. The garden sits on an Umbrian hillside and has little steps leading to hidden corners and a large aviary, whose birds escape and return at night. There are lovely views across to old Abbazia, and other, more edible delights: breakfast brings warm, fresh, homemade bread and tasty jams. Once a week, guests get together for dinner with everyone contributing a national dish. Don't mind the odd bit of peeling paint – this is an individual and joyously eccentric place.

rooms	3 + 3: 3 doubles. 3 apartments for 3-5.
price	€50-€60 (€250-€300 per week). Apartments €60-€120 (€300-€600 per week).
meals	Many restaurants nearby.
closed	Rarely.
directions	From Perugia-Cesena exit Massa Martana (316) to Foligno/Bastarelo; left to San Terenziano; 1km; right to Viepri; 100m, track on left; 1st on right.

	Carolina Bonanno
tel	+39 075 8947347
email	camporo@libero.it
web	www.casalecampodoro.it

B&B & Self-catering

Map 12 Entry 242

Tenuta di Canonica

loc. Canonica m.75/76, 06059 Todi

The position is wonderful, on a green ridge with stunning views, and the house is special. It was a ruin (17th century, with medieval remnants and Roman foundations) when Daniele and Maria bought it in 1998. Much creativity has gone into its resurrection. There's not a corridor in sight – instead, odd steps up and down, hidden doors, vaulted ceilings, enchanting corners. Cool, beautiful reception rooms are decorated in mellow, muted colours, then given a personal, individual and exotic touch: family portraits, photos, books. The bedrooms are vast, intriguingly shaped and alluring, with lovely rugs on pale brick or wooden floors and gorgeous beds and fabrics. All in all, it's a house that reflects its owners' personalities: Daniele and Maria are vivid, interesting people, well-travelled and good company. Meals are cooked by a couple of chefs from the Cordon Bleu school in Perugia. The dining room opens onto a covered terrace surrounded by roses and shrubs, a path sweeps down to the pool and there are many good walks over the 24-hectare estate. *Minimum stay two nights, one week in August.*

rooms	11 + 2: 11 doubles.
	2 apartments for 3-4.
price	€130-€220.
	Apartments €800-€950 per week.
meals	Dinner €30.
closed	January-February.
directions	Florence-Roma A1, exit Valdichiana; E45 Perugia-Terni exit Todi-Orvieto; SS448 for Prodo-Titignano; 2km, Bivio per Cordigliano; 1km, signed.

	Daniele Fano
tel	+39 075 8947545
fax	+39 075 8947581
email	tenutadicanonica@tin.it
web	www.tenutadicanonica.com

Agriturismo & Self-catering

Map 12 Entry 243

Le Logge di Silvignano
fraz. Silvignano 14, 06049 Spoleto

Wrought-iron gates swing open onto a courtyard... and there is the house, in all its unruffled, medieval beauty. Thought, care and talent have gone into its restoration. And the setting: the Spoleto hills with views to Assisi! Alberto's love of roses has been awoken in Diana and is wonderfully evident, while the recent planting preserves as many of the old inhabitants as possible: prune, Japanese persimmon and two ancient figs, source of breakfast jams. The graceful open gallery with octagonal stone pillars dates from the 15th century but the main building has its roots in the 12th. Guest suites, big and charming, have Amalfi-tiled bathrooms, pretty sitting rooms with open fireplaces, tiny kitchens for snacks and drinks; sumptuous fabrics woven in Montefalco look perfect against stone walls and massive beams. Diana and Alberto are delighted if you join them for a glass of wine before you set off to dine, or a nightcap on your return. They're warm, interesting people, genuinely happy to share their corner of paradise. *Minimum stay two nights. Children over 12 welcome.*

rooms	5 suites.
price	€190-€250.
meals	Good restaurants 1.5-4km.
closed	10 January-20 February.
directions	A1 Florence-Bologna, exit Bettolle-Sinalunga, then E45 for Perugia-Assisi-Foligno. SS3 Flaminia until Fonti del Clitunno, then for Campello-Pettino; 3km after Campello right for Silvignano, 1.5km. Unsigned.

	Alberto Araimo
tel	+39 0743 274098
fax	+39 0743 270518
email	mail@leloggedisilvignano.it
web	www.leloggedisilvignano.it

B&B

Map 12 Entry 244

Il Castello di Poreta
loc. Poreta, 06049 Spoleto

You approach via a steep and winding track through oak woods where truffles are found. The crumbling, ruined walls of the 14th-century village (which took a tumble after the 1703 earthquake) enclose the church and restored buildings that make up the Castello di Poreta. All was revived when a co-operative from the village won the right to transform the ancient stones and rafters into a country-house hotel – and a very special one at that. Simple, comfortable bedrooms – the loftiest in the old priest's house, the rest in a new part off the terrace – reflect the pastel shades of the sun-bleached, olive-growing hills outside. There's a soothing and elegant sitting room, and a light, airy restaurant (open to all: do book) with stunning views, interesting modern art and sophisticated Umbrian food. Donatella, the young chef, is enthusiastic and creative: the menu changes often and is seasonally aware. There are small jazz concerts in the church in summer, young and cheerful service, wild boar safaris, birdsong and wild flowers. An unusual and delightful place to stay, well off the beaten track.

rooms	8 twins/doubles.
price	€85–€115.
meals	Dinner €35 à la carte, with wine (restaurant closed Monday evening).
closed	Rarely.
directions	Signposted on via Flaminia between Spoleto & Foligno.

	Luca Saint Amour di Chanaz
tel	+39 0743 275810
fax	+39 0743 270175
email	castellodiporeta@seeumbria.com
web	www.seeumbria.com/poreta

Convento di Agghielli Country Resort / Agriturismo

fraz. Pompagnano, 06049 Spoleto

More than a thousand years old, its ancient walls exude monastic calm. Deep in 100 hectares of wooded estate, you feel blissfully isolated, although the town of Spoleto is only five kilometres away. Marinella and Dario are justly proud of the old monastery, which they restored using environmentally friendly materials. Be treated to home-grown, homemade organic food in the restaurant (both your hosts are passionate chefs); sleep under organic bed linen in the warmth of the beautifully decorated and superbly equipped bedrooms; sink into voluptuous sofas by the hearth in the living and dining area. The ceilings are terracotta or wood-panelled, the walls honey-coloured stone or painted in a wash of soft, earthy shades. All is expertly done, but the masterstroke of the Convento is the on-site Creative Wellness Centre, run exclusively for guests, which offers every form of relaxation under the sun: hydromassage, reiki, yoga, Turkish baths… you are even invited into the woods for sensorial perception treatments. Hard to conceive of a more peaceful or delectable place to stay.

rooms	16: 5 doubles, 11 suites.
price	€124–€155.
	Suites €140–€230.
meals	Half board €78–€135 p.p.
closed	Never.
directions	From Spoleto south on Flaminia; right to Pompagnano; signed on right at bottom of gravel track, 700m.

	Marinella De Simone
tel	+39 0743 225010
fax	+39 0743 225010
email	info@agghielli.it
web	www.agghielli.it

Agriturismo

Map 12 Entry 246

Arthouse Spoleto

via Cecili 26, 06049 Spoleto

Climb to the top of the marble staircase… and the 16th-century palazzo opens into a cool, minimalist space. You might feel inspired to paint, make music, create Italian dishes. Wallace would be delighted; once a fashion designer for Donna Karan among others, he's settled here from his native Glasgow, to run creative courses and share his love of Spoleto. In what was once the Archbishop's palazzo, built around a rare, 800-year-old tower, rooms are light, elegant and airy. The salon, originally the loggia, has beautiful arched windows and a black fireplace; contemporary sofas and chairs team charmingly with white walls. High-ceilinged bedrooms are sleek with modern furniture, funky lighting and polished parquet, and all have glorious views over Spoleto's sun-bleached roofs. Breakfast in the kitchen – the original chapel – on Wallace's lovely homemade bread and perfect coffee and preserves. Your host, who has his own separate apartment, is irrepressible company; warm, enthusiastic, creative, in love with Italy and Italian life. A B&B that is soothing, stimulating, special. *Minimum stay two nights.*

rooms	4 doubles.
price	€95–€125.
meals	Restaurants 1km.
closed	December–January.
directions	Florence-Roma A1, exit Valdichina, Trasimeno, Asissi, Spoleto. Roma-Firenze A1, exit Orte, Terni, Spoleto.

C. A. Wallace Shaw

mobile	+39 347 4639198
fax	+39 0743 202067
email	be@arthousespoleto.com
web	www.arthousespoleto.com

B&B

Map 12 Entry 247

Photo Torre Tenosa, entry 253

le marche
abruzzo molise

Villa Giulia

via di Villa Giulia, Località San Biagio, 40, 61032 Fano

Pines, cypress oaks and roses surround the Napoleonic villa, wisteria billows over the lemon house wall. The gardens merge into the family olive farm and an ancient wood. No formality, no fuss, just an easy, calm and kind welcome from Anna, who moved here a year ago with her youngest son. The villa was named after an indominatable great-aunt (the first woman to climb Mont Blanc!) and the family furniture remains – large wooden mirrors, stunning antiques – along with a candle burn on the mantelpiece left by the Nazis. Bedrooms, the best and most baronial in the villa, have shuttered windows and old-fashioned metal beds; one noble bathroom has its own balcony, another is up a winding stair. The two suites in La Dependence have kitchenettes, while the apartments proper are divided between the Farmhouse and the Casa Piccola. Sitting rooms are grand but easy, the dining room's chairs are gay with red checks and summer breakfasts are taken at pink-clothed tables on a terrace whose views reach to the Adriantic (the beach is a mile away). Atmospheric, historic, beautiful and good for all ages.

rooms	10 + 5: 3 doubles, 7 suites. 5 apartments for 3-6.
price	€90-€230. Apartments €800-€1,800 per week.
meals	Dinner €20-€40. Restaurants nearby.
closed	Rarely.
directions	SS16 from Fano for Pesaro, 3km north of Fano turn left; signed.

	Anna Passi
tel/fax	+39 0721 823159
mobile	+39 347 0823935
email	info@relaisvillagiulia.com
web	www.relaisvillagiulia.com

B&B & Self-catering

Map 10 Entry 248

Le Marche

Studio Apartment
via Piave 7, 61029 Urbino

Open the gate in the wall of the tiny, brick-paved alley and enter an enchanting terrazzo garden. A fabulous sun trap, even in winter and spring, it stands above the city ramparts with superb views to the south. Double-shuttered French windows lead from the garden to the apartment – sweet rather than roomy, and ingeniously created from an old chapel. The courteous owners live above. The crisp lines of contemporary furniture and fittings harmonise well with the gentle curves of the apse; white walls and floors offset the odd colourful fabric and pretty picture. Storage separates the living from the sleeping area (no windows); a teensy kitchen and bathroom have been fashioned on either side. Make yourself at home and relish the fact that you are in the heart of Urbino, the most delightful of university cities; the ducal palace, a Renaissance gem housing the National Gallery of the Marches, is almost next door. There are several Adriatic coastal towns nearby, always a pleasure to explore out of season – stay as long as you can. *Owners happy to ferry guests to & from bus station.*

rooms	1 apartment for 2.
price	€550 per week.
meals	Restaurants nearby.
closed	June-15 November.
directions	In *centro storico* of Urbino.

	Signora Adriana Negri
tel/fax	+39 0722 2888
mobile	+39 335 6915141
email	gsavini@supereva.it

Locanda della Valle Nuova
La Cappella 14, 61033 Sagrata di Fermignano

An unusual, unexpectedly modern place whose owners have a special interest in the environment, organic farming and horses. This conversion has given La Locanda the feel of a discreet modern hotel, where perfectly turned sheets lie on perfect beds, as crisp and as clean as new pins. Ask for one of the bigger rooms, preferably with a view. In gentle hills surrounded by ancient, protected oaks and within sight of glorious Urbino, this 185-acre farm produces organic meat, vegetables and wine. Signora Savini, a force to be reckoned with, and daughter Giulia make a professional team and cook delicious meals presented on white porcelain and terracotta; all the breads, pastas and jams are homemade. Water is purified and de-chlorinated, heating is solar, truffles are gathered in autumn from the woods nearby. The riding school has a club house for horsey talk and showers; there are two outdoor arenas, and lessons and hacks. And a good pool. If you arrive at the airport after dark, Giulia kindly meets you to guide you back. *Children over 12 welcome. Minimum stay three nights.*

rooms	6: 5 doubles, 1 twin.
price	€100. Half-board €75 p.p.
meals	Dinner €30, set menu.
closed	Mid November-May.
directions	Exit Fano-Rome motorway at Acqualagna & Piobbico. Head towards Piobbico as far as Pole; right for Castellaro; signed.

	Giulia Savini
tel	+39 0722 330303
fax	+39 0722 330303
email	info@vallenuova.it
web	www.vallenuova.it

B&B

Map 9 Entry 250

Le Querce

loc. Calmugnano, 61020 Frontino

Take a break from Tuscany! The countryside is as captivating as the house; behind soars the Monte Carpegna. The rooms of this delightful, mellow, country-house B&B are in two buildings. White muslin flutters at the shuttered windows of the barn where everything is well-crafted and has a light and airy feel. There's a cosy sitting room with an open fire where you breakfast, and a kitchen where longer-staying guests can make their own meals. Rooms in the Casa Vecchia are bigger, ideal for families holidaying together: a two-room suite with homely kitchen on the first floor; above, three bedrooms and a bathroom. The Blue Room, a sitting/music room with a fireplace dated 1580, is full of lovely things acquired by Federica. If organic dinner is as delicious as organic breakfast, eat in. (Music and dancing may follow.) Alternatively, the local restaurant is a short, winding drive. A great place for families: resident cats and children, summer activities, a big open lawn and no fences to break the view... stroll out onto the footpath, through the meadows, to Frontius for an idyllic half-hour walk.

rooms	6 + 2: 6 doubles (with kitchen for groups). 2 apartments: 1 for 4-5, 1 for 6-8.
price	€62-€72. Apartments €124-€186.
meals	Dinner €15-€25. Restaurant nearby.
closed	Rarely.
directions	From Rome-Umbria exit A14 at Orte, E17 to S. Giustino; for Bocca Trabaria to S. Angelo in Vado; for Piandimeleto. Thro' Piandimeleto; 10km; ignore left to Frontino; 3km on, then signed left.

Antonio Rosati & Federica Crocetta

tel	+39 0722 71370
email	lequerce32@hotmail.com
web	www.locandalequerce.com

B&B & Self-catering

Map 9 Entry 251

Locanda San Rocco
fraz. Collaiello 2, 62020 Gagliole

Decent, honest, without a whiff of pretension, the *locanda* is a summer-only agriturismo. Built in the late 1700s, the building has kept its purity of style: brick walls, exposed beams and expanses of quarry tiles remain delightfully intact. A lift (no stairs) transports you to five pleasing bedrooms (one, less good, downstairs); beds are of wrought iron or handsome wood, the furniture is properly old-fashioned and the walls rustically bare. Bathrooms have baths and are spotless. Heaps of space here: two country-characterful sitting rooms with billiards and piano, and a dining room with white-clothed tables. The 55-hectare estate supplies the guest house with fresh vegetables and fruit, wine, olive oil, cheese and poultry; throughout the summer, a Palestinian chef cooks superbly. Amazing views not from the house but nearby; the countryside is lusher than Tuscany's and the area less well-trodden. There are mountain bikes for exploring, riding nearby and great opera at Macerata in August and July. Delicious food, lively hosts, comfortable B&B. *Minimum stay two nights.*

rooms	6 doubles.
price	€85.
meals	Dinner €26.
closed	Mid-September-June.
directions	From SS361 left 1km after Castelraimondo for S. Severino Marche. In Gagliole signs for Collaiello & Locanda.

Signora Gisla Pirri

tel/fax	+39 0737 642324
mobile	+39 338 8461123
email	locandasanrocco@libero.it

Torre Tenosa
loc. Santa Lucia 13, 62032 Camerino

Hard to believe this is the old watchtower – it's so peaceful now. The wooded hills and pastures of Sibillini National Park end in the snow-tipped southern Appenines; a gentle breeze ruffles the trees and grass. Drink in the stunning view (and a glass of local wine) from the terrace. Inside is open plan, with ruddy terracotta tiles underfoot and solid beams overhead. Downstairs you have a well-equipped kitchen area, a good-sized dining table and a jolly red sofabed. The bedroom is up on the wide open mezzanine. At night, sink into a red-striped, down-filled duvet; in the morning, peer out of a dear little stone-framed window from your bed. A smart, clean shower room and small utility room are up on a further level. Environmentally-sound behind-wall heating keeps everyone snug, the internet keeps you in touch. Karen, Frank and their young family live next door but you feel nicely private here, and have your own drive. Karen runs yoga retreats nearby, and the National Park is ten minutes – hike, bike, ski, or just tuck into delicious local food. Perfect for a couple, or close friends.

rooms	House for 2-4.
price	€475-€550 per week.
meals	Self-catering. Restaurants within 10km.
closed	Never.
directions	From Camerino SE for Sfercia; left after 2km; right-hand bend signed 'Strada Condominiale'; phone Frank from there.

Frank Schmidt

tel	+39 073 7633500
mobile	+39 334 1846842
email	colletenosa@libero.it
web	www.torretenosa.it

Self-catering

Agriturismo Contrada Durano

Contrada Durano, 63020 Smerillo

Spend a few days at this tranquil agriturismo and you'll never want to leave. The hillside farm, built in the late 18th century as a refuge for monks, has been lovingly restored by two generous, delightful and energetic owners: Englishman Jimmy and Italian Concetta. No clutter, no fuss, just tiled floors, white walls, dark furniture. The bedrooms are simple and some are small, but the bar and sitting areas give you masses of space. And if you're after a room with a view – of olive groves, vineyards and perched villages – ask for rooms 1 or 2. There's dinner most evenings: food to make your heart sing – home-grown or local organic ingredients, prosciuttio, pecorino, their own bread and wine. As you feast your eyes from all three dining rooms on distant mountains you may ask yourself, why eat elsewhere? In spring and summer, walk through wild flowers up to the village of Smerillo. And do visit the 'cantina' and stock up with Durano bounty: olives, preserved apricots and beetroot, wines from the Marche region and homemade passata – an Italian summer in a bottle. *Minimum stay two nights.*

rooms	7 doubles.
price	€85. Singles €60.
meals	Dinner with wine €28.
closed	Rarely.
directions	A14 Ancona-Bari exit Porto San Giorgio for Amandola, 38km. 10km after Servigliano, sign on left; house 2km off road.

	Maria Concetta Furnari
tel	+39 0734 786012
fax	+39 0734 79359
email	info@contradadurano.it
web	www.contradadurano.it

Agriturismo

Map 10 Entry 254

Borgo Storico Seghetti Panichi

via San Pancrazio 1, 63031 Castel di Lama

Princess Giulia is passionate about her ancestral home, her garden and her red setters. Her country house started life as a medieval look-out tower and the façade was added in 1742; the gardens were planted in the 19th century by a German botanist. The suites are decorated in rich, comfortable colours and some oriental wallpapers; there are stone floors, metal bedsteads, family antiques. The five apartments lie in San Pancrazio, a sensitively converted farmhouse next to the outdoor pool. These rooms are smaller (though far from cramped) and the décor more contemporary: muted colours, pretty kitchenettes, modern paintings – including a striking blue picture by Giulia's daughter. Take breakfast and dinner in the dining room or, should you prefer the services of a uniformed waiter, dine with delightful Giulia in her own grand dining room. The food – home-grown organic vegetables and fruit, local meat – is excellent. On a clear day, the snow-capped Gran Sasso appears like a mirage – if you don't catch it, think about extending your stay. Shops, bus and train are all walkable: the village lies below.

rooms	5 + 5: 4 suites for 2-3, 1 suite for 2-4. 5 apartments for 2-4.
price	€155-€207.
meals	Dinner with wine €40-€50.
closed	Never.
directions	From A14 exit San Benedetto del Tronto; superstrada for Ascoli Piceno; exit Castel di Lama.

Giulia Panichi Pignatelli

tel	+39 0736 812552
fax	+39 0736 814528
email	info@seghettipanichi.it
web	www.seghettipanichi.it

Azienda Agrituristica - Il Quadrifoglio

strada Licini 22, Colle Marconi, 66100 Chieti

'The Four-Leaved Clover' is an auspicious place. Italians in the know travel miles to be looked after by Anna, who cooks beautifully and knows exactly how to make her guests feel at home. The house is new, traditional and red-tiled, not stylish but appealing, high up on the gently farmed slopes of Chieti, with vast views. It sits on the family farm, detached from the other farm buildings but with chickens still. There are four good bedrooms, cosily decorated with stencils, cane and prints, two with terraces, and a nice little flat with a balcony and a log fire, ideal for a family. Guests share a large sitting/dining area (one dining table), and a balcony. The garden has walled terraces, arbours, wooden gazebo and swing. Anna used to cook for families in the South of France and now does lunches and dinners: no menu, no choice and, sometimes, the animated (Italian!) accompaniment of TV. Beaches are nearby; Sulmona, the jewel of Abruzzo, is a must by train. In fact, come by train direct to Chieti from Pescara Rome. Good value. *Gourmet cookery courses, 100 per day including B&B.*

rooms	4 + 1: 4 doubles. Extra beds for children. 1 apartment for 2.
price	€50. Apartment €70 (€400 p. w.).
meals	Breakfast €4. Lunch or dinner €15, on request.
closed	Rarely.
directions	From A25 exit Chieti; right onto SS5 direction Popoli and Monopello, 1.7km; left for Chieti; 4km, right for Colle Marconi; right onto Strada Licini; right again; 1st drive on right.

Signora Anna Maria D'Orazio

tel	+39 0871 63400
fax	+39 0871 63400
email	info@agriturismoilquadrifoglio.com
web	www.agriturismoilquadrifoglio.com

Agriturismo & Self-catering

Map 13 Entry 256

Casa Leone
24 via degli Archi, S Stefano di Sessanio, 67020

In this stunning, glowing, hilltop village, along a narrow, arched street and up some steps, is the wool merchant's house, its 13th-century honeystone façade enlivened by red and pink geraniums dancing in the breeze. The owners have converted one wing into a self-catering set-up of simple cottage charm: little windows, white-washed walls, terracotta tiles, wooden floors. Bedrooms are spread across the three storeys, with one in the low-ceilinged attic; furniture is unfussy, curtains pretty and flowered and two good bathrooms ease queues. There's a cosy sitting room with cream and blue sofas, a supply of books, games and puzzles for rainy days, and a great view of the Medici tower (and a peep of the valley beyond). The kitchen is a convivial room with solid wood cupboards and a chunky table – you won't mind squishing up a bit if there are lots of you. It's well-stocked with crockery, utensils and appliances, and Anna will make sure the fridge is full of breakfast goodies every day. Glorious in summer; skiing a 40-minute drive. *Special deals for small self-catering groups & short breaks.*

rooms	4 doubles.
price	B&B: €70.
	Self catering: €700–€1,400 per week.
meals	Restaurants 3-minute walk.
closed	B&B October-May.
	Self-catering never.
directions	From L'Aquila SS17 for Popoli/Pescara; 15km; left to S.Stefano; ask in village.

	Wendy Sudbury
tel	+44 (0)207 723 1627
fax	+44 (0)207 723 7077
email	wsudbury.camangroup@btinternet.com
web	www.santo-stefano.org

B&B & Self-catering

Map 13 Entry 257

Cantone della Terra 22
67020 Fontecchio

Bon viveur Alessio is the inspiration behind this environmental project which, after two years, is nearing completion. Off a narrow street, hanging high on the walls of a lovely medieval village, the house's big wooden doors open to guests in 2006. Come not for unbridled luxury but for wholesome simplicity and a sensational location. High up, overseeing the green valley and the wooded hills, the house has glorious views in fine weather and feels cosy when the winds whistle and the snows drift. The tower of this (in parts ramshackle) mid 17th-century house was one of many that controlled the valley; now the building has been nudged into the 21st century and promises solar panels, cork-insulated walls and sustainable heating. In small, simple bedrooms, original floor bricks and oak ceiling timbers remain, while plaster walls have been rendered with a traditional calcium and earth mix. Bedsteads have been welded by local craftsmen and bed covers woven in muted colours. There will be cookery and environmental courses to inspire you and bikes to keep you fit: a special place with an offbeat style.

rooms	6: 4 twins; 2 twins sharing bathroom.
price	€52. Singles €38.
meals	Restaurants nearby.
closed	Opening March 2006.
directions	From Rome, A24 to l'Aquila Est; SS17 to Pescara/Popoli; exit at fork with SS261 for San Demetrio/ Molina; Fontecchio 15km. Call mobile 30 mins before arrival: meet in Piazza del Popolo, in front of Bar La Fontana.

	Alessio di Giulio
tel	+39 0862 85441
mobile	+39 328 0617948
email	info@ilexitaly.com
web	www.ilexitaly.com

B&B

Map 13 Entry 258

Villa La Ruota Bed & Breakfast
Colle Massarello 3, 67032 Pescasseroli

The floors are so beautifully polished they squeak. Elegant Adele, welcoming, unflappable, runs a super-organised B&B – a great place to stay on a walking holiday in the Abruzzo National Park. It's a balconied, shuttered, 60s-built chalet house, surrounded by a large garden and many pines. The sitting room is homely with an open fire and simply decorated bedrooms are comfortable. Doors have blue and red painted frames; basement rooms take an extra bed; two rooms share a balcony. There's a nice big dining room – and a garden terrace – for meals: warm rolls and packeted butters and jams at breakfast; straightforward regional dishes at dinner. Picnics can be arranged. In spite of the romance of early morning cow bells, you are only a mile outside Pescasseroli and far from isolated. You are in the oldest national park in Italy, there are maps in every room and you can book a mountain bike and a guide. Pescasseroli is well set up for skiers too, with a cable car and five lifts. *Easily accessible by bus and train; owner will pick up.*

rooms	6: 1 twin, 1 double, sharing bathroom; 4 doubles.
price	€60-€80. Half-board €47-€57 p.p. Full-board €62-€68 p.p.
meals	€20-€25.
closed	Never.
directions	A24-A25 Rome-Pescara exit Pescina; SS83 for Pescasseroli. On central piazza, follow sign for skiing attractions; at r'bout, 3rd exit; signs for Villa.

	Adele Gentile
tel	+39 0863 910516
fax	+39 0863 910516
email	bnb@villalaruota.it
web	www.villalaruota.it

B&B

Map 13 Entry 259

Dimora del Prete di Belmonte

via Cristo 49, 86079 Venafro

The old palace hides among the cobbled streets of the medieval centre – a gem once you step inside. Venafro, a Roman town, lies in the lovely valley of Monte Santa Croce, ringed by mountains. The first thrill is the enchanting internal garden with its lush banana palms and citrus trees, where a miscellany of Roman artefacts and olive presses lie scattered among tables and chairs. Next, a frescoed interior in an astonishing state of preservation; painted birds, family crests and *grotteschi* adorn the walls of the state rooms and entrance hall. Bedrooms are furnished in simple good taste, one with a big fireplace and a sleigh bed, another with chestnut country furniture, most with views. Shower rooms are small – bar one, which has a bath. Dorothy is a wonderful hostess and has fantastic local knowledge; she and her son are a great team. They also run an organic farm with 1,000 olive trees (many of them over 400 years old), vines, walnut-trees and sheep. An area and a palace rich in content – and relaxed, delicious dinners do full justice to the setting. Breakfasts are as good. *Easy access by train.*

rooms	6: 4 doubles, 1 suite for 4, 1 suite for 3.
price	€110. Singles €95. Suite €150.
meals	Lunch or dinner with wine, €25.
closed	Rarely.
directions	Exit Rome-Naples m'way at S. Vittore for Venafro, Isernia & Campobasso; palace signed from Venafro centre.

	Dorothy Volpe
tel	+39 0865 900159
fax	+39 0865 900159
email	info@dimoradelprete.it
web	www.dimoradelprete.it

B&B

Map 13 Entry 260

Photo www.paulgroom.com

lazio

La Bougainville
via Montecagnolo 50 (ex 44), 00045 Genzano

Rome is 25 miles and yet this renovated farmhouse sits in its vineyards and olive groves with views rolling out in every direction. And it's just a hop, skip and a jump to the Pope's Summer Palace at Castelgandolfo Lake. Diane has lived in Italy for four decades, she's a delightful hostess and her Anglo-Italian touches are everywhere. Airy, light rooms, a sheltered pool lit at night – stretch out your legs and enjoy it all. If you want to venture further then Diane is a walking, talking tourist office. Need a rail ticket to Rome?, she will organise it for you, and even run you to and from the station. The rooms are full of antiques and some ceilings are oak beamed; two bedrooms have a lovely terrace. At night, when the weather's cold, you can draw your chair up to one of the open fires with a book before retiring to your room and snuggling down between crisp, cotton sheets. Two rooms have a walk-in shower, one a bath, the views are to the terrace or the pool and the delicious four-course dinner is traditional Italian. *Minimum stay three nights. Children over five welcome.*

rooms	4: 2 twins/doubles; 2 twins/doubles sharing bath (let to same party only).
price	€80–€90.
meals	Dinner with wine €30.
closed	Rarely.
directions	From Rome SS7 south; at r'bout in Genzano, right down road with oleanders; at junc., right for Lanuvio & pass sign; right fork for Landi; next fork, right into via Mennone; left at x-roads; 1st on right.

Diane Semple-Baldascini

tel/fax	+39 06 9370689
mobile	+39 338 3258997
email	labougainville@hotmail.com
web	www.labougainvillerome.com

B&B

Map 12 Entry 261

Villa Ann

via Mole del Giardino 4, Velletri, 00049 Rome

Gentle, charming Lismay and John, so eager to ensure you go home with good memories, are reason enough to stay here. She is a trained cook so Italian dinners and breakfast jams are delicious; John is a golfing enthusiast and will let you in on all the secrets… and who would guess Italy's oldest golf course was so near? Indeed, the whole family is sports-mad which is why they chose this area: it's perfect for sailors and windsurfers, hand-gliders, hikers and bikers. The modern villa, named after John's mother, sits in its own olive grove and palm tree-studded gardens, with a large fenced pool in the orchard – yours for early-morning or pre-dinner dips. There's a private entrance and a sitting room for guests, and simple, pleasant bedrooms with good comfy beds. Bathrooms have baths – a rare treat – and plenty of towels. Best of all, bedroom French windows open to a large and lovely balcony, full of morning sunshine and views to the hills. Wine-tastings at Frascati are a short drive, and the Rome express train gets you to the city in 20 minutes; your hosts will drive you to and from the station.

rooms	2 twins/doubles sharing bathroom. Whole house available during holidays.
price	€60. €80 sole use of bathroom.
meals	Dinner with wine €15.
closed	Rarely.
directions	Directions on booking.

John & Lismay Garforth-Bles

tel	+39 06 96453398
fax	+39 06 96453398
email	j.garforth@tiscali.it
web	www.villa-ann.com

B&B

Map 12 Entry 262

Hotel San Francesco

via Jacopa de' Settesoli 7, 00153 Rome

You are on the edge of the 'Greenwich Village' of Rome. Trastevere is at its best on a sleepy Sunday morning when the flea market unfurls and the smell of spicy *porchetta* infuses the air. But first, enjoy one of the most generous breakfasts Rome has to offer, served in a long, light room that overlooks a 15th-century cloister complete with friar, garden and hens… Built in 1926 as a training school for missionaries, this young hotel runs on well-oiled wheels thanks to Daniele and his hospitable staff. There's a black and white tiled sitting room with contemporary black armchairs, big white lilies and a piano, and a stylishly furnished roof garden with canvas parasols and views to the Aventine Hill – delightful by day, ravishing by night. Marble stairs lead to carpeted corridors off which feed small, smart, very comfortable bedrooms – lined curtains at double-glazed windows, fabulous bathrooms, garden views at the back. Pop into the Santa Cecilia next door for a peep at Bellini's *Madonna*, stroll to the Forum, cycle along the Tiber. A delightful launch pad for discovering the Eternal City.

rooms	24 doubles.
price	€135–€205.
meals	Restaurants nearby.
closed	Never.
directions	From Termini station, bus 75, 44 or line H. Airport train to Travestere (35 mins).

	Daniele Frontoni
tel	+39 06 5830 0051
fax	+39 06 5833 3413
email	info@hotelsanfrancesco.net
web	www.hotelsanfrancesco.net

Hotel

Map 12 Entry 263

Hotel Lord Byron

via G. de Notaris 5, 00917 Rome

Down a peaceful cobbled street is an unexpected edifice of imposing proportions and immaculately dressed windows. The Lord Byron is shamelessly exclusive, extraordinarily hushed (is this Rome?) and not terribly Italian – but for luxuriousness it cannot be beat. The service is professional, generous, discreet, the sitting room is grand and inviting with huge sofas, big lilies and gilt-framed oils, and the basement dining room sparkles at night. Cocoon yourself in the Art Deco splendour of it all – the food is as good as it gets. Walls are strokeable, colours are bold, the Art Deco décor is in impeccably good taste. In your smallish but delightful double room, pad across a sumptuous wine-red carpet from cocoa velvet chair to cream marble bathroom to vast bed. If you want a view, book the suite on the top floor: it has the roof terrace. The hotel is not bang in the centre, but there's a private shuttle to the swish Via Veneto six days a week and you are on the edge of the 'museum park' of Villa Borghese, Rome's most special green space. Be pampered big time! *Secure parking.*

rooms	32: 23 doubles, 9 suites.
price	€305–€450.
	Suites €550–€950.
meals	Dinner from €50.
closed	Never.
directions	A1 for centre, exit via Saleria; right at Viale Liegi, follow tram tracks & left at end; after Residence Aldrovandi, right at lights onto via Mangili; cont. to Piazza Don Minzoni; via Giuseppe De Notaris; up hill, on left.

Amedeo Ottaviani

tel	+39 06 3220404
fax	+39 06 3220405
email	info@lordbyronhotel.com
web	www.lordbyronhotel.com

Hotel

Map 12 Entry 264

Hotel Modigliani
via della Purificazione 42, 00187 Rome

There's a sense of anticipation the moment you enter the marble hall, with its deep, pale sofas and fresh flowers. Marco's wide smile and infectious enthusiasm reinforce the feeling and a glance round the hotel confirms your pleasure. This is an unusual, delightful place, hidden down a side street just five minutes' walk from the Spanish Steps and Via Veneto. The house belonged to Marco's father, and Marco and Giulia (he a writer, she a musician) have turned it into the perfect small hotel. Marble floors and white walls are a dramatic setting for poster-sized, black-and-white photos, their starkness softened by luxuriant plants. The dining room – it was a bread oven in the 1700s – has vaulted ceilings, whitewashed walls, cherrywood tables and more fabulous photos taken by Marco. Grey and white bedrooms are restful, fresh and elegant; some have balconies and wonderful views, all have small, perfect bathrooms. The whole place has a sweet, stylish air, it's amazingly quiet for the centre of the city and there's a patio scented with jasmine. Marco and Giulia will tell you about Rome's secret corners.

rooms	23: 20 twins/doubles, 2 suites, 1 family suite for 4-6.
price	€150-€195. Suite €208-€340. Family suite €330-€440.
meals	Restaurants nearby.
closed	Rarely.
directions	5-minute taxi from Termini station. 5-minute walk from Spanish Steps.

Giulia & Marco di Tillo

tel	+39 06 42815226/42014864
fax	+39 06 42814791
email	info@hotelmodigliani.com
web	www.hotelmodigliani.com

Hotel

Map 12 Entry 265

Caesar House Residenze Romane

via Cavour 310, 00184 Rome

A calm, comfortable oasis above the Roman din. The Forum can be glimpsed from a bedroom window, elegant cafés, shops and restaurants lie below, and the Colosseum is a five-minute stroll. Charming, stylish Giulia and son Giuseppe live here and run things with the help of sister and Grandma: a family affair. On the second floor of the ancient palazzo, grand reception doors open to a huge, bright, welcoming space. Bedrooms, named after celebrated *italiennes*, have warm red ceramic floors, heavy curtains in maroon or blue, matching sofas and quilted covers, a choice of blankets or duvets, vestibules to keep luggage out of the way and every modern gadget: air con, minibar, internet, safe, satellite TV. The suite also has a kitchenette with a hob. You breakfast in your room – it's big enough – or at the round glass table in Giulia's living room, stylishly dotted with contemporary art. The service here is exemplary – maps, guided tours, airport pick up, babysitting, theatre booking, bike hire. It's thoroughly professional, and, thanks to Giulia, who loves her guests, personal too.

rooms	6: 4 doubles, 1 twin, 1 suite for 4.
price	€180–€230.
meals	Restaurants nearby.
closed	Never.
directions	Metro: line B from Termini station to Cavour, then 5-minute walk.

	Giulia & Simona Barela
tel	+39 06 6792674
fax	+39 06 69781120
email	info@caesarhouse.com
web	www.caesarhouse.com

Hotel

Map 12 Entry 266

Casa Trevi I & II

via in Arcione 98, 00187 Rome

A hop, skip and a jump from Italy's most famous fountain, the Casa Trevi is a treasure. Find yourself in an astonishingly peaceful courtyard, all olive trees, scented oranges and a fountain inhabited by small turtles. Though you're in Rome's most vibrant heart, not a sound penetrates from outside. The apartments are on the ground floor of one of the old buildings and open directly off the courtyard. Interiors are bright, soothing and minimalist in the most beautiful way: white walls and terracotta, glass shelving and concealed lighting, a mix of modern and brocante finds. There are no windows as such but the double glass-paned doors let in plenty of light. Hobs and fridges are provided in the airy, white kitchens, but serious cooking is not catered for (who wants to eat in in Rome?). Shower rooms are gorgeous. On three sides are 17th-century buildings in yellows, ochres and reds; on the fourth, a modern monstrosity. Marta could not be sweeter, and the security – a big plus – is excellent, with a porter and security camera in the main entrance. Good value for central Rome. *Minimum stay four nights.*

rooms	2 apartments: 1 for 2-3, 1 for 4.
price	€130. €160 for 4.
meals	Self-catering.
closed	Rarely.
directions	Directions on booking; no parking in pedestrianised area. 10-minute taxi from Termini station. Metro: Piazza di Spagna.

	Signora Marta Nicolini
tel/fax	+39 06 69787084
mobile	+39 335 6205768
email	info@casatrevi.it
web	www.casatrevi.it

Self-catering

Map 12 Entry 267

Casa Trevi III
via dei Maroniti 7, 00187 Rome

This, too, is five minutes from the Trevi Fountain – most breathtaking by night –
but in a separate street from Casas Trevi I and II. Marta – full of warmth, a busy
bee – has waved her stylish wand again and created a deeply desirable place to
stay. She employed one of the top restoration experts in Rome to make ceiling
beams glow and terracotta floors gleam – and the result? Old Rome meets new.
Up a tiny lift to the third floor and into an open-plan sitting, dining and kitchen
area – black, white, grey, chic, with a polished wooden floor. A discarded shutter
for a frame, an antique door for a bedhead, air con to keep you cool, double
glazing to ensure quiet. The white-raftered twin and double rooms share a
sparkling, 21st-century shower in beige marble. Modigliani prints beautify cream
walls, mirrored doors reflect the light, silk cushions sprinkle the sofa and shutters
are painted dove-grey. Never mind the tourists and the street vendors, Rome lies
at your feet. And you have the unassuming Trattoria della Stampa, where the locals
go, in the very same street. *Minimum stay four nights.*

rooms	1 apartment for 3-4.
price	€130-€155.
meals	Self-catering.
closed	Rarely.
directions	Directions on booking; no parking in pedestrianised area. 10-minute taxi from Termini station. Metro: Piazza di Spagna.

	Signora Marta Nicolini
tel/fax	+39 06 69787084
mobile	+39 335 6205768
email	info@casatrevi.it

Hotel Santa Maria

vicolo del Piede 2, 00153 Rome

All around are cobbled streets, ancient houses and the evening bustle of cafés, bars and tiny shops that is Trastevere. And just behind the lovely Piazza de Santa Maria – whose church bells chime every 15 minutes – is a pair of green iron gates that open to sudden, sweet peace and the fragrance of honeysuckle. On the site of what was a 17th-century convent is this secluded single-storey hotel, its courtyards bright with young orange trees. The layout is a tribute to all those earlier cloisters: rooms open onto covered, brick-pillared terraces that surround a central, gravelled courtyard – and you can sit out here in summer. Authentic materials have been used throughout – Peperino marble for the floors, walnut and chestnut for the ceilings – while the breakfast room has the original terracotta floor. Bedrooms, decorated in soft yellows, have high ceilings and big, floral beds. Stefano runs a courteous staff and you are looked after well. There's no sitting room but a good bar; free internet; free bikes. Stefano is a qualified guide, too, and will organise private tours of the ancient city.

rooms	18: 12 doubles, 2 triples, 3 quadruples, 1 suite for 6.
price	€155–€210. Triple €200–€250. Quadruple €220–€320. Suite €250–€450.
meals	Restaurants nearby.
closed	Never.
directions	10-minute taxi from Termini station.

Stefano Donghi

tel	+39 06 5894626
fax	+39 06 5894815
email	info@hotelsantamaria.info
web	www.htlsantamaria.com

Hotel

Map 12 Entry 269

Hotel Villa San Pio

via Santa Melania 19, 00153 Rome

The Hotel San Pio is pristine. It was a residential villa, one of the many that gives the Aventine hill its air of serene calm and makes an evening stroll up here – past the Church of Santa Sabina to the orange gardens – such a joy. This large hotel congregates around a central space crammed with bougainvillea, camellias, roses and palms. An elegant, verdigris conservatory is where you breakfast, sometimes to the live accompaniment of a minuet or sonata; the new dining room is also conservatory-style, to pull the lovely leafiness in. Bedrooms have pretty painted furniture, brocade bedcovers and frescoed or stencilled walls – all gorgeous. There's much comfort, bathrooms are immaculate, the larger rooms have balconies filled with flowers and views and the family rooms are really special. The conveniences of the modern city hotel are all here – minibar, air conditioning, parking – and Signora Piroli rules the roost. A short walk to the metro whisks you into *centro storico* yet you wake to birdsong and the scent of orange blossom.

rooms	78: 61 doubles, 3 singles, 14 family rooms.
price	€140–€240. Singles €98–€140. Family €170–€270.
meals	Dinner à la carte €45.
closed	Rarely.
directions	5-minute walk from Metro Piramide.

	Signora Roberta Piroli
tel	+39 06 5783214/06 5745174
fax	+39 06 5741112
email	info@aventinohotels.com
web	www.aventinohotels.com

Hotel

Map 12 Entry 270

Casa in Trastevere

vicolo della Penitenza 19, 00165 Rome

If you're feeling independent, and are lucky enough to be planning more than a fleeting trip to Rome, this apartment is a great base, deep in the fascinating old quarter of Trastevere. The area, though residential, has a great buzz at night and the shops, bars and restaurants are a treat to discover. And you're a short walk from St Peter's. Signora Nicolini, once a specialist restorer, has furnished the sunny first-floor flat as if it were her own home. She has kept the original 19th-century brown and black terrazzo floor and has added contemporary touches: a cream sofa, an all-white kitchen, kilims and modern art. You have a big open-plan living/dining room with screened kitchen, a double and a twin bedroom, each with a white bathroom, and an extra sofabed. All is fresh and pristine, and the big bedroom is very inviting with its hand-quilted bedspread. Marta is a delight and does her best to ensure you go home with happy memories. Put your feet up after a long day, read a book... then set off to explore some more of this magical city. *Minimum stay four nights.*

rooms	1 apartment for 2-6.
price	From €130 for 2; from €160 for 4; from €180 for 5-6.
meals	Self-catering.
closed	Rarely.
directions	From Ponte Sisto cross Piazza Trilussa. Right into via della Lungara, right into via dei Riari, right into Vicolo della Penitenza.

Signora Marta Nicolini

tel	+39 06 69924722
fax	+39 06 69787084
email	info@casaintrastevere.it
web	www.casaintrastevere.it

Self-catering

Map 12 Entry 271

Hotel Fontana

Piazza di Trevi 96, 00187 Rome

Near chic shops, the Spanish Steps, Piazza di Spagna, Piazza Navona, the Panteon, the Colosseum, and overlooking the most fabled fountain in the world. With the help of a small staff Elisabetta runs this romantic, quirky hotel with a smile. The 14th-century convent has an unassuming front door and the lovely large floor tiles remain. Simple windows are shuttered; in the day, when guests are out, it is a sweet retreat in a pulsating city. Updated bedrooms are cosy but simple, with pale wooden floors, whitewashed walls, cream linen drapes. More traditional rooms have classic colours, flowers in silver bowls, curtains falling to the floor. Bathrooms are tiny, bedrooms small; the quietest rooms, away from the fountain, are at the rear. (The latter have air con – a plus in summer.) On the fifth floor is the dining room – a special place for breakfast, cocktails and afternoon tea. Round tables are dressed in white and topped with flowers, cushioned bench seats grace one wall and you may have a table that overlooks the baroque glories below. Breakfast on the terrace is best – there everyone gets the view.

rooms	25: 18 doubles, 3 twins, 3 singles.
price	€180-€260.
	Singles €180.
meals	Restaurants nearby.
closed	Never.
directions	Metro: line A to Barbernini.
	Private parking 10-minute walk.

	Signora Elena Daneo
tel	+39 06 6786113
fax	+39 06 6790024
email	info@hotelfontana-trevi.com
web	www.hotelfontana-trevi.com

Hotel

Map 12 Entry 272

Hotel Villa del Parco

via Nomentana 110, 00161 Rome

The frenzy of Rome can wear down even the most enthusiastic of explorers, so here is a dignified place to which you can retreat: a 19th-century villa in a residential area, surrounded by shrubs and trees. Inside the mood is relaxed, charming and friendly – the Bernardinis are quietly proud of the hotel that has been in the family for over 40 years. Good-sized bedrooms – the quietest at the back – are cosy and fresh, with colourwashed walls and wrought-iron beds. All have good lighting, crisp cotton, double glazing and carpets (unusual so far south). Shower rooms are tiled from top to toe – beautifully. The remnants of frescoes on the stairs are a comforting reminder of Italy's past, though the house is fin de siècle in spirit. A pretty terrace with white-painted, wrought-iron tables and big parasols is the setting for summer breakfasts; the bread basket is full of delights and the cappuccino delicious. There are a vaulted dining room and a pretty reading room, too. Delightful staff provide umbrellas for rainy days – and will help you negotiate the buses into town. *Special weekend rates.*

rooms	30: 14 doubles, 11 singles, 5 triples.
price	€125–€165.
meals	Restaurants 200m. Snack service available.
closed	Never.
directions	From Termini station right into via XX Settembre; past Piazza di Porta Pia into via Nomentana. Bus: in square in front of station, no 36 or 84; 2nd stop after Villa Torlonia.

	Signora Alessandro Bernardini
tel	+39 06 44237773
fax	+39 06 44237572
email	info@hotelvilladelparco.it
web	www.hotelvilladelparco.it

Hotel

 Map 12 Entry 273

Casa Plazzi

via Olivetello 23, 00069 Trevignano Romano

The ever-sociable Gianni gives you free run of the house. The building is modern, set on a terraced olive grove high up above the Lago di Bracciano. Bedrooms are comfortable, some with lake views, and are individual: Margherita's and Mimma's gently floral with matching bedcovers and drapes, Marco's with a plain, wrought-iron bed. The suite is swisher, with a CD player, a bathroom of Peperino marble, a jacuzzi and a rooftop terrace. There are two sitting rooms, one with a fireplace and a grand piano, and a kitchen sometimes open for cookery lessons. The terraces and the pool have fabulous lake views. Like any good host, Gianni gets the measure of your needs and provides accordingly; his staff too are helpful. Gianni will cook for you if there are sufficient takers, so you book in advance. Alternatively you can cook dinner yourself under your host's guidance, and he'll help you scour the local market for the best buys. The village is a short walk. *Unsuitable for young children. Ask about cookery classes. .*

rooms	7: 4 doubles, 1 single, 1 suite for 2, 1 triple.
price	€100. Singles €50-€65. Suite €140. Triple €120.
meals	Restaurant 1km.
closed	Rarely.
directions	Main road west through Trevignano Romano; before IP service station, right into Strada Olivetello (steep with sharp bends); Plazzi almost at end of road, on left.

	Signor Gianni Plazzi
tel	+39 06 9997597
fax	+39 06 99910196
email	casaplazzi@tin.it
web	www.casaplazzi.com

B&B

Map 12 Entry 274

Villa Monte Ripone
via Civitellese 2, 00060 Nazzano

Slip through glass doors into a cool, welcoming space of fresh flowers, comfy sofas and richly tiled floors. This handsome country house, with its golden colours and olive green shutters, was Anna's family home. The open-plan, ground floor – all vaulted ceilings, polished tiles and beautiful antiques – includes an elegant dining room and comfortable sitting room. Upstairs is a maze of unexpected spaces, little steps up and steps down. Airy, boldly-coloured bedrooms are a mix of much-loved antiques and modern functional furnishings. Some are grander than others but all share dreamy views over fields and the family's olive groves and fruit trees. The views from the pool, hidden below the house, are equally enchanting. There are walks directly from the house and peaceful shady spots in the garden. Eat out in Nazzano (a five-minute drive) or here: it's regional cooking with organic veg from the garden. Anna, Renzo and their two children live next door and the atmosphere is family-friendly and easy. *Minimum stay three nights.*

rooms	5: 2 doubles, 1 twins/doubles, 1 family room for 4, 1 suite.
price	€80–€90. Family €120. Whole house on request.
meals	Dinner with wine €25. On request.
closed	November–March.
directions	A1 Roma-Firenze exit Ponzano Sorrate for Nazzanno; 2km after Ponzano Romano right fork for Rome; ignore turning to Nazzano; on left, supermarket, on right, via Civitellese; 200m on right, signed.

	Anna Clarissa Benzoni
tel	+39 0765 332543
email	monteripone@virgilio.it
web	www.abmonteripone.it

La Chiocciola

Seripola, 01028 Orte

Perhaps the name has something to do with the pace of life here. 'Chiocciola' means 'snail' and certainly this is an unhurried place. Maria Cristina and Roberto have turned a 15th-century stone farmhouse and outbuildings in the Tevere valley into an entrancing small hotel and restaurant. Gardens full of flowering shrubs and peaceful walkways are set in 25 hectares of woods, olive groves and orchards, with a wonderful pool. Indoors, you're welcomed by mellow, gleaming floors and furniture, and the intoxicating smell of beeswax. A beautiful staircase sweeps up to the bedrooms, each of which has its name painted on the door: Mimosa, Coccinella, Ciclamine... They are arresting rooms – big, uncluttered, individual. Terracotta tiles contrast with pale walls and lovely fabrics, family antiques with elegant modern furniture or pieces that Maria Cristina and Roberto have collected on their travels. They're a charming, gentle young couple, proud of what they have created here, and their 'Before and After Renovation' albums show the full extent of that achievement. The food is delicious.

rooms	8: 5 doubles, 2 suites, 1 family room.
price	€100-€130.
meals	Half-board €146-€176.
closed	November-February.
directions	Exit autostrada at Orte for Orte Town. After 3km, right for Amelia. Left for Pennadi Teverina after 300m. After 2.5km, sign for La Chiocciola on left.

	R. & M. Cristina de Fonseca Pimentel
tel	+39 0761 402734
fax	+39 0761 490254
email	info@lachiocciola.net
web	www.lachiocciola.net

Hotel

Map 12 Entry 276

La Meridiana
strada Cimina 17, 01100 Viterbo

Sometimes called Meridiana Strana, on account of the sundial's erroneous habit of recording sun at 11pm, this old farm crouches above the gently sloping hills around Viterbo, facing eastward towards the sea. Its 25 hectares of woodland yield honey and chestnuts – and botanical trails in summer. This is an activity-orientated place, where courses are organised most weekends from June. The nearby stables and riding school are the pride and joy of Salvatore Ranucci, a showjumper himself. His father, Giuseppe (often to be seen about the place sporting the flat cap of the English country gent), knows a lot about family genealogy – if your Italian is up to it! The family love La Meridiana, whose stones and rafters go back some 300 years, and work hard to keep farm and agriturismo ticking over. Self-cater or go B&B. Bedrooms are unmodernised but the best are charming and furnished with old family pieces, bathrooms are new and make simple use of Peperino marble, living rooms are cosy with fireplaces in winter. Fish, walk, mountain-bike ride, play golf; 'photographic trekking' is yet another option here.

rooms	4 apartments for 2-3 & 4-6.
price	B&B: from €50 p.p. Self-catering: €140 for 4.
meals	Restaurants 4km.
closed	Rarely.
directions	From Rome SS2 to Viterbo Sud. In Viterbo, right at 2nd traffic lights to Ronciglione & Lago di Vico. on for 2km, after petrol station, right into country lane, signed.

	Signor Salvatore Ranucci
mobile	+39 347 17 35 066
email	b.b@lameridianastrana.com
web	www.lameridianastrana.com

B&B & Self-catering

Map 12 Entry 277

La Torretta
via G. Mazzini 7, 08400 Casperia

Casperia is a joyful, characterful, car-free maze of steepish streets in the stunning Sabine hills. La Torretta has the dreamiest views from its terrace, and interior spaces that have been beautifully designed by architect Roberto. A huge, ground-floor sitting room with beautiful frescoes around the cornice welcomes you with fireplace, modern sofas and chairs, books, paintings and piano. The upper room, where meals are taken, opens onto that terrace; it is a stunning, vaulted, contemporary space with open stainless-steel kitchen and views through skylights to the church tower and valley. Maureen, warm-hearted and hospitable, is passionate about the region and its food. She arranges cookery courses and will cook on request using whatever is in season – mushrooms, truffles, wild boar... and the finest olive oil. Whitewashed, high-ceilinged bedrooms are charming in their simplicity; beds are made and towels changed daily; bathrooms are a treat. The apartment is a five-minute walk from the house. Don't worry about having to leave your car in the square below the town: Roberto has a buggy for luggage.

rooms	7 + 1: 5 doubles, 1 single, 1 family room for 4. 1 apartment for 4.
price	€90. Singles €75. Family room €150. Apartment €700 per week.
meals	Dinner with wine €35. Restaurants 5-minute walk.
closed	Rarely.
directions	From North, A1, exit Ponzano Soratte towards Poggio Mirteto. Continue on SS657 for 5km to T-junc. Left on SS313 to Cantalupo towards Casperia.

Roberto & Maureen Scheda

tel	+39 0765 63202
fax	+39 0765 63202
email	latorretta@tiscalinet.it
web	www.latorrettabandb.com

B&B & Self-catering

Map 12 Entry 278

Azienda Agrituristica Sant'Ilario sul Farfa

loc. Colle, 02030 Poggio Nativo

Straightforward good value, and an hour from Rome by car. The approach, along a steep, unmade track, is marked by that typically Italian juxtaposition of the electric gates and an olive tree of staggering antiquity. This little farm sits on one of the steeply terraced hills above the river Farfa, with views from its terrace to the Sabine hills. Susanna Serafini is a chatty and creative hostess whose dinners – delivered on request, and using farm produce – are brilliant value. The aspect of the place is rather ranch-like, with bedrooms in two single-storey farm buildings, white with wooden shutters. Bedrooms are snug and wood-panelled with some fine antique bedheads, white walls and showers. The two apartments in the main house have small kitchens for simple meals: great for families. A pleasing tangle of trellises extends across the garden – more farmyard than formal. Take a dip in the pool or the river, spin off on a mountain bike, book onto an olive- or grape-harvesting weekend. There are painting classes for grown-ups, cookery and craft classes for children and little ones love it.

rooms	6 + 2: 2 doubles, 4 family. 2 apartments: 1 for 3, 1 for 5.
price	€76. Half-board €53–€58. Apartment €600–€850 per week.
meals	Dinner & Sunday lunch, with wine, €20. Restaurants 2km.
closed	January.
directions	From SS4 Rome-Rieti exit to Poggio Nativo & Monte S. Maria. Just before Monte S. Maria sharp left onto track signed to Sant'Ilario sul Farfa.

	Signora Susanna Serafini
tel/fax	+39 0765 872410
mobile	+39 380 3572303
email	info@santilariosulfarfa.it
web	www.santilariosulfarfa.it

Agriturismo & Self-catering

Map 12 Entry 279

Villa Sanguigni
Bagnolo di Amatrice, 02012 Rieti

The snow-capped Laga mountains, glimpsed from some windows and seen as full-blown panoramas from others, are a constant reminder of how close you are to some of Italy's most spectacular scenery. Yet, even though this tiny mountain village stands like Horatius at the gates of Umbria, the Marches and the Abruzzi, the temptation to stay indoors at Villa Sanguigni is strong. The delightful owners, the Orlandi Sanguigni, have restored their ancestral home with unusual sensitivity and care. The five good-sized double bedrooms are beautifully furnished with 18th- and 19th-century bedheads, old washstands, chests, rugs and pictures, and the main rooms are even more delightful: the grand *sala* with huge fireplace, rafters and cream sofas; the elegant dining room, reminiscent of a banqueting hall, with long table and lovely pale stone walls. Best of all, perhaps, is the library, which guests are free to use: curl up with a book, or choose from Signor Sanguigni's vast collection of classical music CDs. *Minimum stay two nights.*

rooms	5 doubles.
price	€90. Singles €50.
meals	Restaurants 3km.
closed	Rarely.
directions	Take SS4 (via Salaria) for Ascoli Piceno to Bagnolo. At km129.400 before lake turn for Bagnolo. Villa on right just inside village.

	Anna Maria Orlandi Sanguigni
tel/fax	+39 0746 821075
mobile	+39 360 806141
email	sanguigni1@libero.it
web	www.primitaly.it/bb/villasanguigni

B&B

Villa Il Noce
via Antica 1, 03040 Picinisco

Countrywoman Marialuisa runs joyfully down-to-earth B&B and serves wonderful food; even her *biscotti* are homemade. She is the dynamo behind Il Noce, though her daughter and grandchildren often pop by, and she has help in the kitchen and garden. The chalet was built in the Sixties, is wrapped with balconies potted with herbs, strewn with geraniums, and has an endearingly lived-in feel. Small bedrooms are simple, clean, cluttered and cheerful, all bar one with big balconies and wicker chairs from which to catch the sun. The huge vegetable garden is gloriously ramshackle, the chickens strut, the outhouses guard logs and bicycles, and trees hang with apples, pears, walnuts and figs. Olives and grapes from surrounding farms are pressed here, then used. You eat on the first-floor balcony in summer, to the background trickle of the river and with views that stretch to distant blue hills. To the north are the mountains of the Abbruzzo National Park – walking country. Families have swings and a pool. It's bliss in good weather and pleasant in bad, with lots of comfy sitting spots inside.

rooms	4: 2 doubles; 1 double, 1 twin sharing bathroom.
price	€60-€80. Half-board €47-€57 p.p. Full-board €62-€68 p.p.
meals	Lunch or dinner €20-€25.
closed	Rarely.
directions	A1 Rome-Naples exit at Cassino for Sora; exit Atina Infiriore for Forca d'Acero, turn right for Borgo Castellone.

	Marialuisa Ponzi
tel	+39 0776 66259
fax	+39 0776 66259
email	bnb@villailnoce.com
web	www.villailnoce.com

B&B

Map 13 Entry 281

Photo Hotel Villa San Michele, entry 294

campania

Azienda Mustilli

Piazza Trento 4, 82019 S. Agata dei Goti

Since ancient times, Benevento and the surrounding area has been famous for its wines; here's is a chance to stay on an estate steeped in the art of viticulture. The Mustilli Wine Company, run by Leonardo and Marilì Mustilli, is housed in a 16th-century palace, one wing of which has been restored and converted for guests' use. Right in the centre of a charming village, on a piazza away from the restaurants and bars, from here you can easily explore the upper reaches of Campania. Comfortable bedrooms up under the roof have tiled floors, antique beds, patterned wallpapers, perhaps a roof terrace. There's a new wine bar in the cellar with music on Saturday nights, and the restaurant is huge, popular for weddings. In an atmosphere of rustic, faded charm, local dishes are prepared by Marilì herself, accompanied by their wines. The family knows a lot about the history of the area, and will help you organise a tour of the vineyards or the historic centre of the town. They will also tell you where to buy local produce and ceramics. A characterful and civilised place.

rooms	5: 4 twins, 1 suite for 4.
price	€70. Half-board €55 p.p. Suite €128.
meals	Lunch or dinner €20. Festive lunch €26.
closed	Rarely.
directions	Leave Rome-Napoli Autostrada at Caianello towards Beneveneto & then Incrocio & S. Agata dei Goti. Azienda Mustilli signposted from *centro storico*.

	Leonardo & Marilì Mustilli
tel	+39 0823 717433
fax	+39 0823 717619
email	info@mustilli.com
web	www.mustilli.com

Agriturismo

Map 13 Entry 282

Il Cortile
via Roma 43, 80033 Cicciano

Arriving here is a memorable moment. The black door in the suburban street opens onto a beautiful flagged courtyard rich in jasmine and oranges – ravishing in spring. The villa was built as a summer retreat for Arturo's forebears, and now includes two self-contained homes facing the courtyard with secluded entrances. Guests have their own sitting room / library filled with family antiques, comfortable sofas and pictures, and cool, spacious bedrooms, with pale washed walls, tiled floors and some good antiques; shower rooms are crisply white. Access to one bedroom is through the other, making this absolutely perfect for families with children. Dutch Sijtsken is charming and thoughtful, serves truly delicious food and brings you little vases of flowers from her and Arturo's lushly lovely garden. This *giardinello delle delizie* – a little garden of delights – is surprisingly large. Three tall date palms, two ancient magnolias, beds stuffed with calla lilies, hedges of glistening roses and camellia, paths that meander... choose a deckchair and dream. Special people, special place.

rooms	2: 1 suite for 2-3, 1 suite for 4-5.
price	€60-€70.
meals	Dinner €25.
closed	Rarely.
directions	A1 Rome-Naples towards Bari; exit Nola direction Cimitile/Cicciano; 10-minute drive.

	Arturo & Sijtsken Nucci
tel	+39 081 824 8897
fax	+39 081 824 8897
email	dupon@libero.it

B&B

Map 13 Entry 283

Megaron Rooms & Breakfast
Piazza Dante 89, 80135 Naples

In the fashionable-funky heart of Naples, a stylish, minimalist B&B. The sober frontage of the 1900 palazzo conceals a luxurious interior and the whole feel is one of serenity and calm. A lift glides up to the seventh floor, glass doors reveal a smart 24-hour reception and noble double doors open to each large, light-filled bedroom or suite – each a symphony in cream and black. Imagine muslin curtains at tall windows, big beds, deep sofas which convert into extra beds and antique tables and chairs. Bathrooms are exquisite in grey marble, with every little luxury. The suites have two bedrooms each and two bathrooms; one is on two levels linked by a fine walnut stairway. The breakfast room is similarly splendid. At your feet lies the enchantingly faded grandeur of one of Europe's liveliest cities; the bohemian Piazza Bellini comes alive at night and the street musicians play. Find an outdoor table at the pizzeria of the same name and watch the literati drift by, drop into Cafe Mexico for the best coffee in town. Naples and the Megaron are a treat.

rooms	5 twins/doubles + sofabeds.
price	€125–€169.
meals	Restaurants nearby.
closed	Rarely.
directions	A1 Rome-Naples; follow Tangenziale (ring road) exit Capodimonte; follow 'centro' for Piazza Dante. On right after National Museum.

	Adele Gentile
tel	+39 081 544 6109
fax	+39 081 564 4911
email	bnb@megaron.na.it
web	www.megaron.na.it

B&B

Map 13 Entry 284

Bed & Breakfast Parteno

Lungomare Partenope 1, 80120 Naples

From the Neapolitan courtyard, steps lead to a glass and wrought-iron door and, with luck, Alessandro, who, with Italian charm and impeccable English, settles you in with welcoming words and a cup of tea. (Note, reception may be manned by staff less fluent.) The reception area and bedrooms, some with balcony, are named after flowers; from Petunia to Orchid they spell out 'Parteno'. The décor is charming: wrought-iron mirrors, tables, chairs, beds and chandeliers have been crafted by local artisan Mazzella, the gorgeous hand-painted bathroom tiles by an artist from Vietri sul Mare. The early 20th-century décor has been restored and the raftered ceilings will delight you. Modernity is revealed in air conditioning, small fridges and walk-in showers; with no breakfast room, this feels more like a charming Italian home than a swish hotel. The Parteno is in a lovely part of Naples, almost on the waterfront, near bustling cafés, restaurants and beautiful squares. Choose the room at the front: what a joy to eat breakfast looking out over the bay of Naples and the ferries heading for Sorrento, Capri and Ischia.

rooms	12: 6 doubles + sofabeds.
price	€125-€169. Singles €90-€110.
meals	Restaurants nearby.
closed	Never.
directions	A1 Rome-Naples; follow Tangenziale (ring road) exit Fuorigrotta for centre. Parteno 1st building right off Piazza Vittoria, across from sea.

	Alessandro Ponzi
tel	+39 0812 452095
fax	+39 0812 471303
email	bnb@parteno.it
web	www.parteno.it

B&B

Map 13 Entry 285

La Murena Bed & Breakfast

via Osservatorio 10, 80056 Ercolano

Views from your rooftop terrace stretch to chestnut forests and the Gulf of Naples below. Here, high on the slopes of Vesuvius, the peace is palpable and the air cool and pure. Giovanni and his son live on the ground floor of this modern house, while the guests have the option of self-catering or B&B: the three bedrooms and kitchen are upstairs, and you share Giovanni's living room (with satellite TV) below. There's also a large outside area for children to play in. Breakfast appears each evening in the fridge as if by magic: peaches, apricots and oranges from the garden, cheeses and homemade jams. The larger of the bedrooms has a fancy wrought-iron bed with a golden cover, writing desks are antique with marble tops and floor tiles are patterned blue. The kitchen, too, is prettily tiled, there's blue glassware in a sea-blue cupboard, a white-clothed table, no shortage of mod cons and a good sofa to curl up into. For lovers of archaeological sites the place is a dream: Herculaneum, Pompeii, Torre Annunziata, Boscoreale, Paestum. *Airport pickup. Minimum stay three nights.*

rooms	3 doubles.
price	B&B: €80. Singles €60. Self-catering: €240 (€1,500 per week).
meals	Restaurants nearby.
closed	Rarely.
directions	From autostrada Napoli-Pompei-Salerno exit Torre del Greco; follow signs for Il Vesuvio (via Osservatorio).

	Signor Giovanni Scognamiglio
tel/fax	+39 081 777 9819
mobile	+39 340 2352037

B&B & Self-catering

Map 13 Entry 286

Villa Giusso
via Camaldoli 25, Astapiana, 80069 Vico Equense

This is where Napoleon's brother-in-law spent his last days before his exile from Naples; it has barely changed since. Once a monastery, the villa stands high on a promontory overlooking the Bay of Naples. There are at least five sitting rooms including a wonderful salon (wisely roped-off) full of collapsing 19th-century sofas and silk-covered chairs. Bedrooms have worn 17th-century furnishings and huge paintings; most overlook the ramshackle courtyard where dogs roam. The big gardens and terrace are wonderful for children. You breakfast on figs (in season), fresh ricotta and homemade cakes in the vaulted kitchen, magnificent with fireplace and old Vetri tiles, at tables that seat at least 20. Giovanna has her hands full – she looks after the estate and a young son – but always finds time for guests. She organises Saturday cookery classes, too. Roam the surrounding vineyards and olive groves, drink in the views of the Sorrento coast. It's an adventure to be here and an adventure to arrive – bring a small car with plenty of ground clearance! *Minimum stay two nights.*

rooms	4: 2 doubles, 1 suite for 4; 1 double sharing bathroom.
price	€90–€110.
meals	Dinner €20.
closed	November–Palm Sunday
directions	A3 Napoli-Salerno exit Castellamare di Stabia; signs for Sorrento. At Seiano, after Moon Valley Hotel, left for M. Faito; 4.6km, right after Arola sign, to 'Passeggiate Vicane'; 1.2km.

	Famiglia Giusso Rispoli
tel	+39 081 802 4392
fax	+39 081 403 797
email	astapiana@tin.it
web	www.astapiana.com

B&B

Map 13 Entry 287

Agriturismo La Ginestra

via Tessa 2, Santa Maria del Castello, 80060 Moiano di Vico Equense

There is a fresh, rustic feel to this farmhouse, and its position, 680m above sea level, is incredible. From the flower-rich terraces, sea views stretch in two directions: the Bay of Naples and the Bay of Salerno. The hills behind hold more delights, particularly for serious walkers: the 'Sentieri degli Dei' is a stone's throw away, and some of the paths, especially those down to Positano, are vertiginous and tough. The delightful owners do not speak English but will happily organise guided nature walks; they are also hugely proud of their organic farm status. Bedrooms and shower rooms are charming and mostly a good size, some with their own terrace. Some of the farm's produce – nuts, honey, vegetables, olive oil – is sold from a little cottage; it's also served in the stable restaurant, where delicious Sorrento dishes are served at check-clothed tables to contented Italians. Sunday lunch is a joyous affair. This is quite a tribute to La Ginestra as it is not the most easily accessible of places – but not so inaccessible that the local bus can't make it up the hill. Great value. *Minimum stay three nights*.

rooms	8: 2 doubles, 3 triples, 3 family.
price	Half-board: €80–€90; triples €110–€125; family €145–€165.
meals	Half-board or full-board only. Lunch or dinner €19.
closed	Rarely.
directions	A3 exit Castellamare di Stabia; SS145 coast road to Vico Equense; SS269 to Raffaele Bosco; at Moiano-Ticciano follow road to Santa Maria del Castello.

tel	+39 081 802 3211
fax	+39 081 802 3211
email	info@laginestra.org
web	www.laginestra.org

Agriturismo

Map 13 Entry 288

Le Tore

via Pontone 43, Sant'Agata sui due Golfi, 80064 Massa Lubrense

Vittoria is a vibrant presence and knows almost every inch of this wonderful coastline – its paths, its hill-perched villages, its secret corners. She sells organic olive oil, vinegar, preserves, nuts and lemons on her terraced five hectares. The cocks crow at dawn, distant dogs bark in the early hours and fireflies glimmer at night in the lemon groves. It's rural, the sort of place where you want to get up while there's still dew on the vegetables. The names of the bedrooms reflect their conversion from old farm buildings – Stalla, Fienile, Balcone, and they are simply but solidly furnished. Excellent dinners are served to guests together; breakfast is taken at your own table under the pergola, and may include raspberries, apple tart and fresh fruit juices. You must descend to coast level to buy your postcards, but this is a great spot from which to explore, and to walk – the CAI Alta via di Lattari footpath is nearby. No pool, but Vittoria has arranged a special price with a private swimming club five kilometres away. Le Tore is heaven to return to after a day's sightseeing, with views of the sea.

rooms	6 + 1: 6 doubles. 1 apartment for 5.
price	€82–€110. Half-board €120. Apartment €700–€1,000 per week.
meals	Dinner €22.
closed	November-Palm Sunday (except 26 December-7 January).
directions	A3 Naples-Palermo, exit Castellamare di Stabia for Positano. At x-roads for Positano, by restaurant Teresinella, sign for Sant'Agata; 7km, left on via Pontone; 1km.

Signora Vittoria Brancaccio

tel	+39 081 808 0637
fax	+39 081 533 0819
email	letore@iol.it
web	www.letore.com

B&B & Self-catering

Map 13 Entry 289

Albergo Punta Regina
via Pasitea 224, 84017 Positano

Catch the sea breezes as you sit on the terrace and drink in the views. The superb, rocky coastline disappears into a distant, shimmering haze yet, just across the bay, you can pick out the enchanted island of Li Galli. Beside you, flowers romp over pergolas and tumble out of pots. This typical, white-painted, late-19th-century building – just a short walk from the town centre and approached by steps – clings steeply to the hillside, with terraces and balconies on its upper three floors. Once a pensione, it has been transformed by a local family into a small hotel with big, lovely, spotless rooms and delightful staff. It is a quietly welcoming place, where guests can enjoy B&B, then go off to explore. Some rooms have pretty vaulted ceilings, others have beds set into arched recesses; shower rooms are simple; most have glorious views. Immediately off the cool, attractive reception area is a big shower room, so guests who have checked out but spent the day on the beach below – 300 steps down! – can shower before moving on. And if all those steps get to you, there's the trusty Positano shuttle.

rooms	18: 16 doubles, 2 suites.
price	€170-€265. Singles €150-€195. Suite €340-€380.
meals	Restaurants nearby.
closed	November-March.
directions	Leave coast road, 163, drive right down into Positano. Full directions on booking.

	Benedetta Russo
tel	+39 089 812020
fax	+39 089 8123161
email	info@puntaregina.com
web	www.puntaregina.com

B&B

Map 13 Entry 290

Casa Albertina
via della Tavolezza 3, 84017 Positano

Positano is a honeycomb of houses clinging to the hillside between beach and high coast road – the famous Amalfitana. Among the colourful facades you cannot miss the deep-red Casa Albertina. Mere minutes from the summer-thronged one-way road system, you climb to get here – or catch the bus and walk down! – leaving car and luggage in the able hands of the hotel staff. (There is a charge for this and you need to pre-book, or phone as you approach.) Here is the one-time refuge of the playwright Pirandello – a historic, and unexpectedly peaceful, *casa* with heavenly views. Air-conditioned bedrooms are comfortable and hotel-smart, many with terraces. No bar, no pool, but a wonderful roof deck and a stylish restaurant serving regional food, including the local *azzurro* (blue) fish. The wine list is pricey but long. Lorenzo, whose family owns the hotel, combines impeccable manners and relaxed charm with good English and his staff are absolutely delightful. A charming spot from which to visit Amalfi, Sorrento, Pompeii or Paestum. Or take the boat to Capri.

rooms	20 twins/doubles.
price	€170–€210.
	Half-board €210–€250.
meals	Dinner €20–€30.
closed	Rarely.
directions	From motorway, exit Castellamare di Stabia towards Sorrento & then Positano. Hotel short walk from main street (call staff to pick up car & luggage).

	Lorenzo Cinque
tel	+39 089 875143
fax	+39 089 811540
email	info@casalbertina.it
web	www.casalbertina.it

Hotel

Map 13 Entry 291

Boccaccio B&B

G. Boccaccio 19, 84010 Ravello

No ordinary village house. Slip between the post office and the hardware store, climb the marble staircase, step into the bedrooms and your heart skips a beat. Spread 1,000 feet below, just across the road, is the dizzying curve of the Bay of Salerno. Vineyards, lemon groves, clusters of white houses, all cling to the steep valley sides in defiance of gravity; it's hard to pull yourself away from the window. Fortunately, all rooms share the view. This is a family affair and Bonaventura and his four children have refurbished the house (grandmother had these rooms; the family still live on the upper floor) in an understated modern style that has a welcoming simplicity: beech wood furniture, crisp bed linen, sleek lighting and sunny, hand-painted Vietri floor tiles. All have smart walk-in showers, one room has a private terrace. Two minutes from Ravello's picture-postcard piazza, and the Rufolo and Cimbrone gardens… what a position! Expect some tourist hubbub in season. Your host – who worked 35 years in the film industry – is warm, charming, easy-going. *Discounted parking: book ahead.*

rooms	4 twins/doubles.
price	€75-€95.
meals	Restaurants nearby.
closed	Rarely.
directions	2-min walk from central pedestrian square of Ravello.

Signor Bonaventura Fraulo

tel	+39 089 857194
fax	+39 089 8586279
email	infoboccaccio@hotmail.com

Villa en Rose
via Torretta a Marmorata 22, 84010 Ravello

You really get a feel here of what life must have been like before roads and motorised transport came to these steep hillsides. The position is stunning, halfway between Minori and Ravello on a marked footpath which was once a mule trail. In fact, the only way to get here is on foot, with about 15 minutes' worth of steps down from the closest road. (Getting your provisions up here might be something of a challenge in bad weather!). The open-plan apartment is modern-functional not aesthetic and the bedroom in an alcove off the sitting room, but the views are wonderful and the house is set amid lemon groves. You are miles from the crowds clustering around the coast, and the pool means you don't have to venture down to the beach. The second, much smaller apartment is on the owner's floor above, and has no seating space as such. If you don't feel like cooking, the walk up to the main square in ravishing Ravello would certainly earn you a cappuccino and a brioche. And don't miss the glorious gardens of the Villas Rufolo and Cimbrone. *Minimum stay three nights. Air conditioning extra charge.*

rooms	2 apartments: 1 for 2-4 (+ sofabed), 1 for 2-3.
price	From €104.
meals	Breakfast €6. Restaurants in Ravello.
closed	Rarely.
directions	Details on booking. Valeria will meet you in Ravello.

	Signora Valeria Civale
tel	+39 089 857661
email	valeriacivale@yahoo.it

B&B & Self-catering

Map 13 Entry 293

Hotel Villa San Michele

SS 163 Costiera Amalfitana, 84010 Castiglione di Ravello

Stone steps tumble down – past lemon trees, palms, geraniums, bright bougainvillea, scented jasmine – to the rocks below, and a dip in the deep blue sea. It is a treat to stay in this small, intimate, family-run hotel, with its happy staff and dreamy views. The gardens and bedrooms are terraced, and the dining room and reception are at the top – light, airy, cool. Almost everyone gets a balcony or terrace, everyone gets a view, and at night you are lulled to sleep by the lapping of the sea. Floors are cool and pale-tiled, some in classic Amalfi style, some white, beds have patterned bedspreads, colours are peaceful, shower rooms are clean. It is all charming and unpretentious, from the white plastic tables to the blue stripy deckchairs from which you can gaze on the sea and watch the ferries slip by, heading for Positano or Capri. Delectable aromas waft from a cheerful kitchen where Signora is chef; no need to eat anywhere else. Atrani and Amalfi are walkable – under half a mile; for the weary, a bus stops in front of the hotel. It couldn't be better. *Use of pool at Villa Scapariello nearby.*

rooms	12 doubles.
price	€128-€156.
meals	Dinner €26.
closed	7 November-25 December; 7 January-14 February.
directions	A3 to Salerno exit Vietri sul Mare; follow signs to Amalfi; hotel 1km before Amalfi on left. Discuss parking on booking.

	Nicola Dipino
tel	+39 089 872 237
fax	+39 089 872 237
email	smichele@starnet.it
web	www.hotel-villasanmichele.it

Hotel

Map 13 Entry 294

Azienda Agrituristica Seliano
via Seliano, 84063 Paestum

The *masseria* – the converted farm and stables – is about a mile from Seliano where the warm-hearted, dog-loving Baroness Cecilia Baratta lives. She and her sons keep a 600-strong buffalo herd, the milk from which makes fine butter and mozzarella. The five bedrooms in the old stone barn and pigeon loft are furnished in laid-back country style; more rooms in the villa, where Cecilia cooks for her family and many guests. (Note: it gets pretty busy at times.) You eat – authentically, generously, well – in the dining room, or under pergolas in the scented gardens. There's also a long sitting room to share, charmingly furnished with sofas and country pieces. When he has a spare moment, Ettore is happy to give farm tours; children will enjoy seeing the buffalo up to their necks in a delicious pool of black mud. Cecilia holds cookery courses in the well-equipped kitchen below your rooms, and there's a lovely pool at the main house. The beach is a bike or horse ride away (experienced equestrians only), and the Greek temples at Paestum are not to be missed. *Minimum stay two nights.*

rooms	5 doubles.
price	€70-€115. Half-board €110-€150.
meals	Dinner at sister house Seliano, €20-€25 with wine.
closed	Mid-January-mid-February.
directions	From A3 to Battipaglia, right onto SS18 to Cappacioscalo (20km). Signs to Seliano on right.

	Baroness Cecilia Bellelli Baratta
tel	+39 0828 724544
fax	+39 0828 723634
email	seliano@agriturismoseliano.it
web	www.agriturismoseliano.it

Agriturismo

Map 14 Entry 295

Villa Giacaranda

Cenito, 84071 San Marco di Castellabate

Listen to the gentle rustle of the jacaranda and olive trees as you relax in the vast terraced gardens. The trees were brought by Luisa from Africa and planted here. Having eaten lightly in the day, dine classically on the Franco-Italian cuisine at night. The adorable Luisa loves people as much as she loves food and every year visits Paris to brush up her gastronomic skills. Her 19th-century farmhouse is deeply traditional yet is in part being transformed. Four beautiful, contemporary bedrooms are being created, all grey slate floors, primary colours, internet connections and stunning showers. The existing bedrooms are traditional and more modest, but still have hand-embroidered sheets and their own terraces. The lovely light dining room is a fitting background for the food, and guests of different nationalities are encouraged to mingle – but only if they wish. The next day Luisa delights in showing you how you could recreate the previous evening's dishes. No rush? Wander down to the beach just a kilometre away – and return to Debussy and a deep cream sofa.

rooms	6 doubles.
price	€120.
meals	Dinner, 5 courses, €40.
closed	Rarely.
directions	From St Marco di Castellabate follow signs for Hotel Hermitage. At hotel, left up hill; left track; Villa at end.

Luisa Cavaliere

tel	+39 0974 966130
fax	+39 0974 966800
email	giaca@costacilento.it
web	www.giacaranda.it

B&B

Map 13 Entry 296

La Mola
via Adolfo Cilento 2, 84048 Castellabate

You'll catch your breath at the views as you step onto your balcony. La Mola is perched high up in the old town, way above the tourists who congregate down the hill in Santa Maria. It is a grand old 17th-century palace and incorporates a 12th-century tower – an interesting building in its own right. The balconies are superb and wrap around the house; the terraced garden is lovely; the restaurant a joy. The huge round stone olive press found in the cellars during restoration gives the hotel its name; now it forms the base of a vast, glass-topped drinks table. The sea is everywhere – your room looks onto it, as do the communal sitting areas, and the terrace where you take summer meals. Furnishings are pristine, bedrooms have tiled floors, wrought-iron bedsteads with embroidered linen and the odd antique, bathrooms are charming. La Mola is the ancestral home of Signor Favilla, who spends every summer here with his wife, running the hotel with admirable and amiable efficiency. Away from the seafront resorts the countryside up here is lovely, and Paestum, Agropoli and Velia are a short drive away.

rooms	5 doubles.
price	€114–€124.
	Singles €80.
meals	Dinner with wine €40.
closed	November–March.
directions	From Naples A30 south to Battipaglia, then Agropoli-Castellabate. La Mola is in *centro storico*.

Francesco & Loredana Favilla

tel	+39 0974 967053
fax	+39 0974 967714
email	lamola@lamola-it.com
web	www.lamola-it.com

B&B

Map 14 Entry 297

Il Tufiello

SS 399 Km 6, 83045 Calitri

Sunflowers alternate with wheat and oats in the rolling acres that surround the farm. Tomatoes dry in wicker baskets in the sun, others are bottled with basil; there are chestnuts and honey and vegetables in abundance – all organic. The Zampaglione family have farmed here for generations; wholly committed to ecological principles, they are proud to show guests around the place – and delighted if you help out in the vegetable garden! A white house standing four-square in the fields is the family home, but it is the old, single-storey farmhouse, and Grandfather's House, that have been made over to house guests. The old stable, with its huge fireplace, high rafters, excellent sofas and little library full of local information, serves as a general gathering place. Borrow a bike and set off for a nearby farm to buy fresh ricotta and pecorino, book in for a cookery course, bake bread in a wood oven. This is a fascinating area, where Campania, Basilicata and Puglia meet… don't miss the castle of Frederick II, or Calitri, with its sensational, steeply terraced houses, and its pottery. *Minimum stay two nights.*

rooms	4 + 2: 4 doubles.
	2 apartments: 1 for 2-4, 1 for 4.
price	€60.
	Apartment €80-€120.
meals	Breakfast €3. Packed lunch €6.
	Restaurants 6km.
closed	1 November-Easter; except Christmas.
directions	A16 Naples-Bari exit Lacedonia
	towards Calitri. Il Tufiello midway
	between Bisaccia & Calitri.

	Pierluigi & Nerina Zampaglione
tel	+39 0827 38851
fax	+39 081 5757604
email	info@iltufiello.it
web	www.iltufiello.it

B&B & Self-catering

Map 14 Entry 298

Photo Fototeca ENIT, Vito Arcomano

calabria
basilicata
puglia

La Bouganville

Parco Bouganville, 87028 Praia A Mare

You could spend weeks here, there's so much to do – snorkelling, sailing, swimming in caves. And to see: the town of Praia, the grottos of Dino Island, the Tower of Fiuzzi, waterparks and beaches. Softly-spoken Giovanni will meet you and settle you in; he and his son live in Ercolano (see entry 286) and in August this is their holiday home. On its peaceful residential street you can barely see the house for the flowers and the trees; the garden was established 25 years ago when the house was built. The garden, enclosed and perfect for little ones, is full of scents and shade; a gardener comes several mornings a week and from the terrace is a fantastic view of tiny Dino Island. Inside, rooms are simple and comfortable: cheerful checked bedcovers on plain wooden beds, a gleaming white bathroom and a shower, a well-equipped kitchen and a brightly tiled sitting/dining room with a sofabed, a pine table and chairs and a hearth for winter. You can walk to the resort of Praia a Mare and the beaches are special, with crystal clear water and fine sands. Excellent for families. *Minimum stay one week.*

rooms	Apartment for 4–5.
price	€650–€750 per week.
meals	Restaurants nearby.
closed	August; November–April.
directions	Autostrada Napoli-Salerno exit Lagonegro Nord; continue for Praia A Mare. Ask owner for precise directions.

Signor Giovanni Scognamiglio

tel/fax	+39 081 7779819
mobile	+39 340 2352037

Il Giardino di Iti

Contrada Amica, 87068 Rossano

The farm, peaceful, remote and five minutes from the Ionian sea, has been in the family for three centuries. A massive arched doorway leads to a courtyard and vast enclosed garden (rabbits for the children, pigs, goats and cats too). Meals are served here in summer; at night, the lemon and orange trees glow from little lights tucked into their branches. The large, cool bedrooms have been simply and prettily decorated. Ask for one that opens directly off the courtyard, its big old fireplace (lit in winter) and brick-paved floors intact. Each room has a wall painting of one of the farm's crops, and is correspondingly named: Lemon, Peach, Sunflower, Grape. The bathrooms are old-fashioned but charming, the apartment kitchens basic. Courses are held here on regional cooking; weaving, too. If neither appeals, revel in the atmosphere and the gastronomic delights of the restaurant and atone for the calories later. There's a host of activities on offer in the area, and, of course, heaps of history. Signora is gentle and charming. You'll be sad to leave.

rooms	12 + 2: 10 family rooms; 2 doubles sharing bath. 2 apartments for 3-4.
price	Half-board €40-€55 p.p. Full-board €50-65 p.p.
meals	Half-board or full-board only. Limited self-catering in apartments.
closed	Never.
directions	A3 Salerno-Reggio Calabria exit Sibari. Rossano road (SS106) to Contrada Amica, then towards Paludi.

Baroness Francesca Cherubini

tel	+39 0983 64508
fax	+39 0983 64508
email	info@giardinoiti.it
web	www.giardinoiti.it

B&B & Self-catering

Map 15 Entry 300

Villa Cheta Elite

via Nazionale, 85941 Acquafredda di Maratea

Villa Cheta Elite is a godsend in an area with few really nice hotels. It's a gracious Art Nouveau villa set back from the coast road, with a terraced garden of winding paths, tropical trees, scented plants and exotics in amphora-style pots, and views that keep you rooted to the spot. Relax in the shade of the gardens, or cross the road and plunge down 165 steps for a swim in the clear green waters below. (Then trek up again!). Bedrooms are comfortable, with slightly maiden-auntish furniture, large windows and plenty of light; some are being redecorated in Art Nouveau style. The public rooms, with ornate cornices and mouldings, are more elaborately furnished with antiques, good paintings and a number of portraits of previous occupants. There's also a small sitting room, and a library where you can bone up on the history of the region. Five chefs deliver delicious food, served on the upper terrace in summer with views of the sea and the moon. It's a hugely romantic spot; you may even hear nightingales sing. Stefania and Piero are lovely hosts, their staff courteous and kind.

rooms	20 doubles.
price	€145-€280. Half-board €144-€300.
meals	Lunch or dinner €35-45.
closed	November-Palm Sunday.
directions	From A3 exit Lagonegro-Maratea; 10km, SS104 right to Sapri. In Sapri left onto coast road for Maratea. Villa 9km along coast, above road on left.

	Signora Stefania Aquadro
tel	+39 0973 878 134
fax	+39 0973 878 135
email	info@villacheta.it
web	www.villacheta.it

Hotel

Map 14+15 Entry 301

San Teodoro Nuovo

loc. Marconia, 75020 Marconia di Pisticci

A haven in a green sea of citrus and olive groves. Bougainvillea disguises the lower half of the old rose-tinted mansion; shutters peep from above. Rent an apartment furnished with family antiques in a wing of the house, or choose one of three beautifully converted ones a short stroll away – in the old stables where the restaurant is housed. These rooms are large and light, with marvellous vaulted ceilings, and elegantly and charmingly furnished; they also have small parterre gardens. A whitewashed chapel alongside adds a Mexican feel, and there's a fine pool. You will appreciate the range of Basilicata cuisine here; breakfasts and dinners – candlelit, atmospheric – are unusually good. The Marchesa is delightful and has the perfect manager in Antonio, who's been with the family for years. You are five minutes from the Ionian Sea and white sands, golf courses are nearby and archaeological sites abound. San Teodoro Nuovo runs programmes of varying lengths: follow the routes taken by 18th-century travellers, visit workshops devoted to reproducing classical antiques. *Minimum stay two nights.*

rooms	9 apartments for 2, 4 or 6.
price	€90–€110 with breakfast.
meals	Dinner €20–€25. Self-catering.
closed	Rarely.
directions	From Bari E843 south to exit Palagiano. South to SS106 for Metaponto & Policoro. About 4-5km after Metaponto right at milestone 442km; left at T-junction. On right.

Marchesa Maria Xenia D'Oria

tel	+39 0835 470042
fax	+39 0835 470223
email	info@santeodoronuovo.com
web	www.santeodoronuovo.com

B&B & Self-catering

Map 15 Entry 302

Masseria Agriturismo Il Cardinale

Contrada Capoposto, 70020 Poggiorsini

A hostelry since 1197, it is now a relaxed agriturismo run by Anna – serious, wry, intelligent and kind. Husband Leonardo, a dashing national event rider, introduced her 20 years ago to these deep, wild hills. The main house forms a square with the guest rooms, which resemble a row of stables on each side; the stables housing 30 thoroughbreds lie beyond. The feel is of a slightly shabby South American hacienda: there's a dusty rose garden in the centre and the guest rooms, though spotless, are simple and outdated. The *grande sala* is vast and vaulted and 700 years old, used for dining when large parties are present; the big sitting room is filled with interesting family portraits and numerous pictures of horses, rosettes and silver cups. There's masses of space for children to explore, a good swimming pool, a big fish pond, tennis, billiards and trekking nearby. Come for the atmosphere, the horses, for Anna and her cooking – the food (set menus) is excellent and generous with masses home-produced. If you time it right you could be galloping across the hills with Leonardo at full moon.

rooms	17: 2 doubles, 10 suites, 5 family apartments (without kitchen).
price	€56–€60.
meals	Dinner €30.
closed	Rarely, but book in advance.
directions	From Pioggiorsini, 2km to Il Cardinale. Detailed directions on booking.

	Leonardo & Anna Terribile
tel	+39 080 323 7279
fax	+39 080 323 7279
email	info@ilcardinale.it
web	www.ilcardinale.it

Agriturismo

Map 14+15 Entry 303

Trulli Country House

Contrada Figazzano 3, 72014 Cisternino

More ultra-fashionable trulli towers in Puglia. But wait till you get inside. This is a rare and inspired fusion of the rustic and the minimalist, utterly sympathetic to its origins. Bedrooms have polished cement floors and whitewashed walls, distressed cupboards, sweet raffia, natural hessian. So much imagination has gone into making them special: niches glow with antique lanterns or fresh flowers, a bedstead has been constructed from an olive-tree ladder, spotless shower rooms are arched and curved. Artistic, hospitable Caroline is a mother and photographer whose fine prints dot the house. On cooler days, she serves breakfast at her kitchen table, charmingly fashioned out of two rustic doors. The terrace – shaded by bamboo, scattered with faded blue cushions – is a blissful spot for an evening tipple, the young garden is dotted with olive trees and gay pots of plants, and the small pool, with submerged seating and a whirlpool, is perfect for unwinding. The setting, too, is special: negotiate the external staircase to the rooftop for timeless views of olive groves and the distant Murgia hills. *Minimum stay two nights.*

rooms	5 + 1: 1 double, 1 twin sharing bathroom; 3 doubles. 1 studio for 2.
price	€75-€85. Studio €75-€140.
meals	Dinner with wine €20. Book ahead. Restaurants 2-3km.
closed	Generally closed in winter.
directions	From N379 Bari-Brindisi, exit Ostuni, signs to Cisternino; there, SP134 to Locorotondo; at blue boundary signs of Bari & Brindisi, left into Contrada Figazzano; immed. right; house 2nd on left.

Caroline Groszer

mobile	+39 335 6094647
email	carolinegroszer@tre.it
web	www.trullicountryhouse.com

B&B & Self-catering

Map 16 Entry 304

Acquarossa
C. de Acquarossa 2, 72014 Casalini

It's like a fairytale. You're high in the hills above the quiet Itria valley, looking out over olive groves and orchards. Suddenly the *strada bianca* peters out among scrubby juniper bushes and there, in front of you... an extraordinary cluster of round buildings, their conical roofs topped by stone balls. Acquarossa is a 19th-century trulli settlement and some of the foundations go back 500 years. Timeless and disarming, the restored, white-painted stone buildings stand in courtyards and terraces lavishly planted with clumps of lavender and herbs, surrounded by arches and drystone walls. Their immensely thick walls and pointed roofs make them beautifully cool in summer, and the little rooms have been delightfully, rustically decorated. Delicious country antiques, niches bright with flowers, voile curtains over small, deep windows and arched doorways, flagged floors and wood-burning stoves – an imaginative mix of style and tradition. The bathrooms are simple and pretty; the kitchens tiny and minimalist. And if you have the urge to cook something ambitious, there's an oven in the courtyard.

rooms	6 + 3: 3 doubles. 3 apartments for 4.
price	€90-€102. Apartments €104-€116.
meals	Restaurants 70m.
closed	Rarely.
directions	SS379 for Bari; exit Ostuni-Villanova for Ostuni. At Agip station, left up road to roundabout, signed 'Strada dei Colli'. Left after '200m fine strada' sign. Uphill 1km, left at end of road. Track ends at Acquarossa.

	Luca Montinaro
tel	+39 080 4444093
fax	+39 0831 542280
email	lucamontinaro@libero.it
web	www.acqua-rossa.com

B&B & Self-catering

Map 16 Entry 305

Masseria Il Frantoio
SS 16km 874, 72017 Ostuni

So many ravishing things! An old, white house clear-cut against a blue sky, mysterious gardens, the scent of jasmine and a private beach five kilometres away. Armando and Rosalba spent a year restoring this 17th-century house (built over a sixth-century oil press) after abandoning city life. Inside - sheer delight. A series of beautiful rooms, ranging from the fairy-tale (a froth of lace and toile) to the endearingly simple (madras bedcovers and old desks) and the formal (antique armoires and doughty, gilt-framed ladies)… a gloriously eclectic mix. Dinner is equally marvellous - put your name down. Rosalba specialises in Puglian dishes accompanied by good local wines; Armando rings the courtyard bell at 8.30 and the feast begins, either in the arched dining room or outside in the candlelit courtyard. It will stay in your memory - as will other details: an exterior white stone stairway climbing to a bedroom, an arched doorway swathed in wisteria. And there's a riding school on site, surrounded by olive groves and with a view of the sea. *Minimum stay two nights.*

rooms	8 + 1: 3 doubles, 2 triples, 3 family. 1 apartment for 2-4.
price	€176-€216; €54-€61 for children. Apartment €290-€365.
meals	Dinner €31-€53. Also local restaurants.
closed	Rarely.
directions	From Bari airport superstrada E55 exit for Pezze di Greco towards Ostuni. On SS16, watch for Ostuni until km sign 874. Right into drive.

	Silvana Caramia
tel	+39 0831 330 276
fax	+39 0831 330 276
email	prenota@masseriailfrantoio.it
web	www.masseriailfrantoio.it

B&B & Self-catering

Map 16 Entry 306

Caelia

Contrada S. Anna, Ceglie Messapica

Conical stone houses peculiar to this area – trulli – make a deliciously eccentric contribution to a remote and beautiful landscape; you spot their distinctive round shape and pointed roofs cropping up among the more traditional farm buildings. At Caelia you get to sleep in one. Davide, who works in Milan, has converted part of some old farm dwellings into an apartment for himself and two B&B rooms with a communal kitchen. The exterior, all different levels, is painted dazzling white, the terraces bright with flowers. Both bedrooms are small and vibrant, with well-designed shower rooms. The *trullo* room has narrow ledges running round its curved walls, lit by ceramic lights, and a double bed directly under the cone of the roof. A vase of flowers glows in a deep alcove, a blue stable door leads outside via three stone steps. The arched *lamia*, opening onto the terrace, has a small window set into its thick wall and a painted stone fireplace. The living room is new, with a flagged floor and windows and doors on both sides to allow a through draught. Works by Davide's grandmother add charm.

rooms	2 doubles.
price	€70-€90.
meals	Restaurants 7km.
closed	October-Easter.
directions	Ceglie Messapica to Fedele Grande, after 5km right (sign Padre Pio). After 1km, blue gate on left; house 50m on right.

	Edy Lurani Vincenzi
tel	+39 0831 380977
mobile	+39 335 6649848
email	edylurani@hotmail.com
web	www.caelia.it

Palazzo Bacile di Castiglione

730100 Spongano

The 16th-century palazzo walls dominate Spongano's Piazza Bacile; behind is a secret oasis. The history is interesting, the comfort seductive. The charming *barone* and his English wife offer you a choice of self-catered apartments for couples or families, and B&B accommodation for groups. On the first floor of the palazzo, four rooms open off a vaulted baronial hall – beige check sofas on pale tiles, an open fire, a grand piano – and a series of large terraces. Imagine choice fabrics and new four-posters, pink or marble bathrooms, lofty wardrobes dwarfed by even loftier ceilings, kitchens for serious cooks. Nor have corners been cut in the converted outbuildings at the end of the long garden. Solid olive wood tables, big lamps, framed engravings, oodles of towels, books and CDs; excellent kitchens reveal the owner's passion. The garden is lovely, all orange trees and wisteria, secluded walkways and corners, old limestone pillars and an impressive pool. Beyond: the baroque splendours of Lecce, Gallipoli and Otranto, and the wonderful coastline. *Minimum stay four nights.*

rooms	7 apartments: 2 for 2, 2 for 4, 2 for 6, 1 for 8.
price	€800-€2,464 per week.
meals	Restaurant 500m.
closed	Never.
directions	From Lecce N16, exit Nociglia (after Maglie); to Surano, then Spongano; cross railway into centre; on Piazza Bacile, entrance to left of Farmacia. Please call owners if lost.

	S. & A. Bacile di Castiglione
tel	+39 0832 351131
fax	+39 0836 940363
email	info@palazzobacile.it
web	www.palazzobacile.it

Self-catering

Map 16 Entry 308

La Macchiola
via Congregazione 53/57, 73038 Spongano

The palazzo's courtyard walls drip with creepers and geraniums; in front, across a little road, is a verdant citrus grove worth resting in. This *azienda agricola*, dating from the 17th century, is devoted to the production of organic olive oil (massages available) and the Rizzelli family turn out some of Puglia's finest. Through the massive gates the narrow and unremarkable streets of Spongano village are left behind and you enter, via a Moorish arched portico, a white-gravelled, white-walled courtyard dotted with elegant wrought-iron tables and chairs. Off the creeper-clad inner courtyard, ground-floor apartments have been carefully converted into a series of airy and beautifully furnished rooms. Walls are colourwashed warm yellow and soft blue, sleeping areas are separated by fabric screens, ceilings are lofty and stone vaulted. One apartment for two has a 'dining room' squeezed into an ancient fireplace, bathrooms have pretty mosaic mirrors and most of the kitchenettes are tiny. *Marmellata* and cakes for breakfast, a vast roof terrace, beaches a short drive. *Minimum stay three nights.*

rooms	3 + 5: 2 doubles, 1 family room for 4. 5 apartments for 2, 4 or 6.
price	€70–€100. Apartments €570–€1,500 per week.
meals	Restaurants 10km.
closed	5 November–22 December; 9 January–16 March.
directions	Directions on booking.

	Anna Addario-Chieco
tel	+39 0836 94 50 23
mobile	+39 339 5451307
fax	+39 0832 24 62 55
email	lamacchiola@libero.it
web	www.lamacchiola.it

B&B & Self-catering

Map 16 Entry 309

Puglia

Hotel Palazzo del Corso
corso Roma 145, 73014 Gallipoli

A fascinating maze of narrow streets, hidden entrances, baroque facades and balconies bright with washing and geraniums make up the old part of Gallipoli. Dottor de Donno is a native of the town and loves it all. In 2000, despite also running an organic farm, he decided to buy the 18th-century Palazzo del Corso, near the old quarter, and turn it into a small hotel. It's an elegant, stucco-fronted house close to the waterfront. A small sitting room runs from front to back, with a fine vaulted ceiling, panelling and oriental rugs. The suites, too, have vaulted ceilings and parquet or marble floors. If there's a slight flavour of the gentlemen's club about the brown leather sofas in the sitting rooms, it's redeemed elsewhere by soft colours, pretty bedheads and beautiful linen. Up on the roof is a terrace looking over moored yachts to the harbour and the Gulf of Taranto, and if you don't feel like going down to the private beach, you can bask under big cream cotton umbrellas – or in the hydrotherapy/hydromassage pool. In summer, dinner is served up here by candlelight. *Minimum stay one week, mid-June-mid-Sept.*

rooms	7: 2 doubles, 2 doubles + sofabeds, 3 suites.
price	€155-€205. Suites €180-€310.
meals	Dinner €50. Restaurants nearby.
closed	Rarely.
directions	From Lecce superstrada for Santa Maria di Leuca, exit Gallipoli Centro. Hotel on left side of Corso Roma, a one-way street, parallel to harbour.

	Dottor Pasquale de Donno
tel	+39 0833 264 040
fax	+39 0833 265 052
email	info@hotelpalazzodelcorso.it
web	www.hotelpalazzodelcorso.it

Hotel

Map 16 Entry 310

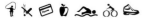

Relais Corte Palmieri

Corte Palmieri 3, 73014 Gallipoli

Brilliant whitewashed walls, square outlines and stone staircases…There's a distinctly Greek flavour to this 17th-century building with its charmingly haphazard levels and unexpected views. It's in the old fishing quarter of Gallipoli, surrounded by narrow, colourful streets where fisher families have lived for generations. Each cool, pretty, newly renovated room is different – some have high arched ceilings, others are lower and beamed. Soft, glazed cotton curtains on iron poles and painted, hand-stencilled furniture give a subdued, country feel – so restful. Most of the rooms open onto their own terrace, where you can breakfast in seclusion among potted palms and flowering shrubs should you choose to eschew the bar. There's a pretty beach nearby, and dinner is a ten-minute walk along the waterfront to the elegant Palazzo del Corso – Dottor Pasquale de Donno's first hotel. Corte Palmieri is his latest venture and very different in style; however, his enthusiastic commitment to ensuring that his guests are comfortable and well looked after is unwavering. *Minimum stay one week August.*

rooms	9 doubles.
price	€100-€180.
meals	Dinner €50 at Hotel Palazzo del Corso.
closed	November-Easter.
directions	From Riviera Colombo south on via Roncella & Corte Palmieri, 3rd street on right.

	Dottor Pasquale de Donno
tel	+39 0833 265 318
fax	+39 0833 265 052
email	info@hotelpalazzodelcorso.it
web	www.hotelpalazzodelcorso.it

B&B

Map 16 Entry 311

sicily

Hotel Quartara

via San Pietro 15, 98050 Panarea, Aeolian Islands

You arrive by boat; waves glitter in the sun, white houses dazzle on the shore. The exterior of this beautiful hotel may be typically Aeolian, but bedrooms are eclectic: Melanesian, Chinese and Indonesian hand-crafted furniture, Sicilian crocheted bedspreads and tiled floors. Four overlook the sea. Bathrooms have soft lighting and a generous supply of lotions and potions, and every room has a terrace. The solarium is a popular late afternoon retreat, wide terraces are equipped with tempting teak loungers, cool shade and endless sea views, and there's a pool to cool off in. Breakfast on figs, pears, honey, prosciutto, yogurt; dine on divine risotti with prawns and saffron. The restaurant is beautiful: arched ceilings, an art collection, crisp white linen decorated with special seashells. This is a genuine family affair: Signor Capelli's garden supplies fragrant basil, lemons and glossy aubergines; attentive Maria and her sisters are on hand; the young children stop by to say hello. The lovely isle of Panarea, a refuge for the rich and famous, has three villages and golf carts for cars.

rooms	13: 10 doubles, 2 singles, 1 triple.
price	€130-€360.
meals	Dinner €30-€40.
closed	November-March.
directions	Pick-up from port of Panarea. By electric shuttle, or on foot; from port, right onto via S. Pietro. Hotel 200m up lane.

	Maria Pia Cappelli
tel	+39 090 983027
fax	+39 090 983621
email	info@quartarahotel.com
web	www.quartarahotel.com

Hotel

Map 18 Entry 312

Hotel Signum

via Scalo 15, Malfa, 98050 Salina, Aeolian Islands

Leave the car and Sicilian bustle behind. Salina isn't as famous as some of her glamorous Aeolian neighbours (though *Il Postino* was filmed here) but is all the more peaceful for that. The friendly, unassuming hotel sits so quietly at the end of a narrow lane you'd hardly guess it was there. Dine on the shaded terracotta terrace with its chunky tile-topped tables, colourful iron and wicker chairs; gaze out over lemon trees to the glistening sea. Traditional dishes and local ingredients are the norm. Then wind along the labyrinth of paths, where plants flow and tumble, to a simple and striking bedroom: cool pale walls, pretty antiques, a wrought-iron bed, good linen; starched lace flutters at the windows. The island architecture is typically low and unobtrusive and Clara and Michele have let the hotel grow organically as they've bought and converted farm buildings. The result is a beautiful, relaxing space where, even at busy times, you feel as if you are one of a handful of guests. Snooze on a shady veranda, take a dip in the infinity pool – that view again – or clamber down the path to a quiet pebbly cove.

rooms	30: 28 doubles, 2 singles.
price	€110-€280.
meals	Dinner à la carte, €30-€40.
closed	1 December-1 March.
directions	By boat or hydrofoil from Naples, Palermo, Messina & Reggio Calabria. If you want to leave your car, there are garages in Milazzo.

	Clara Rametta & Michele Caruso
tel	+39 090 9844222
fax	+39 090 9844102
email	salina@hotelsignum.it
web	www.hotelsignum.it

Hotel

Map 18 Entry 313

L'Appartamento

via Roma 17, Malfa, 98050 Salina, Aeolian Islands

The volcanic archipelago seduces all who visit. Brilliant light, black pebble beaches, clear waters, sea breezes… the islands are named after the Greek god of winds who kept the earth's breezes stuffed in an Aeolian cave. Come to learn the art of *dolce far niente*, the idle life, to sample Malvasia, the sweet golden wine, and *granitas*, iced coffee pureés, the finest in the world. Here in your fisherman's cottage you have all the advantages of the Hotel Signum just up the road – restaurant, bar, pool, Clara and her staff's gentle attention – yet you are private. You have a living room, two smallish bedrooms, a rustic kitchen with pretty tiles, a microwave and a hob. Rent a boat from the local fishermen and explore the coves, seek out the best scuba-diving spot, book the ferry and island hop. On still-steaming Stromboli see the red lava flow, on Alicudi ride a donkey up the hill (what views!). Salina, with its vineyards and lemon groves, is perhaps the most beautiful of all the islands; its restaurants and bars are delectable, its twin peaks extinct. *Minimum stay one week.*

rooms	Cottage for 4.
price	€600-€1,400 per week.
meals	Dinner à la carte, €30-€40 at Signum hotel, 1km.
closed	Rarely.
directions	By boat or hydrofoil from Naples, Palermo, Milazzo, Messina and Reggio Calabria.

	Luca Caruso
tel	+39 090 9844222
fax	+39 090 9844102
email	salina@hotelsignum.it
web	www.hotelsignum.it

Self-catering

Map 18 Entry 314

Chez Jasmine

vicolò dei Nassaiuoli 15, 90133 Palermo

Down by the 27-centuries-old Phœnician port you are enveloped in the ancient history of Palermo and some breathtakingly fine old buildings. Jasmine stands in a 10th-century courtyard in the old Arab town, just reviving from centuries of neglect. Irish-turned-Sicilian (almost), the delightful Mary lives round the corner, leaves fresh breakfast in your super modern kitchen, is involved in conservation, can keep you entertained for hours with her insights into local mores. Her vertical, newly renovated 'doll's house' is adorable. It starts on the first floor (but you can barbecue in the courtyard): a pleasing little all-Italian shower room and the bedroom with its own wicker sofa and writing table; on the second floor, sitting, eating and cooking are cleverly open planned, well-lit and comfortably furnished, marrying northern minimalism and southern colour; finally, an iron spiral leads to a pretty terrace shaded by bamboo blinds, decorated with eager creepers and plants. 'Kalsart', a feast of music, art and many talents, makes summer evenings in La Kalsa so very pleasurable. *Minimum stay three nights.*

rooms	1 chalet for 2-4.
price	€90–€110.
meals	Restaurants on doorstep.
closed	Rarely.
directions	From port road in Palermo go towards La Kalsa; at Piazza Kalsa, right; house off La Chiesa della Pietà.

	Mary Goggin
tel	+39 091 616 4268
mobile	+39 338 6325192
email	info@chezjasmine.biz
web	www.chezjasmine.biz

B&B & Self-catering

Map 18 Entry 315

Palazzo Cannata

vicolo Cannata 5, Palermo

The stone escutcheon over the door justifies the palatial name, the tenderly scruffy yard inside tells today's humbler tale. One of the most exuberantly hospitable men you could hope to meet, Carmelo inhabits the top of the former bishop's palace: you can see Palermo's domes from the terrace. All her treasures are within walking distance – and quite a bit of her traffic. The flat is as full of eclectic interest as Carmelo's captivating mixed-lingo conversation. He teaches mechanics, with deep commitment, and breathes a passion for dance and music. Everywhere are paintings and photographs, bits of furniture and cabinets of mementos, yet there's plenty of space for everything to make sense. One could explore the details for hours, including the madonnas in the high-bedded double room and the painted beds in the twin. A fount of insight into his home town, Carmelo will tell you all, so after the pastry breakfast he has prepared before going to work, go and discover his fascinating city. You will also meet friends Argo, the superb bouncing dog, and Enzo, his sociable master from next door.

rooms	2: 1 double, 1 twin, sharing bathroom.
price	€70.
meals	Wide choice nearby.
closed	Rarely.
directions	West side of Palazzo dei Normanni, a small street off via del Bastione.

	Carmelo Sardegna
tel	+39 091 651 9269
email	sardegnacarmelo@hotmail.com

B&B

Map 18 Entry 316

Green Manors

Borgo Porticato, 98053 Castroreale

Your hosts spotted the remote and dilapidated 1600s manor house years ago; it has been gloriously revived. Bedrooms, some with terraces, are rustic-refined: tiled floors, heavy curtains, Sicilian patchwork, laced linen, family antiques, flowers, tapestries and paintings illuminated by chandeliers and tapered candles in silver candelabra. Bathrooms have huge baths or showers, delicately scented homemade soaps and waffle towels. Chris, Paolo and Pierangela have also been busy establishing their bio-dynamic orchard and you reap the rewards at breakfast – stylish with silver cutlery, antique napkins and linen. The homemade jams are divine – cherry, apricot, ginger; the freshly squeezed juices are worth getting up for. Languid dinners are delicious and served outside behind a curtain of shimmering plants, or by the huge fireplace when the weather is cooler. There are two charming wooden cabins in the olive groves, with outside kitchens and bathrooms; a lush tropical park with peacocks and ponies; occasional summer concerts beneath the mulberry tree. Exceptional. *Minimum stay two nights.*

rooms	10 + 2: 5 doubles, 3 suites, 2 singles. 2 cabins for 2.
price	€100–€180. Cabins €80–€100 (summer only).
meals	Dinner €30. Self-catering in cabins. Restaurants 4km.
closed	Rarely. Cabins available summer only.
directions	Milazzo-Palermo, exit Barcelona; immed. before Terme bridge sharp left. Signed.

	P. & P. Verzera & C. Christiaens
tel	+39 090 9746515
fax	+39 090 9746507
email	info@greenmanors.it
web	www.greenmanors.it

Hotel & Self-catering

Map 18 Entry 317

Hotel Villa Schuler

Piazzetta Bastione, Via Roma, 98039 Taormina

Late in the 19th century, Signor Schuler's great-grandfather travelled by coach from Germany and built his house here, high above the Ionian Sea. He chose the site well – the views of the Bay of Naxos and Mount Etna are spellbinding – and he built on a grand scale. When he died in 1905, Great Grandma decided to let out some rooms and the Villa has been a hotel ever since. Though restored and brought up to date, it still has an old, elegant charm and a cool, quiet atmosphere. Lavish breakfasts are served on an antique buffet with Sicilian lace in the chandeliered breakfast room or out on the terrace. Individual bedrooms vary: older rooms have beautifully tiled floors, antique furniture and stone balconies, more modern ones at the top have new bathrooms and large terraces. All look out to sea or over the garden, which is a delight – vast, sub-tropical and scented with jasmine, and magical when lit up at night. Hidden away behind a stone arch is a delightful, very private little apartment. A path leads through the gardens and out into Taormina's famous, pedestrianized Corso Umberto.

rooms	26 + 1: 22 doubles, 4 triples. 1 garden apartment for 2-4.
price	€118-€184. Apartment €230-€360.
meals	Restaurants 100m (special prices for hotel guests).
closed	December-February.
directions	A18 exit Taormina; 3km; at 'Lumbi' car park into 'Monte Tauro' tunnel; around 'Porta Catania' car park to Piazza S. Antonio; right at P.O. into via Pietro Rizzo; right into via Roma.

	Gerado Schuler
tel	+39 0942 23481
fax	+39 0942 23522
email	schuler@tao.it
web	www.hotelvillaschuler.com

Hotel & Self-catering

Map 18 Entry 318

Hotel Villa Belvedere
via Bagnoli Croci 79, 98039 Taormina

It is aptly named – stunning views sweep down over the botanical gardens to the azure sea. Each front room has a balcony or bougainvillea-draped terrace; tantalizing glimpses of the sea can be caught from every angle. The five rooms on the first floor have beautiful big private terraces (no. 25 is particularly lovely, with arched windows and alcoves), those on the second have pretty little French balconies, and the bright-white 'attic' rooms on the top floor, with smaller terraces, are delightful. The family rooms are at the back with views to the hills. The hotel has been in the family since 1902. Monsieur Pécaut, great-grandson of the founder, is French, his wife Italian, and they are a friendly, helpful and constant presence. There is no restaurant but light lunches of pasta, sandwiches and snacks can be taken by the pool – a cool, delicious oasis shaded by sub-tropical vegetation and dotted with waving, century-old palms. A short walk away is a cable car that takes you down to the sea; medieval Taormina, where Lawrence wrote *Lady Chatterley's Lover*, is enchanting by day and night.

rooms	52: 20 doubles, 23 doubles with terrace, 9 family rooms.
price	€100-€200. Singles €65-€134. Family room €130-€260 for 3.
meals	Lunch €3-€9. Good trattoria 800m.
closed	20 November-10 March.
directions	Signs to town centre, then ringroad. At Hotel Méditerranée, left into via Dionisio. At piazza S. Antonio, via Pietro Rizzo left of chapel, then via Roma. Right into Bagnoli Croci.

	Signor Christian Pécaut
tel	+39 0942 23791
fax	+39 0942 625830
email	info@villabelvedere.it
web	www.villabelvedere.it

Hotel

Map 18 Entry 319

Hotel Villa Ducale

via L da Vinci 60, 98039 Taormina

The ebullient Dottor Quartucci and his family have restored this fine old village house with panache, re-using lovely old terracotta tiles and mixing family antiques with local fabrics and painted wardrobes and chests. Taormina, with its fabulous bays and young clientele, is the chicest resort in Sicily, and rich in archaeological and architectural sites. From the terrace high on the hill, distance lends enchantment to the view. You can see the sweep of five bays and the looming presence of Mount Etna as you breakfast on delicious Sicilian specialities – linger as long as you like. Flowers are the keynote of this romantic little hotel: bunches in every room, pots placed like punctuation marks on the steps, terraces romping with geranium and bougainvillea. Bedrooms, not large, are full of subtle detail, each one with a terrace; fresh shower rooms come with slippers and robes and five of the suites lie across the road. The style is antique-Sicilian; the extras – air conditioning, internet, minibar, satellite TV – entirely modern. The buses don't run very often into Taormina so the shuttle to the private beach is a godsend.

rooms	17: 11 doubles, 6 suites for 2-4.
price	€130-€250.
	Suites €250-€440.
meals	Lunch or dinner €20.
closed	10 January-10 February.
directions	From Taormina centre towards Castelmola. Hotel signed.

	Andrea & Rosaria Quartucci
tel	+39 0942 28153
fax	+39 0942 28710
email	info@villaducale.com
web	www.villaducale.com

Hotel

Map 18 Entry 320

Villa dei Papiri

Holiday Farm & Congress Centre, Contrada Cozzo Pantano, 96100 Fonte Ciane

The river and nature reserve named after Ovid's Ciane are but a few steps from this 19th-century dry-stone Sicilian farm building – an oasis of greenery, elegance and space. And there's more than a passing nod to Greek mythology and its Syracusan heritage inside. Bedrooms – in pretty stone cottages, 200 metres from the main building – are named after Minerva, Zeus, Diana and the other gods, their faces ethereally sculptured into the walls. The main hall (once the stables) is huge and raftered with three fireplaces, couches and divans, oriental rugs, games, books, a music corner… a grand and artistic setting in which to dally over breakfast buffet. The air-conditioned suites are upstairs in split-level loft spaces with a similarly stylish décor: new wrought-iron beds, soft white fabrics, colourful kitchen tiles. Slip into cushioned stone alcoves in the beautiful gardens and relax on wooden recliners under shady palms and Egyptian papyrus (unique in Europe). Or pedal off on a bike (yours to borrow) into the glorious Ciane-Saline nature reserve. Bliss.

rooms	4 + 8: 4 doubles.
	8 self-catering suites for 2-5.
price	€75-€110.
	Suites €90-€220.
meals	Restaurants 1-2km.
closed	Never.
directions	5-minute drive from Siracusa towards Canicattini; signed.

	Attilio Bianchi
tel/fax	+39 0931 721321
mobile	+39 348 5121829
email	info@villadeipapiri.it
web	www.villadeipapiri.it

Agriturismo & Self-catering

Map 18 Entry 321

Hotel Lady Lusya
96100 Feudo Spinagallo

Over the door of this fine Bourbon house is the coat of arms of the family who built it. When Lusya's grandfather acquired it, it was in ruins. Now it has opened as a hotel – an exciting new venture for Lusya and her family. It looks especially lovely lit up at night and the sea views are wonderful (you are a five-minute drive from a beautiful beach). The lovely pool overlooks hills, lemon trees and ancient olive groves; from the roof terrace you can see a cave where the remains of a dwarf mammoth were found. The oldest part of the house is the breakfast room, its 16th-century floor tiles and stone basins used in wine-making intact; breakfasts are very good. Limestone stairs lead to the bedrooms, simply but exquisitely done; their high ceilings give them an air of grandeur, and keep them cool. Other rooms are in a separate building and have terraces. The suites are splendid, with four-posters and rich fabrics; one has a small fresco found during the renovation work. Lusya and her husband are charming, elegant hosts who have lived in the US and speak excellent English. A stunning place.

rooms	17: 9 doubles, 3 triples, 5 suites.
price	€112-€160.
meals	Lunch €20. Dinner €30.
closed	Rarely.
directions	SS114, motorway Siracusa-Gela exit Cassibile; after 2km right, signed.

	Lusya Giardina
tel	+39 0931 710277
fax	+39 0931 710274
email	info@ladylusya.it
web	www.ladylusya.it

Limoneto
via del Platano 3, 96100 Siracuse

Dogs doze in the deep shade of the veranda. In the lemon grove, ladders disappear into trees and occasionally shake as another full basket is lowered down. This is 'rustic simplicity' at its best. The main house is modern and white, with as many openings as it has walls, through which chairs, tables and plants burst out on all sides. Lemon and olive trees (you'll be served homemade *limoncello* after dinner) stop short of the terrace where, not surprisingly, meals are taken throughout the summer. The bedrooms are simple cabin-like arrangements with unapologetically straightforward furniture. Spotless shower rooms, air conditioning, no TV. Those in the main house look out across the garden to a play area; three larger rooms in the pale pink *casa* across the courtyard sleep five, with twin beds on an upper mezzanine level. The lovely and engaging owners, Adelina and husband Alceste, believe in the traditions of the region and are full of ideas for you: visit Noto, Palazzolo and the soft sands of Siracusa. Homemade dinners are good value; tennis, golf and swimming are a short drive. *Discounts for children.*

rooms	10: 4 doubles, 3 triples, 3 family rooms.
price	€70–€90 Singles €55.
meals	Sunday lunch (except July & August) €20. Dinner €20.
closed	November.
directions	From Catania towards Siracusa, when road becomes motorway, take exit for Palazzolo & follow signs for 'Limoneto'.

Signora Adelina Norcia
tel	+39 0931 717352
fax	+39 0931 717728
email	limoneto@tin.it
web	www.limoneto.it

Monteluce Country House

Contradda Vaddeddi - Villa del Tellaro, 96017 Noto

Hiding in deep country just four miles from gorgeous sleepy baroque Noto, Monteluce is a jewel of design and warm-heartedness. Superb architect-designers, Claudio and Imelda have created a discreet wilderness bolthole from the grey urban north and genuinely welcome guests who bring news of the outside world. As carefully as these two houses lie respectfully low among the olive and citrus orchards, their sense of space and style will wrap you gently in colour, texture, excitement (Imelda's paintings, Claudio's gliding shots) and extreme Italian comfort. Brilliant, individually-tiled bathrooms, some fun furniture, superb beds, fine detailing, nothing tacky, and each room with its own garden. If you are self-catering in one of the apartments, your kitchen will be another delight of colour and style, your beds may be on really generous mezzanines. A perfecly complementary couple, they share the caring: Claudio makes a wonderful breakfast (different cake every day) which is brought to your table, inside or out, and Imelda entertains with her fascinating talk of north and south, Sicilian life.

rooms	3 + 2: 1 double, 2 suites with kitchen. 2 apartments: 1 for 3, 1 for 4.
price	€100-€140. Apartments €900-€1,200.
meals	Restaurant 8km.
closed	Rarely.
directions	From Noto take SP19 for Pachino; 5km, SP22 for Vaddeddi; 2km, head for Monteluce.

	Imelda Rubiano
mobile	+39 335 6901871
	+39 347 0890311
email	info@monteluce.com
web	www.monteluce.com

B&B & Self-catering

Map 18 Entry 324

Bed & Breakfast Villa Sara

Contrada Senna, 97014 Ispica

Once the family's summer house, Villa Sara is now a relaxed and friendly place to stay, thanks to gentle Enrico who once worked in city hotels. His parents live nearby; Signora Caruso bakes fabulous cakes and tarts for breakfast, Signor shaped these surroundings, his architect's eye and his attention to detail ensuring the place feels calm, spacious and uncluttered. Cupboards hide flush to the walls, stylish shutters soften the Sicilian light and low round windows are designed to let moonlight play in the corridor. Bedrooms are minimalist with bright white walls and bold bedcovers. Upstairs rooms share a long terrace shaded by a huge carob tree; two rooms interconnect for families. Tiled bathrooms – some huge and with sea views – sparkle and use solar-heated water. A tree was planted to mark the birth of each of the three children and the garden is now luscious and filled with all kinds of tree: banana, orange, lemon, almond… you can idle in their shade, work up a steam on the tennis court, or cool off in the striped pool.

rooms	7: 5 doubles; 2 doubles with separate bathrooms.
price	€60–€90.
meals	Restaurants 1.5-4km.
closed	Rarely.
directions	From Siracusa to Ispica; SP46 Ispica-Pozzallo for Pozzallo, house 4km. Signposted.

Enrico Caruso

tel/fax	+39 0932 956575
mobile	+39 339 3613787
email	villasara2002@yahoo.it
web	www.villasara.it

B&B

Map 18 Entry 325

Hotel Locanda Don Serafino

via XI Febbraio 15, 97100 Ragusa Ibla

The hotel lies in the heart of the stepped city, rich with baroque churches and mansions – a World Heritage Site. The sitting and breakfast room are cool all year round, their rock walls revealing that this part of the 19th-century building was hewn straight from the hillside – and most inviting with their cream couches and bright red rugs. Doubles are small, suites larger… and your bathroom could be as narrow as a corridor or house a bath tub of Olympian proportions. But all bedrooms are delightfully simple, spotless with mod cons, their wooden furniture designed by a local architect, some with balconies, some with direct access from the street. And you'll sleep well: there are deeply comfortable mattresses and a choice of pillows, soft or firm. The staff here are wonderful, thanks to gentle, friendly Guiseppe. Homemade breads and hot chocolate are served for breakfast; for dinner, there's the family's restaurant, a ten-minute walk to the stables of an 18th-century mansion – elegant, intimate and very good. *Flexible breakfasts & check-out.*

rooms	10: 6 doubles, 1 single, 3 suites.
price	€100–€170.
meals	Owner's restaurant 10-minute walk.
closed	Never.
directions	Ragusa-Ibla road. Down Corso S. Mazzini to Piazza della Repubblica; along via della Repubblica; 50m past Chiesa del Purgatorio; right into via XI Febbraio.

	Famiglia La Rosa
tel	+39 0932 220065
fax	+39 0932 663186
email	info@locandadonserafino.it
web	www.locandadonserafino.it

Hotel

Map 18 Entry 326

Agriturismo Gigliotto
C. Da Gigliotto, 94015 S. Michele di Ganzaria

The Savoca family are from Piazza Armerina, famous for its August Palio. They bought the ancient farmhouse 15 years ago – before their children were born – and opened in 2000. They speak English hesitantly but they are delightful hosts. Cypress trees border the property, vineyards and garden surround it, painted Sicilian carts lie in corners, farm labourers come and go. The estate produces, in order of rank: figs, grapes, artichokes, olives, aubergines, tomatoes, peppers, pears, peaches and cherries, many of which you'll taste. Food is important here – look forward to homemade pasta, barbecued roasts, Sicilian cheeses and hams, cakes, honey and homemade jams. The vaulted cellar restaurant caters for 300, much of the produce used is organically grown. The bedrooms, in the characterful old farmhouse or in the outbuildings, have the usual terracotta floors, local wooden furniture and attractive wrought-iron beds, perhaps an antique cot in the corner or a basket of magazines. Shower room are small and spotless. From the pool is a spectacular view, reaching to Mount Etna on fine days.

rooms	15 twins/doubles.
price	€80-€100.
meals	Lunch or dinner €20-€30.
closed	Rarely.
directions	From Piazza Armerina, SS117 to Gela exit Mirabella Imbaccari; 9km from town; first right, follow signs.

	Elio & Laura Savoca
tel/fax	+39 0933 970898
mobile	+39 335 8380324/ 337
email	gigliotto@gigliotto.com
web	www.gigliotto.com

Agriturismo

Map 18 Entry 327

Fattoria Mosè

via M. Pascal 4, 92100 Villaggio Mosé

The town creeps ever up towards the Agnello olive groves but the imposing house still stands proudly on the hill, protecting its private chapel and a blissfully informal family interior. In the main house, high, cool rooms have superb original floor tiles, antiques and family mementos. The B&B room is plainer, has an old-fashioned idiosyncratic bathroom and olive-grove views. Breakfast is in a huge, shutter-shaded dining room or on the terrace, the dumb-waiter laden with homemade jams – lemon, orange, grapefruit, apricot – served on silver. Chiara's family used to come to escape Palermo's summer heat: a blessedly cooling breeze frequently blows. Your hostess, a quietly interesting ex-architect, has converted the stables into six airy modern apartments with high, pine-clad ceilings, contemporary fabrics and good little kitchens, plain white walls, paper lampshades, no pretensions. Most have their own terrace, all spill onto the lovely plant-packed courtyard (with guest barbecue). The Valley of the Temples is a short and hugely worthwhile drive. *Minimum stay two nights.*

rooms	1 + 6: 1 double. 6 apartments for 2, 4 or 6.
price	€80. Apts €434 for 2; €869 for 4; €1,092 for 6. Apt prices per week.
meals	Restaurants short drive.
closed	November-22 December; 7 January-March.
directions	From Agrigento SS115 for Gela-Siracusa. At end of Villaggio Mosè road (past supermarkets, houses) left at sign for Fattoria Mosè; signed.

Chiara Agnello

tel	+39 092 260 6115
fax	+39 092 260 6115
email	fattoriamose@libero.it
web	www.fattoriamose.com

Agriturismo & Self-catering

Map 18 Entry 328

Villa Ravidà
via Roma 173, 92013 Menfi

The unremarkable town of Menfi conceals, behind the pale uniformity of its streets, a rare gem. Still under restoration (scaffolding intact), the four massive columns of its stone portico – approached across a courtyard of patterned paving – are built of that same rose-honey stone as the great neighbouring temples at Selinunte. There is an ethereal elegance to the state rooms with their heavenly frescoed ceilings and their 18th-century furniture; even the light bulbs are old. The stable block, at right angles to the villa and with its own little courtyard, has been converted to make a series of simply furnished bedrooms with high wooden ceilings. The charming and noble Ravidà family, whose summer residence this is, will give you a tour of the farm and provide excellent itineraries. Signora, a fine cook, runs courses throughout the summer in the historic kitchen, or outside, at a huge marble table: carpaccio of tuna, focaccia stuffed with figs, gorgonzola and prosciutto. The food is delicious, the olive oil the finest – the family is a celebrated producer.

rooms	3 twins/doubles.
price	€130. Singles €117.
meals	Lunch or dinner €40, with wine. On request.
closed	5-20 August and December-March.
directions	From Palermo A29 for Mazara del Vallo; exit Castelvetrano; take Agrigento road to Menfi.

	Ing. Nicolo Ravidà
tel	+39 092 571109
fax	+39 092 571180
email	ravida@ravida.it
web	www.ravida.it

B&B

Map 18 Entry 329

Villa Mimosa

La Rocchetta, Selinunte, 91022 Castelvetrano

Not far away are the breathtakingly beautiful Greek temples and ancient city of Selinunte. They overlook the sea, just a short drive along the main road that passes quite close by. The villa was a ruin when Jackie found it crumbling among umbrella pines and olive groves; she has restored and rebuilt it as traditionally as possible. Three of the apartments (you can self-cater or go B&B) stretch along the back of the house and open onto a long, pergola-shaded terrace and a garden of vines, olives and orange trees. In the spring it's ablaze with poppies. The fourth apartment is on the first floor, and has a balcony. Each is open plan, with a shower room and a kitchenette. They are homely, cosy spaces, traditionally furnished with chunky, carved Sicilian armchairs, high antique beds, fine linen and pictures on the walls. If you dine with Jackie, you'll eat out on the terrace on her side of the house – or in her *salotto* if the weather isn't good. She's lived in Sicily for over 25 years and is gentle, delightful and very knowledgeable about the island. Wonderful beaches and nature reserves are close by.

rooms	4 apartments: 3 studio apts for 2-3. 1 apt for 2-3.
price	€60–€80. Studio apartment €300–€350 per week. Apartment €400 per week.
meals	Dinner with wine €30. Restaurants 6km.
closed	Rarely.
directions	From Agrigento SS115 to very end, exit Castelvetrano. At end of slip-road sharp right; 2nd entrance on left.

	Jackie Sirimanne
tel/fax	+39 0924 44583
mobile	+39 338 1387388
email	j.sirimanne@virgilio.it
web	www.aboutsicily.net

B&B & Self-catering

Map 18 Entry 330

Zarbo di Mare

contrada Zarbo di Mare 37, 91010 San Vito Lo Capo

A simple stone-built house, slap on the sea, on a beautiful stretch of coast to the north-west tip of the island, designed to catch the sun. Sun-worshippers can follow the progress of the rays by moving from terrace to terrace through the day; those who seek the shade will be just as happy. A vine-clad courtyard behind the house is a lovely place to take breakfast; you might move to the large shady terrace with a barbecue at the side of the house for lunch… later dine on the front terrace looking out to sea. There are two bedrooms, each with two beds, and an open-plan sitting-room with a pine-and-white kitchen. Below the house are steps down to a private swimming platform, fine for the sprightly; the sea is deep here, and perfect for snorkelling. (Families with small children may prefer to swim from the beach nearby at San Vito, where the water is shallow.) There are some lovely things to see in this part of Sicily; visit the extraordinary Greek temple at Segesta, which stands grave and quiet at the head of the valley as it has done for centuries. *Contact numbers are in Belgium.*

rooms	House for 2-4.
price	€750-€800 per week.
meals	Self-catering.
closed	7 July-20 August.
directions	Approx. 120km from Palermo airport. Motorway to Trapani, exit Castellammare del Golfo. Coast road SS187 to Trapani. San Vito clearly signed. House 4km after village.

	Barbara Yates
tel	+32 25 12 45 26
fax	+32 25 12 45 26
email	barbara.yates@belgacom.net

Self-catering

Map 18 Entry 331

Photo www.paulgroom.com

sardinia

Ca' La Somara

loc. Sarra Balestra, 07020 Arzachena

A short drive to the coast, a far cry from the flesh-pots of Costa Smeralda. Ca' La Somara's white buildings stand out against the peaceful wooded hills and jutting limestone crags of Gallura. And as you'd expect from the name, donkeys feature here – they're one of Laura's passions. She's an ex-architect who gave up city life over a decade ago and has converted the stables with charm and flair; once used to shelter sheep, they are now stylishly rustic. There's a striking, galleried living/dining room, its stone walls decorated with harnesses and lanterns, farm implements, baskets and the odd amphora, while bedrooms are simple and immaculate with whitewashed walls, locally carved beds and shower rooms with hand-painted tiles. Dinner is delicious Mediterranean, served with Sardinian wines. From stylishly cushioned benches in the informal garden and hessian hammocks in the paddock, guests may gaze over the valley and its windswept cork oaks. It's all deliciously restful and undemanding – and there's a sparkling pool. *Relaxation therapy available.*

rooms	8 doubles.
price	€58–€126.
meals	Dinner €17.
closed	Rarely.
directions	From Arzachena towards San Pantaleo. Left at T-junction for S. Pantaleo; signed.

	Alberto & Laura Lagattolla
tel	+39 0789 98969
fax	+39 0789 98969
email	calasomara@tiscali.it
web	www.calasomara.it

Agriturismo

Map 19 Entry 332

Li Licci

loc. Valentino Stazzo, La Gruci, 07023 Calangianus

Twenty years ago this tranquil, lovely place was inaccessible. Deserted for many years after the death of Gianmichele's grandfather, it was rescued by Jane and Gianmichele in 1985. Once they had moved in, the almost nightly entertaining of friends began. English-born Jane is an inspired cook of Sardinian food and the entertaining grew into the opening of a delightful restaurant – with a Michelin mention – that is based on their own, organic produce: pecorino, ricotta, salamis, hams, preserves, liqueur. They have added four simple, white-walled guest bedrooms, each with a basic shower. Jane's approach as a hostess is to look after guests as she would like to be looked after herself, and staying here is like being in the home of a relaxed and hospitable friend. Li Licci has its own wells, producing the most delicious clear water, and a 2,000-year-old olive tree. Breakfast is outside in summer, overlooking the oak woods and hills of Gallura, or by the fire in the converted stables in winter: a delicious start to a day's walking, climbing or sailing… or lazing on the north coast beaches. *Minimum stay two nights.*

rooms	4: 1 double, 2 twins, 1 family for 4.
price	€60–€80. Half-board €65–€75 p.p.
meals	Dinner €30–€35.
closed	Rarely.
directions	Through S. Antonio until roundabout, then towards Olbia. After 3.5km, right at sign; left through gates, house on right.

	Jane & Gianmichele Abeltino
tel	+39 079 665114
fax	+39 079 665029
email	info@lilicci.com
web	www.lilicci.com

B&B

Map 19 Entry 333

Hotel Villa Las Tronas

Lungomare Valencia 1, 07041 Alghero

It could be the setting for an Agatha Christie whodunnit (Hercule Poirot, not Miss Marple): a crenellated, late 19th-century hotel dramatically set on a rocky spit of land jutting into the sea. The outer walls, gate and entry phone give the requisite aloof, cut-off feeling and the atmosphere within is hushed and stately. Originally owned by a Piedmontese count, it was bought by the present owners in the 1950s and they take huge pride in the place. The big reception rooms and bedrooms – formal, ornate, immaculate – have a curiously muted, old-fashioned air. Only the high-ceilinged bathrooms are new – vibrant with modern fittings and green and blue mosaic tiles. On all sides, windows look down at accusatory fingers of rock pointing into the blue Sardinian waters. There's a little lawned garden and a swimming pool poised immediately above the rocks – listen to the waves crashing below as you bathe. Close by is the pretty, interesting town of Alghero and there are fabulous beaches and good restaurants up and down the coast. An imposing place, a matchless setting.

rooms	25: 20 doubles, 5 suites.
price	€210-€350. Suites €410-€520.
meals	Dinner €55.
closed	Never.
directions	Leave Alghero, signs for Bosa/Lungmare. Hotel on right.

tel	+39 079 981818
fax	+39 079 981044
email	info@hvlt.com
web	www.hvlt.com

Hotel

Map 19 Entry 334

Hotel Su Gologone
loc. Su Gologone, 08025 Oliena

Lavender, myrtle and rosemary scent the valley. The dazzling white buildings of Hotel Su Gologone stand among ancient vineyards and olive groves at the foot of the towering Supramonte. The hotel takes its name from a nearby spring and began life in the 1960s as a simple restaurant serving traditional Sardinian dishes – roast suckling pig, wild boar sausages, *dolci sardi* – and the local, potent red wine. It has gradually grown; now the restaurant is famous throughout Europe. Run by the founders' daughter, Giovanna, it employs only local chefs and some of the loveliest waitresses in Italy. (Oliena is as famous for the beauty of its women as for being the home of Gianfranco Zola.) It's an elegant, restrained, magical place in this wilderness region of the island, 30 minutes' drive from the sea. Juniper-beamed bedrooms have intriguing arches and alcoves and make much of local crafts: embroidered cushions, traditional Sardinian fabrics, handmade towels. In the grounds, the enormous pool is fed by cold spring water, and there's an outdoor jacuzzi. *Book in advance May-September.*

rooms	69: 54 twins/doubles, 15 suites.
price	€91–€119. Half-board €105–€145.
meals	Dinner from €40.
closed	Rarely.
directions	From Oliena towards Dorgali. Right at sign for Su Gologone; hotel on right.

tel	+39 0784 287512
fax	+39 0784 287668
email	gologone@tin.it
web	www.sugologone.it

Hotel

Map 19 Entry 335

Glossary

Italian words which appear in our descriptions

affresco	a wall painting (the pigment being applied while the plaster is still wet)	*piazzetta*	little square
		pietra serena	a grey-green type of stone used decoratively in architecture
belvedere	a gazebo or open-sided room, often on the roof	*podere*	farm, estate
borgo	village	*Quattrocento*	fifteenth century
cantina	cellar or winery	*rondini*	swallows
cantucci	almond biscuits	*sala*	hall, room
casa	house	*salone/salotto*	sitting room
casa padronale	manor house	*stemma*	coat-of-arms
casa colonica	farm house	*sala*	hall, room
cascina	originally, a farm	*stuber*	bar (German)
casetta	little house	*tangenziale*	ring-road
centro storico	historic centre, the old part of town	*Vin Santo*	Tuscan sweet wine
		villetta	little villa
Cinquecento	sixteenth century		
digestivo	digestive (usually a drink after dinner)		
dipendenza	annexe		
di lusso	luxury		
duomo	cathedral		
enoteca	a stock of vintage wines		
grotteschi	fanciful ornament in paint or stucco		
limonaia	lemon house		
loggia	gallery open on one or more sides, often with columns		
marmellata	jam		
masseria	originally, a farm		
palazzo	palace/mansion		
pecorino	cheese made from sheep's milk		

Useful vocabulary

Making the booking

Do you speak English?

Parla inglese?

Do you have single/ double/ twin/ triple room available?

Avete una camera singola/ matrimoniale/ doppia/tripla (disponibile)?

For this evening/tomorrow

Per questa sera/domani sera

With private bathroom

Con bagno (privato)

Shower/bathtub

Doccia/vasca

Balcony

Terrazza

Is breakfast included?

La colazione è compresa?

Half-board

Metà pensione

Full-board

Pensione completa

How much does it cost?

Quanto costa?

We will arrive at 6pm

Arriveremo verso le sei

We would like to have dinner

Vorremmo cenare qui

Left/Right

Sinistra/destra

Excuse me

Mi scusi

We are running late.

Siamo in ritardo.

I'm allergic to cats/dogs.

Sono allergica ai gatti/cani.

My wife/ my husband/ my son/ my daughter

Mia moglia/ mio marito/ mio figlio/ mia figlia

Getting there

We're lost

Ci siamo persi

Where is....?

Dov'è....?

Could you show us on the map where we are?

Mi può indicare sulla cartina dove siamo?

We are in Florence

Siamo a Firenze

We will be late

Arriveremo tardi

On Arrival

Hello

*Buon giorno **am-mid-pm***

*Buona sera **mid-pm-evening***

Photo Jill Greetham

May I see a room?
Posso vedere una camera?

I would like to book a room?
Vorrei prenotare una camera

We will stay 3 nights
Ci fermeremo tre notti

Hello! I'm Mr/Mrs Sawday.
Salve! Io sono Signor/ Signora Sawday.

Where can we leave the car?
Dove si lascia la macchina?

Is there a car park/ parking place?
C'è un parcheggio?

Could you help us with our bags?
Potete aiutarci con le valigie?

Could I put these things in your fridge?
Posso lasciare queste cose nel Suo frigorifero?

Could I heat up a baby's bottle?
Posso riscaldare la bottiglia del bambino? (bambina for a baby girl)

Can you put an extra bed in our room?
È' possibile aggiungere un letto nella camera?

While you are there

A light bulb needs replacing
C'è una lampadina fulminata

The room is too cold/hot
La camera è troppo fredda/calda

Do you have a fan?
Ha un ventilatore?

There is no hot water
Non c'è acqua calda

What time is Breakfast/ Lunch/ Dinner?
A che ora c'è la colazione/il pranzo/la cena?

Do you have an extra pillow/towel /blanket?
Avete un altro cuscino/asciugamano/ un'altra coperta?

Can you show us how the AC works?
Come funziona l'aria condizionata?

Do you have a quieter room?
Avete una camera più tranquilla?

Where can I hang these wet clothes?
Dove si può stendere i panni bagnati?

Could we have some soap, please?
Possiamo avere del sapone per favore?

There's no hot water
Non c'è acqua calda

Could you turn the volume down?
Potete abbassare il volume per favore?

Can the children play in the garden?
I bambini possono giocare nel giardino?

Can we leave the children with you?
Possiamo lasciare i bambini con voi?

Can we eat breakfast in our room?
Possiamo fare colazione nella camera?

We need a doctor.
Abbiamo bisogno di un medico.

On Leaving

We would like to pay the bill
Vorremmo pagare il conto

Do you take credit cards?
Accetta la carta di credito?

Are you looking for a new employee by any chance?
Cercate altro personale per caso?

Goodbye!
Arrivederci!

Coffee

Italophile Jill Greetham offers some insights into the intricacies of Italy's coffee culture.

It was the Arabs who invented a way of extracting the drink we know today, and it was in the Islamic countries that the first coffee shops sprang up – the forerunners of today's café bars. Venice takes the credit for the west's first 'coffee shop', sometime between 1640 and 1645. The place, of course, Piazza San Marco. There are several old coffee houses still in existence today, the most famous being the iconic Florian of Venice. Once frequented by sovereigns and courtesans, intellectuals and artists, coffee houses have become fashionable again, and the drink once described as "sweeter far than muscatel wine" has its own vocabulary and culture.

In my search for a good cappuccino, I'm usually successful in the old well-established bars, where a well trained *barista* still follows the traditions.

The cappuccino is the mainstay of Italian coffee culture, and the name is derived from 'hood' – the foam on top of the coffee resembling the hooded robe of the Capuchin friars. A real cappuccino should be one third espresso coffee, one third steamed milk and one third foamed milk, and it must be white at the centre with stronger coffee shades around the rim. The cup is also important – too big is not a good sign – and it must not be boiling hot. (If you want it hot, ask for 'cappuccino caldo.') The Italians do not usually order cappuccino after 11am as it is a breakfast drink, hence the strange looks from waiters when tourists ask for one after a meal! Now Italians are beginning to offer tourists what they think they want – milky coffee.

Espresso is another story – in Italian it means 'quick'. Don't forget, most Italians 'drink and go' and stand at the bar; if you sit down it will cost you more (sometimes double). The International Institute of Coffee Tasters recommends that espresso should always be drunk out of a small cup, with a capacity approximately twice the volume of the drink, allowing the 'cream' on top to convey the aroma to the nose. A well-made espresso gives you a haunting glimpse into the very soul of coffee. The moment of truth. A few sips and then it is gone – but leaving an exquisite aftertaste.

What to order?

Espresso corretto Traditonally combined with grappa, it can also be 'corrected' with cognac, whisky, bitters or sambuca. One rule to be observed: do not drown the espresso with too much liqueur. Purists may argue that it is adding milk or cream that makes it a *corretto*.

Espresso doppio A double espresso. The correct proportions are 60ml of espresso, made the same way but using twice as much ground coffee.

Espresso ristretto Meaning 'restricted' or 'narrow', described by Italians as *poco ma buon* (small but good). This is accomplished by turning the pump off a few seconds early.

Espresso mocha A non-alcoholic verstion of the *corretto*, this is an espresso served over a cup of cocoa, thus accentuating the chocolate flavour.

Espresso lungo Meaning 'lengthened', achieved by leaving the pump on a few seconds longer.

Espresso freddo A refreshing drink on a hot day: a normal espresso with added sugar and ice. Shake well and serve in a tumbler.

Espresso con panna Simply an espresso topped with whipped cream.

Espresso macchiato An espresso 'stained' or 'spotted' with warm or cold milk (according to the client's request).

Latte macchiato A cup of steamed milk, 'stained' or 'spotted' with a spot of espresso.

Mocchaccino A freshly brewed espresso and steamed chocolate-milk, in equal parts. The espresso is added last by pouring it through the foam which leaves the 'mark'.

Caffelatte A shot of espresso with more hot steamed milk than a cappuccino, served with or without foam. If served with foam, make sure that it is no more than 6mm deep. In Italy caffelatte and cappuccino are considered breakfast drinks.

Caffè Americano Either a straight espresso with 30ml water added, or an *espresso doppio* with 60ml water added.

Slow Food & the Italian agriturismo

Wild mushrooms and mascarpone on a bed of delicious pasta *fatto a casa*, delicately sprinkled with fresh local parmesan. Already on my third course and absorbing the mountainous vista of Emiglia-Romagna, I can't help but smile in admiration for my host as he describes how his *agriturismo* has produced or sourced locally all the delicacies on my plate.

Italian *agriturismo*, Remo Giarandoni explains (see entry 79), is the all-important bridge between tourism and the *terra*, offering us a fascinating insight into the traditional artisanal methods of producing good foods and, better still, giving us the opportunity to sample the fruits of their labours, often at a very reasonable price.

Italian cooking is famous for its freshness, tastiness and diversity. The opening of a MacDonalds in the Piazza di Spagna in Rome in 1986 gave rise to the Slow Food movement, Italy's (amiable) protest against the rising trend of fast food that threatens the long and leisurely Italian lunch. Its philosophy has struck a chord across the globe and, with a current membership of 80,000, Slow Food is starting to make a difference. Its snail logo is slowly but surely inching its way into more and more places where food is seasonal, local and, increasingly, organically grown.

Italy has remained very much attached to its traditional rural past. And the Italian *contadino* (man of the country) was celebrated in the 19th-century Italian literature of Manzoni and Verga, thanks to his crucial part in the Risorgimento – the unification of Italy. From the southernmost tip of the country to the borders of Austria you can still find *contadini* – sometimes at the crack of dawn – creating several varieties of salami and salsiccia, crushing tomatoes, picking grapes and tirelessly making all of the delicious cheeses which simply cannot be made in a hurry.

Photo Jill Greetham

It is thanks to Slow Food that the *contadini* of today have found a voice in the public arena. One *agriturismo* owner wrote to us recently to hail the Slow Food movement that has helped save a rare breed of white cow. The Vacca Bianca Modenese produces some of the finest milk, parmesan, ricotta and meat in the country, but, partly due to its relatively low productivity, it was threatened with extinction until Slow Food publicised its heritage and its value. The white cow has been saved and, at Azienda Agrituristica Tizzano (entry 77), you can watch the animals grazing, taste the produce and help boost the rural economy – all at the same time!

Even in the fast-paced Italian cities Slow Food has made an impact: the Città Slow movement has emerged in medieval towns, banishing cars from historic centres and scooters after 10pm. Pedestrian areas are being enlarged and low-energy transport systems and street lighting being introduced... with a bit of luck, we'll all soon be able to see the stars again.

As tourists in Italy, we can contribute to local communities and rural economies in a very simple way. Escape life in the fast lane, relearn the slow.

Kate Shepherd

Photo Fototeca ENIT, Vito Arcomano

FAI – Fondo per L'Ambiente Italiano

(the National Trust for Italy)

Thirty years ago, the thought of their country's great cultural and art heritage falling into disrepair filled Italians with dread...

While famous monuments were in the public eye and cared for by the state, Italy's 'hidden' treasures were under serious threat and deteriorating: uninhabited 13th-century abbeys, privately-owned 15th-centurty castles, 18th-century rococo-frescoed villas, 19th-century newspaper kiosks, Art Deco barber's shops and the smallest theatre in the world, to name but a few.

So, in 1975, taking inspiration from the National Trust in England, Giulia Maria Mozzoni Crespi, Renato Bazzoni, Alberto Predieri and Franco Russoli sprang to the aid of Italy's art heritage. The private, not-for-profit trust FAI was born, providing the legal power to hold property for permanent preservation.

Like the National Trust, FAI acquires sites of historic, artistic and environmental value through donations, bequests or loans for use, restores them, opens them to the public and ensures that everyone can enjoy them.

A descendant of an aristocratic Italian family, unable to cope with the high management costs involved with the upkeep of his or her gothic castle, can therefore approach FAI for help, and if that help is forthcoming, continue to live in a part of their home without bearing all the expenses of taxation, restoration and maintenance.

Members of FAI, "the lifeblood of the Foundation", who contribute to the acquisition and restoration of Italian art heritage, are entitled to free entry into FAI's historic homes, castles, museums and parks and are invited to conventions and on cultural trips with expert guides. From 2006, all members of the National Trust will have free entry to all FAI properties.

FAI is safeguarding the astonishing wealth of heritage loved by all who are enchanched by the rich cultural beauty of Italy. For more information contact: FAI Head office
Viale Coni Zugna 5, I-20144 Milan
tel: +39 02 4676151
fax: +39 02 48193631
info@fondoambiente.it
www.fondoambiente.it

Photo The Villa del Balbianello, Lenno (Como),
© Giorgio Majno, Milan

Special Escapes

A whole week self-catering in Britain with your friends or family is precious, and you dare not get it wrong. To whom do you turn for advice and who on earth do you trust when the web is awash with advice from strangers? We launched Special Escapes to satisfy an obvious need for impartial and trustworthy help – and that is what it provides. The criteria for inclusion are the same as for our books: we have to like the place and the owners. It has, quite simply, to be 'special'. The site, our first online-only publication, is featured on www.thegoodwebguide.com and is growing fast.

www.specialescapes.co.uk

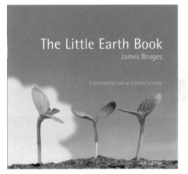

The Little Earth Book

Edition 4, £6.99

By James Bruges

A little book that has proved both hugely popular – and provocative. This new edition has chapters on Islam, Climate Change and The Tyranny of Corporations.

The Little Food Book

Edition 1, £6.99

By Craig Sams, Chairman of the Soil Association

An explosive account of the food we eat today. Never have we been at such risk – from our food. This book will help clarify what's at stake.

The Little Money Book

Edition 1, £6.99

By David Boyle, an associate of the New Economics Foundation

This pithy, wry little guide will tell you where money comes from, what it means, what it's doing to the planet and what we might be able to do about it.

www.fragile-earth.com

Six Days

Celebrating the triumph of creativity over adversity.

An inspiring and heart-rending story of the making of the stained glass 'Creation' window at Chester Cathedral by a woman battling with debilitating Parkinson's disease.

"Within a few seconds, the tears were running down my cheeks. The window was one of the most beautiful things I had ever seen. It is a tour-de force, playing with light like no other window ..."
Anthropologist Hugh Brody

In 1983, Ros Grimshaw, a distinguished designer, artist and creator of stained glass windows, was diagnosed with Parkinson's disease. Refusing to allow her illness to prevent her from working, Ros became even more adept at her craft, and in 2000 won the commission to design and make the 'Creation' Stained Glass Window for Chester Cathedral.

Six Days traces the evolution of the window from the first sketches to its final, glorious completion as a rare and wonderful tribute to Life itself: for each of the six 'days' of Creation recounted in Genesis, there is a scene below that is relevant to the world of today and tomorrow.

Heart-rending extracts from Ros's diary capture the personal struggle involved. Superb photography captures the luminescence of the stunning stained glass, while the story weaves together essays, poems, and moving contributions from Ros's partner, Patrick Costeloe.

Available from Alastair Sawday Publishing £12.99

Order Form

All these books are available in major bookshops or you may order them direct.
Post and packaging are FREE within the UK.

British Hotels, Inns & Other Places	£13.99
Bed & Breakfast for Garden Lovers	£14.99
British Bed & Breakfast	£14.99
Pubs & Inns of England & Wales	£13.99
London	£9.99
French Bed & Breakfast	£15.99
French Hotels, Châteaux & Other Places	£14.99
French Holiday Homes	£12.99
Paris Hotels	£9.99
Ireland	£12.99
Spain	£14.99
Portugal	£10.99
Greece	£11.99
Italy	£14.99
Mountains of Europe	£9.99
India	£10.99
Morocco	£11.99
Turkey	£11.99
The Little Earth Book	£6.99
The Little Food Book	£6.99
The Little Money Book	£6.99
Six Days	£12.99

Please make cheques payable to Alastair Sawday Publishing. Total £ _____

Please send cheques to: Alastair Sawday Publishing, Yanley Lane, Long Ashton,
Bristol BS41 9LR. For credit card orders call 01275 464891
or order directly from our web site www.specialplacestostay.com

Title   First name   Surname

Address

Postcode   Tel

IT4

If you do not wish to receive mail from other like-minded companies, please tick here ☐
If you would prefer not to receive information about special offers on our books, please tick here ☐

Report Form

If you have any comments on entries in this guide, please let us have them. If you have a favourite house, hotel, inn or other new discovery, please let us know about it. You can email info@sawdays.co.uk, too.

Existing entry:

Book title: _____

Entry no: _____ Edition no: _____

Report:

Country: _____

Property name: _____

Address: _____

_____

_____

_____

Tel:

Comments: New recommendation: _____

_____

_____

_____

_____

_____

_____

_____

Your name: _____

Address: _____

_____

_____

Tel:

Please send completed form to ASP, Yanley Lane, Long Ashton, Bristol BS41 9LR or go to www.specialplacestostay.com and click on 'contact'. Thank you.

Booking form

All'attenzione di:
To:

Date:

Egregio Signor, Gentile Signora,

Vorrei fare una prenotazione in nome di:
Please could you make us a reservation in the name of:

Per	*notte/notti*	*Arrivo: giorno*	*mese*	*anno*
For	night(s)	Arriving: day	month	year
		Partenza: giorno	*mese*	*anno*
		Leaving: day	month	year

Si richiede: camera/e sistemazione in:
We would like room/s, arranged as follows:

Doppia/e	*Due letti*
Double bed	Twin beds
Tripla/e	*Singola/e*
Triple	Single
Suite	*Appartamento*
Suite	Apartment

Si richiede anche la cena per . ... persone il ....
We will also be requiring dinner for ...... person on .... (date)

Per cortesia inviarmi una conferma della mia prenotazione al mio indirizzo in fondo pagina.
Please could you send us confirmation of our reservation to the address below.

Nome: Name:

Indirizzo: Address:

Tel No: Email:

Fax No:

Scheda di Prenotazione – Special Places to Stay: Italy

Quick reference indices

Wheelchair
These owners have told us they have facilities for people in wheelchairs. Do confirm what is available when booking.
Piedmont 4 • 5 • 8 • 11
Lombardy 25 • 28
Veneto 41 • 42 • 43 • 44 • 46 • 56 • 66
Friuli-Venezia Giulia 69 • 71
Emilia-Romagna 78 • 83 • 84 • 86
Liguria 95 • 96
Tuscany 110 • 112 • 114 • 122 • 123 • 134 • 142 • 146 • 147 • 148 • 150 • 159 • 172 • 174 • 181 • 187 • 189 • 191 • 200
Umbria 210 • 211 • 214 • 221 • 225 • 227 • 228 • 234 • 239 • 246
Le Marche 248 • 251 • 255
Abruzzo – Molise 256
Lazio 269 • 276 • 277 • 279
Campania 284 • 285 • 289 • 297
Basilicata 302
Puglia 304 • 309
Sicily 312 • 313 • 317 • 320 • 323 • 324 • 325 • 328 • 330

237 • 238 • 239 • 240 • 243 • 246 • 247
Le Marche 248 • 255
Abruzzo - Molise 260
Lazio 274 • 278 • 279
Campania 282 • 283 • 287 • 295
Calabria 300
Basilicata 302
Puglia 305 • 306 • 308 • 309
Sicily 322 • 323 • 325 • 326

No car?
You can stay at these places without a car.
Piedmont 7 • 9 • 11
Valle D'Aosta 12
Lombardy 14 • 17 • 18 • 20 • 21 • 23 • 24 • 25 • 27 • 28
Trentino-Alto Adige 30 • 31 • 32 • 34 • 35
Veneto 37 • 38 • 39 • 41 • 45 • 46 • 50 • 51 • 52 • 53 • 54 • 58 • 60 • 61 • 63 • 65 • 67
Friuli-Venezia Giulia 71 • 72 • 73
Emilia-Romagna 74 • 76 • 77 • 87

Foodies
These places offer tastings of local specialities and/or run cookery courses.
Piedmont 8 • 10 • 11
Trentino-Alto Adige 30 • 32 • 35
Veneto 37 • 38 • 41 • 46 • 63
Friuli-Venezia Giulia 69 • 71 • 73
Emilia-Romagna 74 • 86
Liguria 89 • 90 • 95 • 96 • 98 • 100 • 101 • 102
Tuscany 107 • 109 • 115 • 120 • 124 • 125 • 126 • 129 • 130 • 139 • 142 • 147 • 148 • 151 • 154 • 155 • 157 • 161 • 163 • 165 • 168 • 169 • 170 • 172 • 174 • 178 • 180 • 184 • 185 • 188 • 190 • 191 • 192 • 193 • 200 • 205
Umbria 207 • 210 • 218 • 222 • 225 • 226 • 227 • 229 • 231 • 234 • 236 •

Photo Philippa Rogers

Weddings
These places can organise wedding
receptions.

Mountains
These places are in the mountains.

Photo left Sara Allen
Photo right www.paulgroom.com

Index by town

Index by property name

Index by property name

How to use this book

① Puglia

Trulli Country House
Contrada Figazzano 3, 72014 Cisternino

② More ultra-fashionable trulli towers in Puglia. But wait till you get inside. This is a rare and inspired fusion of the rustic and the minimalist, utterly sympathetic to its origins. Bedrooms have polished cement floors and whitewashed walls, distressed cupboards, sweet raffia, natural hessian. So much imagination has gone into making them special: niches glow with antique lanterns or fresh flowers, a bedstead has been constructed from an olive-tree ladder, spotless shower rooms are arched and curved. Artistic, hospitable Caroline is a mother and photographer whose fine prints dot the house. On cooler days, she serves breakfast at her kitchen table, charmingly fashioned out of two rustic doors. The terrace – shaded by bamboo, scattered with faded blue cushions – is a blissful spot for an evening tipple, the young garden is dotted with olive trees and gay pots of plants, and the small pool, with submerged seating and a whirlpool, is perfect for unwinding. The setting, too, is special: negotiate the external staircase to the rooftop for timeless views of olive groves and the distant Murgia hills. *Minimum stay two nights.*

rooms	5 + 1: 1 double, 1 twin sharing bathroom; 3 doubles. 1 studio for 2.	**③**
price	€75–€85. Studio €75–€140.	**④**
meals	Dinner with wine €20. Book ahead. Restaurants 2-3km.	**⑤**
closed	Generally closed in winter.	**⑥**
directions	From N379 Bari-Brindisi, exit Ostuni, signs to Cisternino; there, SP134 to Locorotondo; at blue boundary signs of Bari & Brindisi, left into Contrada Figazzano; immed. right; house 2nd on left.	**⑦**

	Caroline Groszer
mobile	+39 335 6094647
email	carolinegroszer@tre.it
web	www.trullicountryhouse.com

B&BSelf-catering

⑨ Map 16 Entry 304

 **⑧**

Explanation

1 region

2 write up
Written by us, after inspection.

3 rooms
Assume rooms are en suite, unless we state otherwise. If a room is not 'en suite' we say with separate, or with shared bathroom: the former you will have to yourself, the latter may be shared with other guests or family members. When an entry reads 4 + 2 this means 4 rooms plus 2 self-catering apartments or similar.

4 price
The price shown is for two people sharing a room. Half-board prices are per person. A price range incorporates room/seasonal differences.

5 meals
Prices are per person. If breakfast isn't included we give the price.

6 closed
When given in months, this means for the whole of the named months and the time in between.

7 directions
Use as a guide and travel with a good map.

8 symbols
see the last page of the book for a fuller explanation:

 wheelchair facilities
easily accessible bedrooms
no smoking anywhere
vegetarian dinner options
 guests' pets welcome in bedrooms

 owners' pets live here
 at least one bedroom has air-conditioning.
 pool
bikes on the premises to borrow or hire
tennis on the premises
 information on local walks

9 map & entry numbers

The World Wide Web is big - very big. So big, in fact, that it can be a fruitless place to search if you don't know where to find reliable, trustworthy, up-to-date information about fantastic places to stay in Europe, India, Morocco and beyond...

Fortunately, there's www.specialplacestostay.com, where you can dip into all of our guides, find special offers from owners, catch up on news about the series and tell us about the special places you've been to.

WWW.SPECIALPLACESTOSTAY.COM